DISABILITY, CULTURE, AI

Álfredo J. Artiles, *Series Editor*

Discipline Disparities Among Students With Disabilities

Creating Equitable Environments

Pamela Fenning and Miranda Johnson, Editors

Foreword by Kent McIntosh

TEACHERS COLLEGE PRESS

TEACHERS COLLEGE | COLUMBIA UNIVERSITY

NEW YORK AND LONDON

Published by Teachers College Press,® 1234 Amsterdam Avenue, New York, NY 10027

Front cover photocomposite: Butterfly by Conal Gallagher / Flickr creative commons; Rocks by Aleksandr Simonov / Shutterstock.

Library of Congress Cataloging-in-Publication Data

Names: Fenning, Pamela, editor. | Johnson, Miranda, editor.
Title: Discipline disparities among students with disabilities : creating
   equitable environments / Pamela Fenning and Miranda Johnson, editors.
Description: First Edition. | New York : Teachers College Press, [2022] |
   Series: Disability, Culture, and Equity Series | Includes
   bibliographical references and index. | Summary: "A team of
   interdisciplinary scholars, attorneys, and educators explore the
   disproportionate school discipline and school-based arrests of students
   with disabilities, particularly those who also identify as Black or
   Native American. They suggest promising practices and approaches
   that will reduce discipline disparities and increase the use of
   evidence-supported alternatives"—Provided by publisher.
Identifiers: LCCN 2021062649 (print) | LCCN 2021062650 (ebook) | ISBN
   9780807766422 (Paperback : acid-free paper) | ISBN 9780807766439
   (Hardcover : acid-free paper) | ISBN 9780807780763 (eBook)
Subjects: LCSH: Discrimination in school discipline—United States. |
   Children with disabilities—Education—United States. | Educational
   equalization—United States. | Discrimination in education—United States.
Classification: LCC LB3012.2 .D56 2022 (print) | LCC LB3012.2 (ebook) |
   DDC 379.2/60973—dc23/eng/20220215
LC record available at https://lccn.loc.gov/2021062649
LC ebook record available at https://lccn.loc.gov/2021062650

ISBN 978-0-8077-6642-2 (paper)
ISBN 978-0-8077-6643-9 (hardcover)
ISBN 978-0-8077-8076-3 (ebook)

Printed on acid-free paper
Manufactured in the United States of America

Contents

PROMISING EDUCATIONAL PRACTICES TO ADDRESS DISCIPLINE DISPROPORTIONALITY

LEGAL AND POLICY APPROACHES TO ADDRESS DISCIPLINE DISPROPORTIONALITY

Foreword

The book you are holding now is going to challenge you, like it has challenged me. Listening to the voices of those who have been harmed by our educational systems is troubling, and many will shy away from it. Reading research from a critical theory lens, whether it be critical race theory or DisCrit, can make us feel uncomfortable because it shines light on our failures and how we fall short of our ideals. That is its intent, and it is necessary—through adopting this lens, we can share more equally in this discomfort. Yet we must not confuse feelings of discomfort with feeling unsafe. Instead, this lens allows us to face reality in ways that give us the opportunity to build the educational systems we need.

As the authors of these chapters have shown, our systems far too often fail the students who stand most to benefit from them. Students of color and students with dis/abilities are not inherently more vulnerable than others, but our racist and ableist society makes them so. Unfortunately, we must come to terms with the fact that our systems are working as designed: to perpetuate inequities.

What you are about to read is the product of a catalytic event of shared purpose and learning. Readers of this volume can benefit from the richness that comes from that shared learning and put it to work. This book is needed and tells us what is needed.

We need interdisciplinary research. Racism, ableism, and intersectional oppression are complex problems that are evident across each of our fields. Students do not shed their experiences with oppressive systems when they enter the school building. That insight tells us that this challenge takes all hands, including practice informed by educational and psychological scholarship, policy informed by legal scholarship, and systems change informed by implementation science scholarship. We cut ourselves off from promising solutions when we continue to work in silos.

We need to center student and family voice. This work begins with listening to the voices of those who are being marginalized by our systems. Too often, I have been less effective by assuming I understand the concerns and jumping to action without hearing those who have deep lived experiences in marginalization and can share their expertise. However, the work cannot end with listening. We do better when we co-create a path forward in which we do not ask whether we have listened because those who are most harmed are already at the table with us. The authors of this book provide abundant examples of counternarratives and participatory action research to show the way forward.

We need to take action. For some, the events of racial brutality in the summer of 2020 brought to the forefront what many who had been looking already knew. Before the murders of George Floyd, Breonna Taylor, and Ahmaud Arbery, the racist and ableist killings of Michelle Cusseaux, Elijah McClain, and countless others were there for anyone who cared to notice. In 2020, many of us read books to build our wells of knowledge. The necessary next step is to put that knowledge to use. We can go beyond ignoring or explaining away inequities or documenting but not taking steps to right wrongs. We now have evidence-based tools to achieve equity. This book presents multiple pathways to do so.

—Kent McIntosh

Acknowledgments

The research reported in the book was made possible in part by a grant from the Spencer Foundation (#201800138). The views expressed are those of the authors and do not necessarily reflect the views of the Spencer Foundation. We would like to gratefully acknowledge the insights and contributions of all participants in the working conference held at Loyola University Chicago in June 2019, which strengthened the research resulting in this book. Conference participants greatly benefited from the tremendous knowledge and insights shared by speakers Dean Adams, Malik Henfield, Angel Love Miles, and Markeda Newell. We also sincerely thank Sarah-Bess Dworin from Restoring Community for her wonderful work facilitating the conference using restorative practices, enabling us to build community among conference participants and helping us find synergies in our research. We appreciate the contributions of Emma Healy, whose support of the working conference as a graduate research assistant was invaluable, and Kiley Callahan who provided editorial assistance. We are grateful for the hard work of Mariam Pera and Angelica Vaca, who helped us obtain funding for the conference.

We appreciate the support of the leadership of Loyola University Chicago's School of Education and School of Law, including current and former deans Zelda Harris, Malik Henfield, Michael Kaufman, and Markeda Newell. Pam is thankful for the many Loyola colleagues and students she collaborates with in this work and for the privilege of watching her two daughters, Abby and Alyssa, side-by-side with her partner Jeff, grow into now amazing adults. Miranda would like to thank her colleagues at Loyola's *Civitas* ChildLaw Center for their encouragement and particularly acknowledges Kathleen Hirsman, Eliza Luvianos, Jackie Ross, Griselda Sanchez, and her research assistant Mikaila John for their contributions to this book and its development. She is grateful for the support of her parents and the love and patience of her husband, Dola, and her wonderful children, Amani and Jasmine, who make her work possible and inspire her daily.

INTRODUCTION: FRAMING DISCIPLINE DISPARITIES THROUGH A DISCRIT INTERDISCIPLINARY LENS

CHAPTER 1

Introductory Comments
An Interdisciplinary Lens in Addressing Discipline Disparities of Students With Disabilities

Pamela Fenning and Miranda Johnson

In June of 2019, educational researchers, school-based mental health professionals, educators, child advocates, policy analysts, attorneys, and a funder came together for an interdisciplinary conference held at Loyola University Chicago to discuss the disproportionate impact of exclusionary school discipline practices on students who have disabilities. The two conference co-conveners come to the work of exclusionary discipline from different disciplines and training, one being a psychologist/faculty member in school psychology and the other being an attorney/law school faculty member. The conference was facilitated by a restorative justice practitioner.

The conference intended to build a research and policy agenda to change laws, policies, and school practices to prevent and respond to behaviors of students with disabilities through nonexclusionary means, with the overall aim of promoting greater school inclusion of students with disabilities. The conference format and structure were modeled after a prior successful national summit on discipline disproportionality sponsored by the Center for Civil Rights Remedies at the Civil Rights Project and the Research-to-Practice Collaborative (Losen, 2013).

Leading up to the conference, the co-organizers sought papers that fell within one of the following three strands: (1) research and data, (2) law and policy, and (3) promising practices. Research expertise from a variety of methodological approaches were encouraged, including quantitative, qualitative, and mixed methods. To promote interdisciplinary collaboration, papers were reviewed in advance by conference participants and the two conference co-conveners and coeditors of this book. The conference participants received advanced feedback on their papers from two other preassigned participants, one from within their same strand and the second representing a different strand. During the paper presentations at the conference, a similar format was followed, with time for feedback from participants both within and outside of each presenter's strand.

Following the conference, papers covering all three strands were selected as chapters for this book. Throughout the developing, editing, and completion of the chapters, the coeditors of this book continued to provide feedback through multiple drafts in the spirit of interdisciplinary collaboration.

EARLY LESSONS—DISCRIT FRAMEWORK

While the initial call for paper submissions focused primarily on critical race theory (CRT) (Crenshaw et al., 1995; Ladson-Billings & Tate, 1995), it soon became clear that DisCrit, which attends to both the ableism and racism in educational contexts, was an important framework to bring to this work (Annamma et al., 2018; Connor et al., 2016). A conversation at the conference was held in which conference participants reflected on who is harmed and who benefits from oppressive systems that favor White supremacy. The discussion centered on the importance of considering oppressive school systems as well as other social institutions when thinking about the impact of exclusionary discipline on minoritized students with disabilities. Chapter 2 provides an overview of DisCrit and CRT and how these theoretical frameworks can be applied and adapted when considering how exclusionary practices maintain the status quo of White supremacy and privilege (Annamma et al., 2012, 2014).

MAINTAINING THE STATUS QUO OF DISPARATE EXCLUSIONARY DISCIPLINE

Applying a DisCrit lens to understanding the intersected oppression of racial/ ethnic minority students when exclusionary discipline is meted out in schools is consistent with over 4 decades of research that consistently document the same findings about exclusionary discipline of students with disabilities who also have an individual identity as a racial/ethnic minority. Specifically, Black students who also have a disability consistently face the highest risk for school exclusion through suspension and expulsion. Table 1.1 provides a snapshot of these findings collected from 1975, beginning with the landmark Children's Defense Fund (1975) study to the most recently available U.S. Department of Education (DOE), Office for Civil Rights (OCR) (2021) data. These studies uniformly and categorically show that Black students are at heightened risk of disciplinary exclusion if they also have a disability (Losen et al., 2021). While not exhaustive of every analysis done to date about disciplinary exclusionary disparities by race and disability, the studies described in Table 1.1 paint a consistent and disturbing picture about how schools use exclusionary discipline as a mechanism to deny students—particularly Black students with disabilities—access to education and educational and mental health supports they are entitled to under federal and state laws.

Table 1.1. Snapshot of Studies Documenting Racial/Ethnic and Disability Disparities in Exclusionary Discipline

Source	Type of Disparity Found
Children's Defense Fund (1975)	**Federal civil rights data (national):** Black elementary and secondary students—higher suspension rates compared with White students
Skiba et al. (2002)	**Midwestern urban district middle school data:** Black students received more referrals for subjective and nonviolent offenses (e.g., class disrespect); White students received more referrals for overt behaviors (e.g., smoking)
Skiba et al. (2011)	**National elementary and middle school data:** African American and Hispanic students are more likely to be suspended or expelled compared with White peers—not due to differences in seriousness of behavior
DOE, OCR (2014b)	**2011–2012 Office for Civil Rights data (national):** Black preschool children have higher suspension rates compared to White students; students with disabilities are two times more likely to be suspended compared to students without disabilities; Black girls are suspended at the highest rates compared to girls of any other race/ethnicity; American Indian/Native Alaskan girls are suspended more frequently than White boys/other girls
Camacho & Krezmien (2020)	**Maryland K–12 public school students:** Black students had higher odds of being suspended compared to White students in every school district in the state; students with disabilities had higher odds of being suspended in all counties in the state except for one
Losen et al. (2021)	**2017–2018 OCR data (national):** Students with disabilities across all grades lost approximately twice the instructional days due to suspensions compared to students without disabilities; a much higher percentage of Black (24%) and Native American (15%) students with disabilities were subjected to one or more suspensions compared to White students with disabilities (11%)
DOE, OCR (2021)	**2017–2018 OCR data (national):** Students with disabilities experience a higher percentage of one or more in-school suspensions (20.5%) as well as one or more out-of-school suspensions (24.5%) relative to their overall school enrollment (13.2%); Black students with disabilities show even more dismal outcomes, making up only 2.3% of all school enrollment but being subjected to 6.2% of one or more school suspensions and 8.8% of one or more out-of-school suspensions

In addition to the disparaging data that is evident for Black students who have a disability, Native American/Indigenous students are also at grave risk of school exclusion. While not represented in adequate numbers statistically in national data that has been collected over the years, nonetheless there is more than adequate evidence in data and national studies that Native American/ Indigenous students disparately receive punitive disciplinary measures (Losen et al., 2021; DOE, OCR, 2014b).

These disproportionate findings by race and ethnicity hold consistently across the snapshot of studies reported in Table 1.1, regardless of whether the data were collected at the state, regional, or national level. Further, these data are consistent from the 1972–1973 school year data (Children's Defense Fund, 1975) or every year since, all the way through the most recently available 2017–2018 school year data (DOE, OCR, 2021). Simply put, these findings are unequivocal that racial/ethnic minority students with disabilities, particularly Black students and Native American/Indigenous students, have been and continue to experience exclusionary discipline at rates much higher than one would expect given their enrollment in school. These educational discipline disparities are happening and maintained across two generations, despite the existence of federal laws, such as the Individuals With Disabilities Education Act (IDEA, 2016) and Section 504 of the Rehabilitation Act of 1973 (2016), which have been put in place to offer protections for students with disabilities that simply are not being implemented adequately (Losen et al., 2021).

Considerable effort has focused on attributing the racial/ethnic differences in exclusionary discipline that are so uniformly documented to internal student factors, particularly the false narrative that Black students, who are the most likely to experience disciplinary exclusion, engage in more serious or violent behaviors that warrant suspension and expulsion from school (Fenning & Jenkins, 2018; Fenning & Rose, 2007). However, there is simply no evidence that Black students engage in more serious infractions that warrant such an extreme school reaction (Skiba et al., 2002, 2011).

Evidence stacks up to the contrary. For example, in an analysis of middle school office discipline referral data, Skiba et al. (2002) found that Black students were referred more often to the office for subjective reasons, such as classroom disrespect and disruption, while White students were referred more for overt reasons, such as smoking and vandalism. In a subsequent national analysis of elementary and secondary school discipline referrals generated through the School-Wide Information System (SWIS) (May et al., 2013), Skiba et al. (2011) found that African American and Latinx students were more likely than their White peers to be subjected to suspension and the most extreme exclusionary reaction of school expulsion for engaging in the same type of disciplinary infraction.

A great deal of research time and energy has been expended on documenting the problem of racial/ethnic and disability disparities in exclusionary discipline. Further, the field has centered on looking to student internal deficits to explain these disparities rather than looking to school policy and practice as underlying root cause drivers (Fenning & Jenkins, 2018; Fenning & Rose, 2007). It is perhaps telling that the authors of the Children's Defense Fund report in 1975 directly took on what they expected to be the prevailing narrative that the racially disproportionate data they uncovered would be explained as Black students demonstrating more problematic behavior. They vehemently disagreed with this assertion, citing evidence that racial disparities were not present across all school districts studied and pointing to administrator decision-making as the more likely driver. They explicitly named the role of racial discrimination and implored administrators to look at patterns of referrals in their school districts. They also recommended that the OCR take a much stronger stance on ensuring school districts' compliance with the civil rights protections afforded to students. It is prophetic but tragic that we continue to have the same conversations today. One might imagine how our schools could be more equitable in school discipline if the recommendations made over 45 years ago by the Children's Defense Fund were implemented.

When we look at the current landscape regarding inequitable school discipline practices, we see glimmers of hope. States across the country have enacted legislation designed to limit the use of school suspensions and expulsions (National Center on Safe and Supportive Learning Environments, n.d.; Rafa, 2019). Cities and school districts have voted to reduce or eliminate school police (Sawchuk, 2020). Educators and student activists have been calling for racial justice, including changes to school curriculum, policies, and practices (Domzalski & Saias, 2021; National Education Association, n.d.).

With respect to scholarship, researchers seeking to identify areas for change are increasingly looking to school-driven practices that focus on professional development and consultation with teachers, as classrooms are the primary setting where referrals to the office happen in the first place (Fenning & Jenkins, 2018). For example, McIntosh et al. (2014) have articulated that vulnerable decision points, which are broadly defined as key momentary discipline decisions prone to implicit bias, could be addressed by teaching educators a simple neutralizing routine to help them make more equitable decisions in the moment. In another study, teachers who received a brief online empathy intervention were less likely to suspend students compared with teachers in a control condition (Okonofua et al., 2016). Of critical importance to mitigating racially disparate discipline is that Okonofua et al.'s (2016) findings held for all racial groups, by gender and for students who had previously been suspended. There has been other promising research documenting that a classroom consultation model that incorporates feedback based on videotaped student teacher exchanges had positive outcomes in mitigating racial discipline disparities and improving student engagement (Gregory et al., 2015). These interventions, which are focused on changing educators' mindsets and school or classroom practices, are arguably where the focus should be in changing the 4 decades-long disparate discipline that is summarized in Table 1.1. Still, school-based mental health professionals and those with behavioral expertise are necessary to facilitate school-based implementation work. We concur with recommendations made for federal funding to address the shortage of mental health professionals in schools so that school-based interventions are feasible, adequately supported, and implemented with integrity (Losen et al., 2021).

IMPACT OF INEQUITABLE DISCIPLINE

Suspension is the most commonly used discipline response, even for behaviors unrelated to school safety, such as tardies, truancies, and class disrespect (American Psychological Association [APA] Task Force on Zero Tolerance, 2008; Losen, 2015). There is no evidence that exclusionary measures, like suspension, are effective in promoting prosocial and expected behavior (Sharkey & Fenning, 2012). Unfortunately, there is evidence that suspension does quite the contrary and may fuel increases in the undesirable behaviors it is designed to curb (Mayer, 1995). School suspension and expulsion, by definition, is associated with removal from the classroom and loss of instructional minutes that directly relate to academic achievement (Sharkey & Fenning, 2012). Students who have disabilities have weaker academic outcomes in reading and math when they are on the receiving end of exclusionary discipline, even beyond what one would expect given their specialized instructional needs (Allman & Slate, 2013).

Suspension is a social justice issue due to the racial/ethnic and disability inequities it produces, and it is not an effective means of handling behavior for any student. Suspending a student is not a benign event. Even one suspension in 9th grade can fuel deleterious educational outcomes such as school dropout (Balfanz et al., 2014) and entry into the juvenile justice and/or penal system, a concept increasingly being coined as the "cradle-to-prison pipeline" (Wright Adelman, 2007). For example, Balfanz et al. (2014) found that Florida students who were suspended in 9th grade were more likely to graduate from high school late and less likely to enroll and stay in postsecondary education. Similar to the literature previously summarized pertaining to the disproportionate exclusionary discipline with Black students with disabilities, Balfanz et al. (2014) also found disproportionate numbers and length of suspension for students who were Black, in special education, and with lower socioeconomic status (SES). The racial differences remained even after controlling for SES. The use of suspension and expulsion is a harmful practice that does not work effectively for any student and has a potentially life-altering impact on students who are historically oppressed in schools, particularly racial/ethnic minority students with disabilities.

CHANGING LENS AND PERSPECTIVE IN THE MIDST OF VISIBLE RACISM AND COVID-19

In the relatively 2 short years between the June 2019 interdisciplinary conference and the writing of this chapter, our country and world has arguably transformed. The world has changed in demonstrable ways, particularly in how racism and other forms of oppression, in place for centuries, have been illuminated in the national discourse. Rather than trying to prove that racism and bias exist through our research, conferences, and think tanks, we only needed to turn on the news and see the horrific killing of an unarmed Black man. Connecting the dots to what we see play out in arrests of Black persons, we can see the earlier trajectory of racism and bias in all institutions, including schools. Further, the disproportionately higher rates of COVID-19 infections and deaths and the life-altering impact of the pandemic on historically minoritized persons, particularly those who identify as Asian American, Pacific Islander (AAPI), Black, and Latinx, have magnified existing social determinant drivers of health, along with other forms of individual, historical, and structural oppression (Kendi, 2019; Lopez et al., 2021).

The tragic racist killings of George Floyd, Eric Garner, Trayvon Martin, Michael Brown, Breanna Taylor, Tony McDade, and countless other persons of color across history has fueled a watershed moment in the United States. A discourse about disproportionate racial and ableist discipline policies and practices cannot be divorced from an understanding about how larger systems of oppression across housing, juvenile justice, mental health, and other systems converge to uphold White supremacy (Alexander, 2012; Harris, 1995; Kohli et al., 2017; Ladson-Billings, 2008; Rothstein, 2017; Sullivan et al., 2020).

The COVID-19 pandemic has undoubtedly had a global influence across the world, impacting all facets of human life. The effect has been felt in a more profound manner by the very students and families who also face disparate discipline, particularly persons who identify as racial/ethnic minorities (Lopez et al., 2021; Song et al., 2020) and have disabilities (Brandenburg et al., 2020). Lopez et al. (2021) describe the existing social inequities in health care access, community resources, and living conditions that racial/ethnic minorities experience, which have only become more exacerbated in the throes of COVID-19 and are associated with the disparate rates of COVID-19 infections, deaths, and hospitalizations experienced by minoritized compared to White persons.

WHAT DID WE COME TOGETHER TO SOLVE?

The conference participants came together with the stated purpose of arriving at solutions to the inequitable exclusionary discipline of students with disabilities, particularly those who hold additional intersected identities as racial/ethnic minorities. Fast-forward to 2021, and while our focus is similar, there is perhaps more of an urgency to arrive at interdisciplinary solutions that are viable and address the ableist and racist inequities that play out in schools (Annamma et al., 2014).

Losen et al. (2021) make critical interdisciplinary policy recommendations to address the widening gaps in educational and mental health opportunities that minoritized students who have disabilities are facing at an epidemic level in the age of COVID-19 and visible forms of racism. Losen et al.'s (2021) recommendations stress the critical role of strong civil rights enforcement in addressing racial and disability discrimination, including bolstering protections under Section 504 of the Rehabilitation Act. They also stress the importance of fully funding the IDEA in order to improve the quality of instruction, enhance the diversity of school personnel, build the capacity of teachers, and equip school service personnel in adequate numbers to provide necessary mental health and trauma-informed services. Currently, there is an extreme shortage of trained school psychologists and special educators in the workforce to meet the exacerbated mental health and educational challenges, particularly in the most under-resourced schools in the nation (National Association of School Psychologists [NASP], 2021).

Figure 1.1 shows the interdisciplinary perspective the conference organizers, participants, and chapter authors applied to dismantling the longstanding issue of ableism and racism in exclusionary discipline. The original intent of the conference, the work at the conference, and the writing of the chapters following it were based on the premise that the enduring and complex nature of this issue requires interdisciplinary expertise, experience, and knowledge to address. In the figure, the focal point is the inequitable discipline meted out in schools for years to students with disabilities who hold intersected racial/ethnic minoritized identities. We see the three strands as influencing one another, with the primary goal being reducing exclusionary discipline. With this in mind, each chapter author comes from one of the three strands and was tasked with offering research, policy, and practice implications of their work in their respective chapter. In the next chapter, Markeda Newell and Emma Healy illustrate how DisCrit and CRT can serve as important frameworks for understanding how inequities in discipline are fueled and maintained through the tenets of each theory.

Figure 1.1. Interdisciplinary Perspectives on Ableist and Racist School Discipline

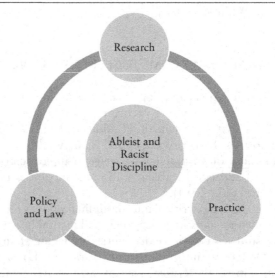

RESEARCH AND KNOWLEDGE THROUGH MULTIPLE
EPISTEMOLOGIES, METHODS, AND VOICES

In Chapter 3, Patrice Leverett provides counter-storytelling consistent with DisCrit (Connor et al., 2016) about the ways in which African American male students experience school discipline and classroom management/behavior practices. Her qualitative methodology offers a fresh approach to interrogating inequitable discipline from the voices of African American students who are most harmed by it. Her recommendations to develop and pilot a student treatment acceptability protocol is an excellent future direction that incorporates the voices of young persons, so research, policy, and practices are construed "with" and not "for" African American students and others who have historically been marginalized by school discipline. Following in Chapter 4, Amy Fisher and Ben Fisher offer an important analysis of 2013–2014 CRDC data that consistently shows students with disabilities (SWD), particularly Black, multiracial, and Hispanic SWD, experience higher rates of exclusionary discipline (e.g., in-school suspension, out-of-school suspension, expulsions with services) when police are present compared with when they are not. Their findings have important implications for the national dialogue about the police presence in schools, the potential harm that befalls SWD and racial/ethnic minoritized students, and how resources are allocated for school safety and mental/behavioral services in schools. Angelina Nortey, in Chapter 5, offers a counternarrative of Black women educators' perspective on school discipline and the ability of minoritized students through a DisCrit and womanist ethics of care lens. She tells the stories of Black women educators through an African American epistemology and Black feminist perspective, highlighting the power of experience these Black women educators bring in seeing ability and not disability in Black students and the importance of interrogating and pushing back on notions of inferiority.

PROMISING EDUCATIONAL PRACTICES IN ADDRESSING
DISCIPLINE DISPROPORTIONALITY

In a transition to educational practices, Chapter 6, contributed by Kristen Pearson, Laura Marques, Monica Stevens, and Elizabeth Marcell Williams describe a day treatment program for students who face substantial trauma and have significant mental health and emotional disorders in a New Orleans context that does not currently have a continuum of supports to address mental and behavioral health needs. The most recent national data available continues to show that Black students receiving special education services under the category of emotional disturbance are at extremely high risk for exclusionary discipline and are the group that is the most vulnerable to have their education in a correctional setting (Losen et al., 2021). Pearson and colleagues offer recommendations for future research, practice, and policy with recommendations that center on building community-based supports that are not currently in place. They make key recommendations for community-based mental health service providers in culturally responsive mental health, educator training in historical racism, and advocacy for equitable access to mental health and educational services in communities of color where minoritized students with disabilities reside. A data-driven, problem-solving framework with educators that specifically focuses on social, emotional, and behavioral supports for students who have a disability classification of emotional disturbances is provided in Chapter 7 by Sandra Chafouleas, Amy Briesch, Kathleen Lynne Lane, and Wendy Oakes. Their work centers on students who are in dire need of educators' attention and support. In Chapter 8 and Appendix A, Lindsay Fallon and Margarida Veiga offer a validated tool—the Assessment of Culturally and Contextually Relevant Supports (ACCReS)—that teachers can use as they engage in self-reflection about their daily classroom practices using a culturally responsive lens. The ACCReS is a tool that can also readily be used by classroom consultants, such as school psychologists, in an efficient manner to mitigate unnecessary referrals to the office that fuel suspensions with Black students who have or are suspected of having a disability. Emma Healy, Michelle Rappaport, and Carly Tindall-Biggins describe the Building Bridges program in Chapter 9, which is an alternative to suspension programs and has been implemented in a therapeutic day school program that serves students with significant emotional and behavioral needs. It is grounded in cognitive behavioral therapy and restorative practices with the goal of addressing day-to-day conflicts that arise in schools. Implications for conducting large-scale evaluations of Building Bridges are offered to better support students with social, emotional, and behavioral concerns along a continuum of educational supports.

In a transition to legal and policy remedies, Heather Hoeschst and Donald Chee make an important contribution in Chapter 10 about the exclusionary discipline of Native American youth in New Mexico. They provide a compelling analysis of how pertinent laws and policies at the national, state, and local levels fail to provide adequate educational protections for Native American youth with disabilities. They provide powerful recommendations for changing federal/state-level policy and legislation to improve the educational experiences of the population they serve as both advocates and attorneys. Thomas Mayes and Perry Zirkel report findings in Chapter 11 from their analysis of publicly available case law about school resource officer (SRO) conduct, finding that most of the cases involved students eligible under IDEA. They provide important considerations for school administrators when making decisions about if and under what conditions SROs should be placed in their schools.

Finally, in Chapter 12 Miranda Johnson and Pamela Fenning describe a path forward in the areas of research, policy, and practice in addressing discipline disparities that students with disabilities and those who have additional intersected minoritized identities experience in schools. In the 2 years since the interdisciplinary conference that fueled this book was held, the world seems like a different place. We argue that equity in school discipline, along with other forms of educational equity, are a needed collective focus now more than ever. Given the events of the past 2 years—including the extrajudicial killing of unarmed Black persons and the COVID-19 worldwide pandemic—it seems abundantly clear that we cannot carry on with business as usual. It is not an understatement to say that students' lives depend on it, particularly those who have faced longstanding oppression, only laid bare and exacerbated by the historical times we are experiencing.

Looking at School Discipline From the Perspective of Critical Race Theory and DisCrit

How Multiple Identities Intersect to Create Inequities in School Discipline

Markeda Newell and Emma Healy

The purpose of this chapter is to provide a theoretical framework for reexamining how intersecting minoritized identities can impact school discipline practices, particularly for Black students with dis/abilities. Given the long history of excluding Black students and students with dis/abilities from school settings through discipline practices, we are proposing the use of dis/ability critical race theory as a framework to conceptualize and analyze school discipline practices impacting Black students who have dis/abilities.

Data about exclusionary discipline, specifically suspension and expulsion, are often reported using single identity demographics (e.g., Black students, students with dis/abilities). However, when school discipline data is examined and reported based on the intersection of multiple minoritized identities (e.g., Black students with dis/abilities, Black male students with dis/abilities), another important pattern emerges (see Chapter 1). Students who hold multiple minoritized identities experience the highest rates of exclusionary discipline compared to students who hold no minoritized identities or only one minoritized identity (see Losen et al., 2015; U.S. Government Accountability Office, 2018). This consistent pattern reveals that Black students with dis/abilities are excluded from school through discipline practices more than other groups, which begs the question, "Why are Black students with dis/abilities experiencing exclusionary discipline at such a high rate in U.S. school settings?" Researchers have already learned that Black students, generally, do not misbehave at higher rates compared to their peers (see Chapter 1; Skiba & Williams, 2014). It is more accurate to say that Black students are referred to the office for behavioral infractions more often than their peers.

Relatedly, Black students are more often referred for special education evaluations, oftentimes by more novice teachers (see Losen et al., 2014). Further, when they are placed in special education, they may not receive adequate support that could prevent disciplinary problems (see Losen et al., 2014). Taken together, the evidence suggests that the greater risk to Black students with dis/abilities lies in how educators perceive their identities in relationship to their behavior in schools. Thus, the purpose of this chapter is to provide a theoretical framework that aims to help readers reexamine how intersecting minoritized identities can impact school discipline practices, particularly for Black students with dis/abilities, as this is the group who has faced disparate rates of exclusion and pushout, spanning from 1975 to the most recently available national data (see Chapter 1). Although the focus of this chapter is largely on the marginalization of Black students with dis/abilities, it is important to highlight that dis/ability critical race theory is useful frame to understand the experiences of all students who have multiple minoritized identities, including Native American students with disabilities and additional minoritized groups, such as students who identify as multiracial (see Chapters 1, 10, and Chapter 4).

THE CASE FOR USING THEORY TO DISMANTLE INEQUITIES IN SCHOOL DISCIPLINE

The significant disparity in the use of exclusionary discipline practices between Black students with dis/abilities and their peers is clear. Given that the research evidence indicates that the disparities begin at the point of referral (office referrals and special education referrals), we propose that educators and researchers begin their analysis by asking why educators are referring Black students more often. This is essential to understand the outcome (i.e., disproportionate use of exclusionary discipline practices). By starting our examination at the point of referral, we can better identify and understand the factors contributing to this outcome, as opposed to trying to postulate based on the outcome. As Skiba and Williams (2014) stated, "Simply showing a difference in the rates of suspension between two groups is not proof of discrimination" (p. 3). We must have a strong theoretical framework to structure our analysis of school discipline to more accurately understand the problem.

IMPORTANCE OF THEORETICAL FRAME

Coupling theory with empirical data is ideal because theory helps researchers more precisely and accurately explain their findings. The limited use of theoretical frameworks, coupled with the inadequate representation and voice of minoritized persons in educational research (Newell et al., 2020), significantly narrows the ability of the field to understand the lived experience of minoritized students in schools. Beyond this, of the research that has been conducted, the use of theory in research with minoritized populations in education and psychology has been fraught with problems.

For example, Newell and Chavez-Korell (2017) examined the evolution of multiculturalism in psychological research and identified how theories of inferiority have been used to explain the psychological and social conditions of minoritized populations. Although there has been some movement away from using theories of inferiority in applied fields like school psychology, the types of theories used when conducting research with minoritized students remains restricted. Recently, Newell et al. (2020) found that most researchers were not offering a specific theory when conducting research with minoritized youth. The field of education and psychology simply lacks critical theories, which contributes to poor insight into how minoritized populations are positioned in research. That is to say, minoritized students have historically been positioned as the problem. More specifically, they have been conceptualized as having within-person deficits that contribute to and/or create academic, behavioral, social, and/or psychological difficulties (Valencia, 1997). Ecological and cultural difference theories move the field further away from within-person deficit conceptualizations of minoritized students, but they often do not go far enough to challenge and interrupt the ways traditional theories and research have identified the problem (Newell et al., 2020). This is why the use of critical theories is essential in applied educational fields, especially when aiming to understand the disproportionate use of exclusionary discipline practices with multiply marginalized students, such as Black students with dis/abilities.

According to Richardson and Fowers (1997), "One of the main thrusts of critical psychology is to expose the ways modern psychology and psychologists—even if they mean well—help to maintain a social and cultural status quo that is unjust, shallow, or in some way harmful to human welfare." (p. 266). Hence, critical theories are designed to challenge, disrupt, and dismantle historical constructs and theories that have served to maintain systems of oppression and marginalization. Within a critical theory perspective, the identities of those who are marginalized are not the problem. Rather, the problem is how the identities of those who are marginalized are viewed and acted on by people and systems around them. Thus, the problem lies in how teachers, school psychologists, and administrators view Black students, how they view students with dis/abilities, and how they view Black students with dis/abilities. Further, the problem lies in how these views translate into discipline policy, special education policy, academic policy, and so on. Even further, the problem lies in how research and theory have contributed to these views and translated to policy that ultimately informs day-to-day practices. With that being said, critical theories provide a framework that shifts the focus away from the identity as the problem and instead draw attention to the ways in which the world treats persons who hold minoritized identities.

CRITICAL RACE THEORY AND DIS/ABILITY STUDIES

Two key critical theories that are most relevant to helping inform the disproportionate use of exclusionary discipline practices with Black students with
dis/abilities are critical race theory and dis/ability studies. Critical race theory
(Crenshaw, 1995) teaches us that a Black person's race is not the problem;
rather the problem lies in how racism persists throughout society to contribute to and/or create unfair, unjust treatment of Black people. Relatedly, dis/
ability studies (Adams et al., 2015) teaches us that a person's ability is not
the problem. Rather, the problem lies in how society has been constructed to
limit or restrict how individuals with different abilities can navigate the world
and live their lives. With the increased recognition of intersectionality (i.e.,
the experience of people who hold multiple minoritized identities) (Crenshaw,
1989), theorists were interested in creating a theoretical framework that
could better explain the intersection of race and dis/ability, which led to the
creation of dis/ability critical race theory (DisCrit) (see Annamma et al., 2018
for a review of the history of DisCrit).

DIS/ABILITY CRITICAL RACE THEORY (DISCRIT): A BRIEF OVERVIEW

Created in 2013, DisCrit is a theoretical and methodological tool that can be
used to better understand "the mutually constitutive nature of race and ability" (Connor et al., 2016, p. 3). At its core, DisCrit theorists oppose the viewing
of disability or race through a singular lens and "seek[] to complicate notions
of race and ability by recognizing ways they are intertwined" (Annamma
et al., 2013, p. 21). In offering a theoretical framework that examines the
intersection and interdependency of racism and ableism in Western society,
the authors of DisCrit aim to honor the experiences and voices of people facing dual marginalization and ultimately support an inclusive society. To do
this, DisCrit theorists explore structural power, both historical and present,
that has been socially constructed to oppress people of color and people with
disabilities. Moreover, DisCrit theorists recognize that racism and ableism
reinforce each other, which provides for unique experiences of oppression
that are different from both racism and ableism on their own.

    As critical special educators, Annamma et al. (2018) recognized a need
for a deeper consideration of race and ability in special education research.
Moreover, they observed a deadlock in special education research resulting in
the examination of the same issues with little change, particularly as it relates
to the disproportionate representation of Black students in special education.
Racial disproportionality in special education has become a routine topic
of discussion, often based on a student deficit model, yet there has been no
meaningful work toward dismantling the oppressive system. Connor et al.
(2018) recognized that academics and researchers were utilizing disability
studies (DS) or critical race theory (CRT) to examine issues within education,

but very few were theorizing about the interaction and unique impact of the combined forces of racism and ableism. Given the longstanding racial and ethnic disproportionality in special education and the subjectivity in disability categories and evaluations, Connor et al. (2018) declared it "irresponsible" to leave race out of research involving special education (p. 12). Annamma et al. (2018) set out to create a new framework for considering the racialized context of special education and through their efforts, DisCrit was born.

ORIGINS

The roots of DisCrit are deeply entrenched in Black feminist thought, CRT, and disability studies (Annamma et al., 2018).

Black feminist thought. Although DisCrit takes inspiration from a variety of activists and theories, it was born from Black and critical race feminist scholarship and activism (Annamma et al., 2018). The core principle of Black feminist thought is to not only detail the myriad and pervasive ways Black women have been marginalized in society, but to also elucidate the contributions, voices, and perspectives of Black women. Anna Julia Cooper (1892) was a fierce advocate for the education of Black women, and Black people more broadly. Her analysis of the racialized experience of Black women in her book, *A Voice From the South: By a Black Woman of the South,* became a seminal text on understanding the lived experiences of Black women. Patricia Hill Collins drew attention to the intellectual work of Black women scholars in her 1990 book *Black Feminist Thought.* Kimberlé Crenshaw (1989) coined the term *intersectionality,* which provides a framework for examining and understanding the connection between different forms of oppression that work together to uniquely marginalize women of color. Anna Julia Cooper, Patricia Hill Collins, and Kimberlé Crenshaw are a few of the Black women who have been instrumental in bringing understanding to the intersection of race and gender for Black women in the United States. From Black feminist thought, DisCrit scholars came to understand the important concept of intersectionality (Annamma et al., 2018). In addition to learning from Black feminists, DisCrit scholars also embraced core tenets of CRT. Although there is some overlap between Black feminist thought and CRT, it is important to understand that these two traditions are distinct and contribute uniquely to the examination of the lived experiences of Black people (see Johnson, 2015 for a review).

Critical Race Theory (CRT). In the 1970s, legal scholars, concerned with the slow pace of progress on racial reform in the United States, proposed CRT as a way to more adequately consider the lived experiences of racially minoritized populations, particularly Black people. Derrick Bell, Alan Freeman, and Richard Delgado were particularly influential in the creation of the theory, and they aimed to demonstrate that racism is not just interpersonal, but structural and integral to Western society (Delgado & Stefancic, 1998; Matsuda et al., 1993). CRT acknowledges that White supremacy is central in the laws, policies, and regulations of American society. Thus, racism is pervasive and impacts the daily lives of Black people (Bell, 1993). Although CRT has its genesis in the work of these critical legal scholars, CRT has been applied to education, illuminating how racism impacts educational policies and practices (Ladson-Billings & Tate, 1995). For example, CRT acknowledges that the White Eurocentric perspective is the predominant perspective from which history is viewed. Consequently, when CRT is applied to education, scholars can trace the past and present practices that have perpetuated racial inequities in areas such as disproportionate discipline (Wilson et al., 2020), the racial achievement gap (Love, 2004), and school funding (Vaught, 2009) in order to identify pathways to dismantle these inequities.

For many years, much of the CRT scholarship did not explicitly address the lived experiences of people with dis/abilities. However, after decades of research on the disproportionate representation of racially minoritized students in special education, scholars began to take notice of the high rate at which racially minoritized students, especially Black students, were being identified with educational dis/abilities and placed in special education (see Annamma et al., 2013). CRT scholars conceptualized disproportionate representation of Black students in special education as another form of historical segregation that Black people long experienced (Beratan, 2008). Moreover, the Black race had long been socially constructed as genetically inferior and less capable than White people (Smedley & Smedley, 2005). This social construction became intertwined with the social construction of dis/ability, which contributed to the disproportionate identification of Black students in special education (see Annamma et al., 2014; Watts & Erevelles, 2004). Therefore, DisCrit scholars learned of the centrality and pervasiveness of racism and how racism influences the identification of Black students with dis/abilities. This view of dis/ability aligned with the notion that dis/abilities are socially constructed, which is the dominant view within dis/ability studies.

Disability studies (DS). Dis/ability studies is an area of study that aims to reconceptualize the definition of dis/ability as a social construct that is designed to limit opportunities and access for people (see Linton, 2005). Dis/ability has been defined through a medical model, which means that dis/ability was understood to be a within-person deficit that should be fixed. In Tom Shakespeare's (2006) social model of disability, he suggests that the problems people with dis/abilities face are the result of how the social world does not accommodate difference and instead excludes and marginalizes those who have differences in ability. In other words, ableism is more harmful than the differences in ability. Thus, the focus of scholars in DS is to break down the socially constructed barriers between "normal" and "abnormal," "abled and disabled." Instead, advocates in DS challenge us to embrace a range of ability and to redesign our social and physical contexts to better accommodate a range of ability rather than marginalizing differences. DisCrit scholars understood and embraced the social construction of dis/ability, and this became a foundational tenet of DisCrit (Annamma et al., 2013).

Summary. The connective tissue across these three traditions (i.e., Black feminist thought, CRT, and DS) is the exclusion, rejection, and marginalization of Black women, Black people, and people with dis/abilities based on the social construction of their identities. That is, the historical and contemporary treatment of these minoritized groups is based on how people in society define them, perceive them, and interact with them, which has been from a within-person, deficit perspective (see Jones, 1996; Smedley & Smedley, 2005). Dis/ability CRT was borne out of the recognition that these marginalized identities intersected to create an interlocking system of oppression that was best evidenced by the disproportionate placement of Black students in special education and the disproportionate exclusionary discipline these students experience (Annamma et al., 2014).

CONCEPTUALIZING SCHOOL DISCIPLINE WITHIN A DIS/ABILITY CRITICAL RACE THEORY FRAME

It was evident that scholars in DS were concerned about the social construction of dis/abilities and how that impacted people's lives, and race scholars were concerned with the educational experience and outcomes for Black students. However, the two traditions did not necessarily intersect to understand the intersectional experience of Black students with dis/abilities. Over time, it became clear that the two forms of oppression are made more complicated when experienced together, as they have separate and combined effects because "racism validates and reinforces ableism, and ableism validates and reinforces racism" (Annamma et al., 2013, p. 6). In using DisCrit as an analytic tool, scholars can reveal new knowledge about the way racism and ableism interact and impact specific individuals and contexts. It was in the seminal work of Annamma et al. (2013) that the intersection of race and dis/ability came together to form DisCrit. Both CRT and DS challenge scholars to answer questions about who is privileged in our society. Who benefits and is advantaged from the current societal norms? Who is exploited and discriminated against? How are people of color and people with dis/abilities represented in society? Who has a platform for their voice to be heard and who is silenced? While CRT and DS ask these questions and focus on a singular dimension, DisCrit accounts for race, ability, and the interaction of the two. By framing these questions in an intersectional lens, DisCrit complicates the analysis and challenges us to hear the voices of those who are marginalized, honor their experiences, and change our policies and practices.

Annamma et al. (2013) outlined the seven key tenets of DisCrit. These tenets provide a useful heuristic for researchers, scholars, and practitioners to understand ways in which DisCrit can be used to examine the complex intersection of race and dis/ability as well as racism and ableism. For the purpose of this chapter, five of the seven tenets are introduced to help use DisCrit as a framework to understand the school discipline practices with Black students who have dis/abilities. For a more in-depth review of all tenets, please see Annamma et al. (2013, 2018).

Tenet 1: "DisCrit focuses on ways that the forces of racism and ableism circulate interdependently, often in neutralized and invisible ways, to uphold notions of normalcy." (Annamma et al., 2013, p. 11)

Racism and ableism are social constructions founded on the belief that White people and people without dis/abilities, respectively, are superior to those who are not White and have dis/abilities (Annamma et al., 2013; Smedley & Smedley, 2005). From a DisCrit perspective, examining how racism and ableism have normalized is essential because they position persons of color and persons with dis/abilities as being inferior or deviant due to their identities. Thus, the more racism and ableism are the norms (i.e., commonly accepted belief systems), the more likely people of color and people with dis/abilities are going to be deemed a problem that should be fixed as opposed to the problem being how people perceive people of color and people with dis/abilities (see Newell & Kratochwill, 2007). Thus, when applying a DisCrit perspective to school discipline with Black students who have dis/abilities, one must first ask, "Where is the problem being located?" If the problem is being located within the student, then stop and consider the following: How have the people and environment around the student created and/or contributed to the concern? For example, if a teacher does not have effective classroom management skills, then might that lack of skill be the problem as opposed to the student's behavior? If yes, the problem lies in the lack of management skills instead of within the student. Hence, when using a DisCrit perspective, one must always seek to understand how the environment (e.g., implicit bias of educator, lack of high-quality instruction, under-resourced schools) is the source of the problem rather than the student.

Tenet 2: "DisCrit values multidimensional identities and troubles singular notions of identity such as race or dis/ability or class or gender or sexuality, and so on." (Annamma et al., 2013, p. 11)

Intersectionality is the core underlying principle of tenet 2. Coined by Crenshaw (1989), the concept of intersectionality recognizes that people who hold multiple marginalized identities not only experience multiple forms and levels of oppression, but intersectionality also creates unique, individualized experiences of oppression. Therefore, the different experiences people have with identity-based oppression cannot be compared. More broadly, DisCrit theorists recognize that a wide range of identities (i.e., culture, sexuality, language, immigration status, class, gender) contribute to society's idea of dis/ability. Therefore, to understand the lived experience of any person with a dis/ability, one must understand how all of their identities intersect to create their unique lived experience. Thus, when applying a DisCrit perspective to school discipline with Black students who have dis/abilities, educators should examine their data to identify how students who hold multiple minoritized identities are being disciplined. For example, educators should examine their data to determine if there is a difference in the suspension rates for Black, male students as opposed to White, male students, or if there is a difference in rates between Black, female students who live in poverty and White, male students who do not live in poverty. The purpose of this type of analysis is to identify first if students with multiple minoritized identities are experiencing more exclusionary discipline. Second, if the data indicate this is true, then one must examine why this phenomenon is occurring, keeping in mind that the intersection of multiple marginalized identities places students at greater risk for unfair or unjust treatment (Annamma et al., 2018; Crenshaw, 1989).

Tenet 3: "DisCrit emphasizes the social constructions of race and ability and yet recognizes the material and psychological impacts of being labeled as raced or dis/abled, which sets one outside of the western cultural norms." (Annamma et al., 2013, p. 11)

While DisCrit theorists acknowledge that race and ability are socially constructed and have no meaning without the labels that society has created, they also acknowledge that these labels have real-world impacts on the daily lives of people of color and people with dis/abilities. To explain, although the concept of race was socially created, there are significant differences in life experiences and outcomes among different racial groups (Smedley & Smedley, 2005) as well as for people with dis/abilities. For example, there are longstanding racial achievement gaps (Gopolan & Nelson, 2019), racial health disparities (Smedley et al., 2003), and income inequality among races (Salazar et al., 2019). As Carter et al. (2017) explained, "Racial discipline disparities are a consequence of U.S. history, of the biases and stereotypes created by that history, and of the still-strong divisions in lived experience between groups that we call 'races'" (p. 208). Similar disparities exist between people with and without dis/abilities with regard to income (Jajtner et al., 2020), health disparities (Krahn et al., 2015), and employment (Rothstein, 2015). Even more illustrative of this tenet is the significant difference in the use of exclusionary discipline practices across racial groups as well as between students with and without dis/abilities (Losen et al., 2015). Thus, when applying a DisCrit perspective to school discipline with Black students who have dis/abilities, educators should examine their own views of race and dis/ability and how those views inform their decisions and actions.

For example, if they hold biases against Black people and or people with dis/abilities, then they make decisions that tend to exclude or marginalize Black students with disabilities in the school environment. In this way, their beliefs about race and ability have real-world consequences for students who are members of these groups. The degree to which educators can recognize their biases allows them to hold their biases at bay so that they do not adversely impact the lived experiences of minoritized students.

Tenet 4: "DisCrit privileges voices of marginalized populations, traditionally not acknowledged within research." (Annamma et al., 2013, p. 11)

A key principle of CRT is counter-storytelling (Bell, 1992). Counter-storytelling is premised on the view that our collective history and experiences are told from a White, more specifically White supremist, perspective. Consequently, racially minoritized groups are positioned as inferior, their achievements and contributions to progress are erased or minimized, and their unique views and experiences are silenced (Bell, 1992). Counter-storytelling aims to disrupt this traditional narrative and elevate the voices and perspectives of those who have been marginalized to provide a more comprehensive, accurate view of the world. From a DisCrit perspective, educators must speak to, listen to, and include the voices and perspectives of Black and Native American students with dis/abilities in order to better serve them. Patrice Leverett offers a counternarrative of how African American males with disabilities view classroom management and behavioral practices (see Chapter 3). Heather Hoescht and Donald Chee, in Chapter 10, describe the ways in which Navajo, or Diné, culture contrast with the authoritarian structure of school discipline in schools and the perspectives of student advocates. Counter-storytelling applies to educators as well. In Chapter 5, Angelina Nortey shares Black women teachers' counternarrative about the intentional ways they create classroom environments that honor and validate their students' multiple identities.

Educators should take steps to ensure the perspective of the student is included whenever there is the possibility of taking disciplinary action. The goal is not to get a student's perspective just for the sake of doing it; rather, the goal is to understand how the student experienced the incident, which may change the action. For example, a Black student may exhibit more disruptive behavior because they are one of a few Black students in the classroom and notice difference in their treatment. One would expect a person to feel upset in that situation, and instead of punishment, the action would be to build more community and fair treatment. As another example, a Black student may be able to explain how White students in the same classroom engage in similar behavior but with no response from the teacher. Again, this would be an opportunity to address that difference in treatment rather than using discipline.

Tenet 5: "DisCrit requires activism and supports all forms of resistance." (Annamma et al., 2013, p. 11)

DisCrit ultimately supports "unqualified belonging and full inclusion in schools and society" (Connor et al., 2016, p. 23), and this necessitates dismantling the current system that segregates individuals based on their identity. To do this, DisCrit embraces all forms of activism, including pedagogical, theoretical, and scholarly. If educators only observe the discipline disparities for Black students with dis/abilities, in many ways, they become complicit. DisCrit scholars challenge us to not only recognize injustice, but to take steps to remedy it. An act of resistance can be as basic as pointing out the disparities in discipline data to your team. It can go further to conduct a review of discipline policy and practices to identify where there is subjective use that is leading to disparities. One can go even further to identify patterns in how Black students with dis/abilities are receiving lower quality supports and services. All of these steps are acts of resistance and activism that can interrupt systems of oppression. The best indicator of whether a system of oppression is working is *to do nothing.* If we do nothing, then the cycle continues, uninterrupted.

IMPLICATIONS FOR FUTURE DIRECTIONS

Decades of research indicates that Black students with dis/abilities are excluded from school through school discipline practices (see Chapter 1). The evidence also suggests that this high rate of exclusion is not by chance. When presented with this reality, many educators become defensive and claim they would never push students out of school. Most of the time, we believe this is true. Most educators are working tirelessly in schools to help students achieve and would never intentionally harm students. However, the expressed beliefs and intent of educators are not always the primary drivers of their decisions and actions. From research on implicit bias, we know that educators can hold explicit egalitarian beliefs but still hold implicit biases that influence their decisions (see Kirwin Institute for the Study of Race and Ethinicity, 2017; McIntosh et al., 2014). We also know that many of the decisions educators make are well intended (e.g., "We need to place this student in special education so they can get help"). However, having good intentions does not mean you cannot do harm; we have to consider the impact of the decision.

Dis/ability CRT offers educators a framework to not only understand how members of minoritized groups are marginalized, but this framework also provides tools to reduce marginalization and create more equitable, just discipline policies and procedures. Foremost, DisCrit guides us to recognize how racism and ableism situates Black and Native American students with dis/abilities as the problem so that we can reject that notion and situate the problem outside of the student and in the environment. DisCrit requires us to identify the increased risk of students with multiple minoritized identities to experience greater levels and more forms of unfair treatment so that we can disrupt this pattern of marginalization. DisCrit helps us to recognize that our beliefs have real-world impacts on the students we serve, so we must become aware of these beliefs to ensure they do not lead us to further marginalize students. Finally, DisCrit challenges us to listen to Black and Native American students so that we can understand their experience and perspective and take action to create more equitable treatment and systems of support. In sum, DisCrit calls us to become educators who are learners and can disrupt traditional theories, policies, and practices in order to center the experiences and voices of those who are most vulnerable, our students.

RESEARCH AND KNOWLEDGE THROUGH MULTIPLE EPISTEMOLOGIES, METHODS, AND VOICES

CHAPTER 3

Let the Students Speak

African American Males With Disabilities' Perspectives of Behavior Intervention Acceptability in Schools and the Implications for Cultural Validity

Patrice M. Leverett

One in six African American students was suspended from 2009 to 2010 (Adams et al., 2012). Compared to the suspension rate of 1 in 20 for their White counterparts, there is an evident racial gap in discipline outcomes. In addition to these racial discipline disparities, students of color are also overrepresented in special education due to emotional and behavioral disorders (ED/BD), learning disabilities, and mild intellectual disabilities, which are based on subjective guidelines or professional judgment (Annamma et al., 2013; Children's Defense Fund, 1975; Skiba et al., 2008). The overrepresentation of African American students in the ED category may also contribute to the disproportionate discipline of these students. Based on a U.S. Government Accountability Office report, students with disabilities are more likely to be suspended than their peers without disabilities (Norwicki, 2018). Students with disabilities make up 11.7% of the K–12 population but comprise 25% of suspensions rates and 30% of students referred to police. African American students with disabilities experience high rates of being disproportionately punished, comprising 19% of students with disabilities but 36% of suspensions. These gaps in suspension translate directly to persistent gaps in the loss of educational opportunities across the United States. As of the 2015–2016 school year, the five states with the most significant gaps in loss of instruction were the following: Nevada, Nebraska, Ohio, Missouri, and Tennessee, with gaps in days lost ranging from 153 days to 103 days; these gaps appear to be widening across states (Losen, 2018).

Not only do we see these discipline disparities among students with disabilities who have intersected identities as racial minorities in school systems across the country, but they are equally paralleled in the juvenile justice system. Wiggin (2016) highlights the disproportionate number of children in the juvenile justice system who are African American and/or in special education. African American youth aged 10 to 17 years comprise 31% of all juvenile arrests, 40% of detentions, 34% of adjudications, and 45% of cases transferred to adult criminal courts. The majority of children in the juvenile justice system, estimated at 70%, have disabilities under the Individuals With Disabilities Education Act (IDEA, 2016) with most having specific learning disabilities or emotional disturbances. These alarming statistics show that systems of oppression operate through ableism and racism across school and juvenile justice settings, with ableism supporting the argument for racism and vice versa (Annamma et al., 2013).

HYPOTHESES OF DISPROPORTIONALITY

Many hypotheses have been suggested to explain the gap in behavioral outcomes, including low socioeconomic status (SES), poor parenting skills, and living in high crime environments, which are all explanations tied to a "deficit perspective" about students, families, and the communities in which they reside (Fenning & Jenkins, 2018; Trent et al., 1998). Research indicates that these factors do not explain the disparities seen in school discipline outcomes. In a study conducted by Kincaid and Sullivan (2017), parents' income and prestige were unrelated to special education identification, though parent educational attainment was related to a reduction in identification. SES alone does not account for the disproportionate rates in Black and White students and cannot be used as a proxy for the gaps in discipline referrals (Skiba et al., 2011).

Additional explanations for disproportionality in discipline referrals include a cultural mismatch between Black students, educational institutions, and teachers, who are predominantly White women (Stephens, Fryberg et al., 2012; Stephens, Townsend et al., 2012; Villegas, 1988). This mismatch perpetuates the status quo by reinforcing White supremist cultural norms as more valuable and ultimately maintaining the power differentials within a society (Ogbu, 1985, 1987). The systematic racist framing of Black males as inferior and aggressive "brutal bucks" and Black girls as sexualized property is considered within the structure of punishment and policing of Black bodies in and outside of schools (Doane & Bonilla-Silva, 2003; Koonce, 2012; Lewis & Diamond, 2015; Morris, 2016; Shedd, 2015; Smedley & Smedley, 2005). The stereotypes are rooted in the capitalist desire to use African people as commerce throughout the 300 years of enslavement and were used to justify differential treatment from the civil rights movement to the murders of persons such as George Floyd and Breonna Taylor. This history is embedded in the racialized language used today, impacting all aspects of society, including schools (Neville et al., 2005; Smedley & Smedley, 2005). Therefore, it is not surprising to see statistics showing that African American students with disabilities are pushed out of school through exclusionary discipline practices. By looking at structural systems of oppression, including ableism and racism, schools can begin to center solutions that are more likely to mitigate longstanding systematic bias and inequities in school discipline rather than continuing to "blame" students for misbehavior (Annamma et al., 2013; Connor et al., 2016).

DISCRIT

DisCrit, a unification of CRT and disability studies, provides a space to explore the intersection of racism and ableism integrated into education in a way that normalizes them and results in the perpetuation of them in the educational process (Annamma et al., 2016). Further, the practices of segregating students based on the intersection of minoritized status and ability have longstanding roots in the American special education process for male and female children alike (Annamma et al., 2020). To actively combat these undercurrents of racism and ableism, we must examine existing practices, particularly those related to the control of the Black body (Carter et al., 2017). Newell and Healy in Chapter 2 provide a detailed overview of DisCrit and CRT and how these theoretical frameworks apply to discipline disparities.

POSITIVE BEHAVIOR INTERVENTIONS AND SUPPORTS AS A REMEDY

One approach to address discipline in school settings is positive behavior interventions and supports (PBIS). While PBIS is commonly utilized to address school-based behavior, the research is on its effectiveness to mitigate racial disparities in school discipline outcomes. PBIS is an intervention framework proposed to support prosocial behavior and reduce problematic behavior, such as aggression. By examining student interaction with the PBIS framework, we can identify and address issues at the intersection of race and ability. Schools have also developed other interventions with similar goals to PBIS, particularly those developed to address overall high rates of behavior referrals. Second Step is an example of one such intervention that is centered on teaching social skills (Frey et al., 2000). Further work to explore the impact of these interventions across the intervention of race and disability status is warranted.

Schoolwide positive behavior support (SW-PBS) is a three-tiered model that seeks to address student needs proactively and at critical stages of behavior response (Dunlap et al., 2009). PBIS is housed in a multi-tiered systems of support (MTSS) model, which aims to blend behavioral, socioemotional, and academic support. Despite the growing use of this framework in many school districts, there is a dearth of research demonstrating that PBIS effectively closes behavior gaps with historically minoritized students. Researchers suggest that the PBIS model is a promising start to addressing behavior referrals and suspension rates but needs to be embedded in a setting that embraces a culturally responsive way of life (Hershfeldt et al., 2009) and one centered on mitigating systems of oppression through an examination of educator biases (McIntosh et al., 2014).

Studies that examine the impact of PBIS across racial and diversity lines are also slim. In existing studies, it appears that while PBIS may reduce the gap in discipline outcomes in some cases, the disparate impact based on race remains (Baule & Superior, 2020; Vincent et al., 2009). Recommendations to integrate culturally responsive practice into PBIS exist, highlighting the importance of cultural identity formation in promoting school success (Bal, 2018; Vincent et al., 2011). More recently, McIntosh et al. (2014) have proposed working with teachers to identify vulnerable decision points in which implicit bias may be present when making disciplinary decisions.

Further, the hypothesized impact of PBIS as a method of decreasing discipline disproportionality presupposes that disparities in school discipline reside in the child rather than the system. By proposing interventions targeted at changing student behavior, schools, teachers, and administrators are absolved from considering the role of schools as institutions of indoctrination, which serves to promote, perpetuate, and protect the interests of the oppressive dominant majority group culture (Annamma et al., 2014). Disproportionality is inherently a byproduct of the White supremacist structures of oppression present in all facets of American and Western society. The often-invisible influence of assumptions, stereotypes, and biases replicate historical inequalities, becoming self-fulfilling prophecies.

The intersection of race and ability adds additional complexities to the educational landscape, which comes to the surface as we examine the gaps in behavioral outcomes for students of color, particularly African American males. Historically, special education has been associated with deviance or stigma, which has led to differential and unjust treatment (Artiles, 1998; Minnow, 1990). The intersection of being Black, which is stigmatized *and* labeled with a disability, can lead to more stigma or perceived deviance than just being ascribed as Black *or* just being labeled with a disability (Cole, 2009). For this reason, Dunhamn et al. (2015), at the National Black Disability Coalition, called for the development and implementation of Black disabilities study pedagogy (BDSP). The focus of this work is to

> help students understand how racism and ableism collude in a variety of ways in contemporary society, not only in the lives of Black disabled people, but also Black people collectively as discourses of disability continue to be used as means to control and do harm to racialized populations. (p. 7)

BDSP considers the social and historical context of Black people with disabilities in the United States and across the African diaspora. This work is fluid to meet the variety of voices housed within the intersection of Blackness and ability that were excluded from the voices leading the charge for disability rights or in the formation of existing disability studies frameworks. Among its recommendations, the coalition calls for the future of BDSP to be led by Black students with disabilities. Following this model, it is imperative to include these students' voices in developing intervention plans, programs, frameworks, and theory development. DisCrit offers a theoretical framework for interrogating racist and ableist structures that have plagued education since its inception (Connor et al., 2016).

There are evident differences in the types of offenses that students of color are disciplined for compared to their peers (Skiba et al., 2011). In a closer examination of discipline data of schools participating in the PBIS data collection system, students of color were found to receive more discipline referrals and suspensions for minor subjective offenses prone to implicit bias (Skiba et. al., 2011). These include low-intensity defiance, low-intensity disruption, inappropriate language, disrespect, and inappropriate physical contact.

Several researchers have proposals for how to close gaps in student outcomes. For example, Liberman (1998) suggests using the environment as an integrated learning context to close the gaps in educational achievement. Ladson-Billings (2009) attributes positive student outcomes of students of color to culturally competent teachers attuned to their students. Cook et al. (2018) and Legette (2020) point to training teachers to engage with students in prosocial ways. Limited research addresses African American male students' perspectives across abilities in behavior practices and policies. To that end, the study presented in this chapter seeks out a point of view—the voice of students themselves—most impacted by exclusionary discipline practices, which is often unheard in the development, implementation, or assessment of intervention effectiveness to increase the cultural responsiveness of existing practices.

TREATMENT ACCEPTABILITY

Treatment acceptability is the perceived appropriateness, fairness, reasonableness, and intrusiveness of intervention, as determined by the client or other stakeholders, such as parents or teachers (Kazdin, 1980). Typically, treatment acceptability studies are done with adults (Elliott et al., 1984). Seeking participants' perspectives on adopting a particular treatment or intervention protocol increases the likelihood of implementation and buy-in. By assessing treatment acceptability, school psychologists can ensure that interventions are culturally appropriate and acceptable for the specific target populations, ultimately reducing disparities (Cooper et al., 2002). The present study identifies themes related to students' perception and acceptability of school positive behavior support and develops a theory of Black males' experience under this framework, which is understudied. Despite a wealth of research on interventions, very few studies consider the student perspective in the design, selection, or implementation of interventions for those most directly impacted by this work, specifically African American males. As a result, the primary question posed in this study is as follows: Do the existing behavior practices adequately address the needs of African American male students with disabilities from the students' own perspective?

CULTURAL VALIDITY

Bal et al. (2012) propose that positive behavior support, while addressing the increase in behavior referrals, must be implemented in a culturally responsive way if it is going to be used to close the gaps in discipline outcomes for students viewed as having disabilities and/or identifying as African American. One way to address this gap is to address issues of cultural validity in the design of interventions and supports with African American students. Quintana et al. (2001) posit that there are also cultural validity and internal, external, construct, hypothesis, and statistical conclusion validity. Leong and Brown (1995) introduce cultural validity as focused on the construct, concurrent, and predictive validity of theories and models across cultures. Quintana et al. (2001) expanded on Leong and Brown's definition of cultural validity. They define it as

> the authentic representation of the cultural nature of the research in terms of how constructs are operationalized, participants are recruited, hypotheses are formulated, study procedures are adapted, responses are analyzed, and results are interpreted for a particular cultural group as well as the usefulness of the research for its instructional utility in educating readers about the cultural group being investigated, its practical utility in yielding practice as well as theoretical implications about the cultural group, and its service utility in "giving back" to the community in important ways. (p. 617)

By including cultural validity in school psychology research, interventions may be more effective for a broader range of students. Similarly, as we field test interventions, it is valuable to get feedback from our participants that interventions match the development stage's intent.

RESEARCH FRAMEWORK

Students, like all humans, are complex. Including students' voices in the development of theory, research, and interventions maintains the human aspect of the work we do as scientists and practitioners. With this in mind, I use constructivist grounded theory to examine the African American public middle school male experience with discipline practices in schools and identify parallels and gaps between existing literature on student perceptions (Charmaz, 2014).

METHOD

Qualitative methods allow us to study processes and phenomena in a natural setting (Lincoln, 1995). In this study, a qualitative methodology was selected to capture the contextual nuances of participants' experiences. The interview protocol was semi-structured and open-ended. Interviews lasted approximately 45 minutes and were conducted one-on-one by an African American female researcher. Interviews focused on students' experiences in public school settings related to rules, routines, and expectations. Students reflected on their experiences around classroom behavior, their peers' observed treatment, the interventions or strategies implemented, and their willingness to engage in those activities. The researcher was the primary coder, with three secondary coders for validity and reliability. Line-by-line coding is a heuristic device used to engage with the text to define experiences and implicit meanings or actions to identify emergent themes (Gibbs, 2018). In the first round of coding, there were 58 in vivo codes (i.e., "favoritism, favoritism"). The codes were grouped into what made the most logical sense to understand students' perception of behavioral interventions and identify factors that influence PBIS (treatment) acceptability.

Based on the categories that emerged, integrative memos were created to integrate the subcategories (Sarker et al., 2001). Subcategories were organized into two main categories: (1) barriers to acceptance of those protocols and (2) facilitators for compliance with school protocols. Themes were the result of grouping in vivo codes into eight topics based on similarity. Five themes pertained to barriers to engaging in school behavior practices: changing rules, letting kids off easily, racism, favoritism, and doesn't help me learn. The three themes that emerged as facilitators were trust in staff, connection to cultural identity, and caring.

Additionally, through member checking, the researchers shared the findings with the students to determine if they agreed that the summary matched their perspectives and experience and helped ensure trustworthiness (Korstjens & Moser, 2018).

Through line-by-line coding, memo-ing, and then grouping the data into themes, the researchers developed a theoretical understanding of students' experiences in teaching relationships and the impact of those experiences on educational outcomes (Charmaz, 2014). New concepts from interviews were continuously compared to the burgeoning theory during data collection, adapting to the new information and solidifying paradigms. During data analysis, categories are developed as axioms of the theory. Axioms emerge from a series of coding strategies (Strauss & Corbin, 1990). For the clarification of themes, students were interviewed a second or third time.

Trustworthiness

To establish trustworthiness, the researcher kept thorough memos of field observations that describe the decisions made throughout the study and how the data guided those decisions (Korstjens & Moser, 2018). The primary researcher sought to maintain *authenticity* to the students' experience, maintaining original language, dialect, and grammatical accuracy. Additionally, quotes were selected to reflect the range of perspectives offered by students (Polit & Beck, 2014). *Credibility* was established through prolonged engagement with participants via multiple sessions over a year, peer debriefing, and member checking by sharing the data in a small group format (Connelly, 2016).

Measures

The researcher developed the interview protocol to explore students' understanding of existing school behavior expectations and practices. The researcher received feedback on the questionnaire from school psychologist researchers and school-based personnel. Revisions were made to align with language similar to school settings. The students were asked open-ended questions about their day-to-day experience (e.g., "What is your classroom like?" and "What are the rules in your classrooms?"). Also, they shared information about issues they had in school (e.g., "Are there teachers you do not listen to in school? Why?" and "Tell me about a time when a friend had a problem with a teacher."). The questions covered specific classes, teachers, and schoolwide norms. Additionally, students were asked directly about their knowledge of PBS practices in their school environment.

Participants

The participants consisted of 12 African American male middle school students in the original study. Sampling was done based on convenience. Students were recruited in after-school and community center locations, with the assistance of the site staff. Then students who returned the parental consent were included in the study. The researcher met with parents and students during an information session to outline student participants' roles.

During the study, the students could disclose if they were receiving special education services either in separate classroom settings or in the general setting; of the 12 students, five identified as receiving special education services. One student identified that his special education services were through the gifted and talented program. All students in the sample were between the ages of 10 and 14. The students were in public education schools in urban environments. This age group was selected due to the disproportionate number of referrals for "disrespect" in middle school in comparison to elementary and high school settings (Kaufman et al., 2010; Theriot & Dupper, 2010). The rates of Black students who received discipline referrals in this age group was also at a consistent high rate in comparison to their peers. The intersection of these voices is underrepresented in the existing literature.

RESULTS

The results of this study are organized into two sections: (1) barriers and (2) facilitators that students experienced regarding school disciplinary practices in settings utilizing PBIS. Barriers for the students included themes such as changing rules and favoritism, while themes for facilitators included connection to cultural identity and teacher trust.

The study's initial results indicate that the students were aware that there are rules and consequences related to behavior in their schools. However, the Black students with individualized education plans (IEPs) in this study did not believe that the consequences they received matched the treatment others experienced or that the response to behavior was consistent between teachers or environments. The students found these inconsistencies to be frustrating and ultimately a barrier to behavioral success. Facilitators, such as having meaningful relationships with school staff, increased students' reports of belonging.

Barriers

Changing Rules

> It kind of depends on the teacher's patience, I guess. Like, if they're—you're, like, the last class and a whole bunch of people have been bugging the teacher, probably the first thing you do is get a detention, 'cause she—he or she—is dealing with enough of that today and just start getting rid of people. Like, if they're goofing off or just, like, not being appropriate, then just send them out. I've already had too much of that today. —Ben

According to Ben, whether a student gets the PBIS model or outright punishment is dependent entirely on the mood of the teacher and the time of day. Overall, the boys in this study felt that teachers' abilities to maintain the classroom environment were variable. While this student did not specify if the students with disabilities received differential treatment, he expressed that students with a higher level of activity and perceived poorer behavior were treated preferentially in some circumstances. Additionally, he later discussed how the other Black males in his class were often excluded. What Ben noticed was consistent across students and aligns with the work of Vavrus and Cole (2002) in which students of color were more likely to be removed from classrooms when overall classroom management was lacking. Students' perception of the school services and practices were informed by the level of consistency students experienced within the learning environment.

Letting Kids Off Easily

Letting kids off too easily was seen by students as the teacher lacking control in the room. A teacher's difficulty keeping a class on track in the lessons was a major deterrent to engagement and rule adherence. Students perceived that some teachers did not know how to keep students on task because they ignore behavior instead of addressing it head-on. According to students, this lack of classroom management could be a barrier to the implementation of interventions.

George explains:

> It's just, like, sometimes, some kids—she'll let you off too easily sometimes. That just makes me real mad, 'cause, like, the one kid, like, in 6th grade—the most irritating kid is in my chorus class, and he gets let off so easily.

For other students, this lax management style was seen as not taking students seriously. According to Harris:

> Some teachers like to play around a lot that I know. So, some teachers, they like to play a little too much. I just don't trust them that much like I do my other teachers that take stuff more seriously.

This aligns with Ladson-Billings's (1994) discussion of the "warm demander." Students in her study preferred teachers who were "mean" to encourage them to behave and work harder, as they found that these behaviors in combination with a surrogate mindset was an indication of care.

Racism

> Some teachers are not like you know; some teachers are like the same to all the kids. Like they're different to different kids of a different race.
> —Ian

The boys in this study were aware that race might impact their treatment in the classroom, particularly in relation to their treatment regarding behavior infractions and academics. Leo provides this example of a time when he was treated differently than a White peer:

> It's, like, when one of the White kids, once they got a thing wrong, he's like, "Oh, that's okay. Just try harder next time." Then, once he went to me and he saw I got it wrong, he was like, "I'm gonna give you a referral. You never do your work," and I'm like, "I do my work." Then he was like, "You got it wrong; you're getting a zero for this assignment." And I'm like, "because I got one wrong? That's like 99%." Then he was like, "Well, we don't accept 99%." I'm like, "If you don't accept 99%, then how come that kid over there got one wrong and you said, 'Okay, it's fine?'"

Leo felt the teacher held views of race that were negatively affecting the teacher's views about his work, his motivation, and his follow-through in comparison to his White peer. He felt this treatment was unfair, and he questioned the teacher about the difference. While he did not mention race to the teacher, it is clear in his recalling of the events that Leo believed race was an underlying factor in this treatment. As a result, the student perceived that his connection to a particular racial group might negatively impact his ability to engage with work in that classroom environment. This racism cut across the ways in which students were disciplined, the expectations of the boys' abilities and behavior, and the ways their disabilities were addressed, or in some cases not attended to, in learning environments.

Favoritism

I never be a teacher favorite, and I don't care. —James

James then proceeded to talk about the injustices of favoritism for approximately 10 minutes, "They always believe the smartest kid, and then don't believe the other kid, like, 'no lying.' Stop favoritism," he said. Students identified ways in which they were overlooked, ostracized, or singled out in favor of others. The students identified the reasons for this as either because of another student being viewed as good, younger, or smarter. Students felt that teachers had clear preferences of students, making the other students who are not favorites less likely to accept or engage in the interventions presented by staff.

Doesn't Help Me Learn

In addition to the lack of structure or support in their classroom environment to facilitate the successful implementation or fidelity of these interventions, students felt that many times the barriers to compliance were a lack of support or engagement between the students and teachers. Students pointed to academics as a reason they chose to engage in the rules or systems of the classroom; it is also the reason they offered for defection from school behavioral expectations.

Students identified a need for structured academic support to ensure adherence to school policies, practices, and interventions:

Like the science teacher. I can't get the work. I kept asking her for help, and she was like "We went over this," but we really didn't. I just like put my head down cause I was frustrated. So, I put my head down, and she was like "Get out my class." —Adam

Students were able to clearly articulate the ways that their needs were not being addressed and could connect that to their getting in trouble in school. James expressed his frustration over lack of academic support, "Like, he just hands out a packet, and he expects that you get all of that done. I hate teachers. Well, I don't hate them, but I just hate what they [do], but, yeah."

By recognizing these behaviors, we can begin to train teachers and school staff to first acknowledge and second address these behaviors. The implications of these student perspectives is that the teachers assumed that the students were incapable or unworthy of educational support. These assumptions for these students could be indicative of implicit or explicit bias toward these students at the intersection of ability and racial marginalization. Through the exploration of these concepts in training we might see an increase in meaningful engagement for these learners.

Facilitators

Students also offered ways for teachers to increase their prosocial interactions in schools. The following themes highlight strategies or factors that facilitate acceptance of the behavioral interventions and practices.

Trust in Staff

> I trust the guidance counselor. He's a good guy to talk to. I know he'll listen, and I know he won't, like, blow me off, like whatever. I know he'll listen and probably take action if there's something really wrong going on. —Ben

Many of the students in this study reported access to one or more trusted adults in their school environment. These trusted adults helped them establish a safe learning environment or were able to help them access the strategies needed for school success. The trustworthy adults included classroom teachers, school psychologists, social workers, principals, behavior support specialists, principals, janitors, and security guards.

Connection to Cultural Identity

Students identified several "nice" teachers with positive qualities, including general skills such as keeping a calm voice or permitting breaks. Several students also identified a more culturally specific definition of a nice teacher that included recognizing and uplifting the students based on race or cultural connections. When asked what teachers could do to support students in adhering to school practices, students identified that conversations with staff about their expectations, in conjunction with a message of cultural esteem, were effective in making a change. For the sake of this paper, cultural esteem is defined as the capacity to connect positively in one's cultural identity to the point of using cultural identity as a point of personal motivation or uplift based on Phinney's (1991) work on ethnic minority development and self-esteem. Eric provided this example:

> They just pretty much explain to you how 'cause we have a lot of Black teachers (lowers voice), so they're just like you just can't keep on doing

this kind of makes us look a type of way. . . . You have to represent us. Because yeah, because you guys are our future, and we don't want to be known for bringing a bunch of people that don't know how to handle theirselves.

Eric recognized that the teachers were addressing a sense of communal hope in the future generation and the desire to facilitate cultural esteem through the direct vocalization of historical perspective and a familial expectation of the student. The shared lineage of this student to the teacher permitted the acknowledgment of higher expectations based on the students' impact on a broader cultural context.

Caring

But one time she pulled me to the side, she told me, she's like, "The other students, I don't . . ."—it's the way she said it—she said, "I don't really care about them, but I want you to pass. I want you to meet your purpose." Nice to hear that. —King

Cultural complexity becomes most evident in the ways individuals show and receive care. The young men in this study expressed the ways in which they felt cared for or understood by their school environment. It is a belief in this care system that increased the likelihood of engagement with the behavior plan in place in the school.

King offers this example of care:

Like, my school—it tries to bring you up, like, if you're down or something. Like, my teacher, he'll like take you to, like, a therapist and you sit down, and you have to tell her why you acting how you acting, and you try to make it better, and call your mom and stuff.

By taking the time to connect him with appropriate resources she was "bringing him up," or making him feel better.

Adam offers this insight as to why his reading intervention teacher is his favorite:

Like the teacher makes me feel comfortable and the class. She can relate to what we are doing. . . . She will like take us out the room . . . talk to us. Um tell us like what we need to work on and like what's been going on.

By the teacher taking individual time with the student, he felt cared for or considered. Making genuine connections with students and taking time to hear them out or to assist them when they need additional support highlights the connection between students' desire to do well in the school environment and the teacher's belief that the student is capable and worthy of support.

Students identified that the likelihood of their following directions is directly linked with the connection to or identification with the staff member delivering the intervention. They need to feel a personal connection, which was facilitated by the interventionist sharing information about themselves in a way that showed understanding or connection.

DISCUSSION

This chapter examines the experience of youth who sit at the intersection of race, disability, and gender as it pertains to school behavior and discipline. This thematic analysis speaks to the connection, or in some cases, disconnect from school experienced by African American students. These perspectives impact the behavior of and consequences experienced by these young boys. It is essential to humanize their experience in the research by including their voices and perspectives, to address the gaps in discipline disproportionality for African American males, particularly students in special education. The boys identify facilitators of their understanding and engagement with behavior practices in their school: a trusting relationship with staff, a connection to their home or cultural identity in the school environment, and feeling cared for by school staff. Additionally, the boys highlight barriers hindering their experiences around discipline: changes in rules, letting kids off too easily, racism, favoritism toward their peers, and not aiding students in academic need.

The concepts of care and support are readily discussed in the literature (Green, 2012; Rogers & Webb, 1991; Velasquez et al., 2013). Yet, there is limited research about how these map onto students' experiences in special education programs, particularly when it comes to students with multiple minoritized identities. Care is often discussed as a tool to develop positive relationships with students. However, that care may look like being identified for a positive reason, like King, who was pulled aside and told he mattered, or making time to connect students to the right person to talk. These are ways that teachers can actively close the gap in students' negative experiences and ultimately impact school behavior. On the other hand, teachers who believe care means being lenient may be creating a space that feels unsafe or too chaotic for children to learn, and these spaces foster further disconnect from expected behavioral norms. Well-run classrooms are essential to providing equitable experiences for learners. Promising interventions exist that focus on the development of positive student–teacher relationships, such as GREET–STOP–PROMPT (GSP), transformative social and emotional learning for teachers, and the establish–maintain–restore model (E-M-R) (Cook, Coco et al., 2018; Cook, Duong et al., 2018; Legette et al., 2020). Additionally, restorative justice practices have the potential to shift from punishment to healing if done in a way that honors the voices of the students as well as the staff involved in the process.

Overall, the students expressed the need to be in an environment that elicits feelings of care and connectedness. Feelings of care can then foster a sense of trust that is essential to the student's acceptance of the school's needs and supports. Finally, the students needed to be grounded in a sense of cultural esteem to counter their experiences of racism in the school environment. The boys in this study were aware of and responded to racial bias in their daily experiences. As a result, addressing race, racism, and its potential impacts on the school process and experience was essential. In their germinal article, "Toward a Critical Race Theory of Education," Gloria Ladson-Billings and Tate (1995) argued that race is not only salient but also under-theorized in the field of education. Moreover, they suggested racism is a persistent and permanent aspect of education and society at large. In the face of these experiences, the need for validation, particularly around academics, is particularly important. The students suggested that the lack of diversity in school staffing may impact their engagement around discipline, the perceptions of the rules, and the intention behind actions.

Research demonstrates a widening gap in the removal of African American males with disabilities from the classroom, especially in comparison to their White, abled peers. The research suggests these gaps continue despite the increased use of evidence-based behavioral interventions. The literature is relatively silent about the experience of African American males in special education and their experiences with school-based discipline practices and interventions. By including students' voices, this chapter begins to close the gap in perspectives that the field of behavioral intervention is missing and moves toward a more culturally responsive and more culturally valid way of thinking about existing interventions.

FUTURE IMPLICATIONS

Research

There are several areas that this study can expand and develop. This study can serve as a pilot for increasing student voice in academic research around discipline and create the groundwork for future research. This research could lead to developing a culturally sensitive treatment acceptability protocol to assess a student's willingness to engage in the behavior systems and to inform team planning. The finding of this study also lays the groundwork for a second study in developing a culturally grounded and sensitive treatment acceptability protocol to assess a student's willingness to engage in school behavior systems and to inform treatment planning based on what they outline as important to having a positive experience with behavior management. The inclusion of student voice in the selection of behavior interventions as a practice in the field increases students' self-advocacy skills and potentially student buy-in. As such, the inclusion of treatment acceptability measures or interviews in practice has promising possibilities for the reduction of suspension and expulsion.

An expansion of this study to diversify the sample of African American males would be beneficial to determine if a theory of Black male experience can be formalized and how Black students with disabilities experience these interactions in a larger context. While students in this sample did not talk about their experience in terms of masculine identity, additional data about student identity pertaining to gender will increase understanding about the intersection of masculinity and Blackness for adolescents in the school environment. Finally, studies should be developed to examine the experiences of African American females in special education, expanding on the work of Morris (2016) and Blake et al. (2011), who identified that Black girls have a higher rate of discipline referrals in comparison to their White peers.

Practice

In terms of school practice, relationship building is an essential component of the work we do in schools. As practitioners, we have to engage in authentic relationships with the students we serve. This practice, for psychologists in particular, is against the culturally White perspective of distance presented in training. When taken out of context, this recommendation could sound like a call to befriend students, which is not promoted as helpful by students. Students seek clear, consistent communication from caring yet authoritative adults.

Schools must provide explicit training to their staff members in classroom management. Milner et al. (2018) discuss the need for co-constructed culturally responsive and equitable teaching strategies that can be used to reimagine school discipline. Strategies such as positive framing, self-reflective practices, and building classroom community are just a few ways we can move from punitive environments to educational spaces where students who are typically sidelined can feel more connected and included in their classroom environment. Training in equity-forward classroom management techniques for all educators regardless of years of experience could increase responsiveness to the gaps in discipline outcomes. It may be possible for teachers to conduct training for their peers, demonstrating strategies that have been effective in supporting learners in their classroom in order to increase parity across the school building. Research demonstrates that culturally competent teaching strategies can be learned when supported by training and adequate support (Brantlinger & Danforth, 2013).

Policy

The chapter offers insights into changes needed to address policy at a local and federal level. Existing educational policies do not specify ways to collect disaggregated data about the students within the district. What is more, it is rare that the data districts do collect account for the intersection of identities (i.e., race, disability, and gender). Without these data, it becomes very difficult to track the needs of these students over time. Further, the data needs to be shared in a transparent way with schools and community members to increase the accountability of governing bodies. Additionally, state educational systems can incentivize professional development pertaining to antiracism and culturally relevant pedagogy by linking it to criteria for promotion and raises. Lastly, there is an opportunity for federal and state officials to call for educational equity standards tied to state and federal funding to address gaps found at pivotal points in student outcomes such as discipline and educational access. These policies can be informed by student voice. Examples of student-led policy work include the Rethinking Safety campaign in Illinois, where youth from Voices of Youth in Chicago Education (VOYCE) (n.d.) developed recommendations for the elimination of the school-to-prison pipeline. Such models can serve as a way forward to eradicate the disparate outcomes of students of color who have disabilities in discipline practices as well as across educational factors.

CONCLUSION

Engagement in the practices and interventions in a school environment must be built on a platform of trust and a general belief that these universal systems are, in fact, applicable to all students. When students feel that they are treated differently from peers, they immediately begin to disengage from the intervention as well as from academic experiences. We must examine our own biases and the way they shape our responses to students. This study offers a way of sharing student experiences with staff so that we can continue to work on checking our biases related to race, gender, and ability. Further, the development and use of a treatment acceptability protocol for regular use in intervention selection and utilization will hold us accountable to the students and their experiences.

CHAPTER 4

School Discipline at the Intersection of Race and Ability

Examining the Role of Police in Schools

Amy E. Fisher and Benjamin W. Fisher

In April 2020, Grace, a Black female student with a disability, was expected to participate in online instruction during the spread of COVID-19. Grace was overwhelmed with expectations from home and school and struggled to keep up with her homework. Instead of being provided with support to enable her to meet school expectations, Grace's difficulty in completing her virtual homework during a pandemic resulted in removal from her home and incarceration in a juvenile detention center (Cohen, 2020). This example highlights how the educational and criminal justice system negatively impact students at the intersection of race and ability. Not only did Grace's incarceration put her at greater risk for contracting COVID-19, but it also caused her to lose instruction designed to address her disability. Grace's story exemplifies the inequitable adult responses to student behavior, particularly those driven by ableism and racism, that continue to support the school-to-prison pipeline (Connor et al., 2016).

Grace's story is one of countless examples highlighting the deep connection between schools and the criminal justice system, particularly among students with multiple oppressed, intersecting identities. This connection is exemplified by the presence of police officers within school buildings. Police presence within schools and the disproportionate impact on Black students gained national attention after Minneapolis police officers were caught on tape brutally killing George Floyd, an unarmed Black man. Since then, the Black Lives Matter movement has called for more increased accountability and an end to police brutality, which fueled advocacy from organizations like the Advancement Project to remove police from schools. On one side of the debate, racial justice organizations and some state education organizations are leading the way in working toward completely removing police from schools (Superville, 2020). Conversely, many organizations argue for the need to maintain police in schools. For example, in August of 2020, the National Association of School Psychologists (2020) issued a joint statement with the National Association of Secondary School Principals, the American School Counselor Association, the National Association of School Resource Officers, and the National Parents and Teachers Association recommending that police not be removed from schools but rather that there be more training, accountability, and clarification of roles.

More broadly, the role of police in schools highlights systemic inequities within the education system, especially for Black students who have been historically displaced in alternative school settings by both racism and ableism (Connor et al., 2016). DisCrit helps to explain how the social constructions of race and ability must be understood as interconnected within the school system and tied to larger systems of oppression. Historically, schools were designed to meet the needs of the White supremacy status quo and, therefore, discipline or displace those who do not fall in line with the standards, particularly Black and Brown students and those with additional intersected marginalized identities, such as having a disability. Racism and ableism in the school system continue to show up through policies and procedures that assume students of color have less ability to succeed than their White counterparts (Annamma et al., 2014). Therefore, discipline procedures and alternative placements through special education for Black and Brown students contribute to disparate outcomes and are sustained through structural racism and ableism. Following the framework of DisCrit and the larger national discourse, the presence of police in schools is likely to heighten the surveillance and targeting of marginalized students, especially Black and Brown students with a disability.

Police Presence In Schools

Estimates suggest that 30% of elementary and 58% of secondary schools nationwide have some form of police presence on at least a part-time basis (Musu-Gillette et al., 2018). Many scholars consider police in schools to be part of a broader paradigm shift toward making schools more punitive, following broader trends in criminal justice policy (Kupchik & Monahan, 2006; Simon, 2007). More than just being punitive, however, Hirschfield (2008) argued that this shift criminalizes students—particularly students of color—and socializes them into lives of limited opportunity and loss of freedom through incarceration. School-based police officers represent physical and visible manifestations of the increasingly close ties between education and criminal justice.

Outcomes of Police in Schools

Existing research provides evidence that having police in schools is associated with higher rates of punishment, including exclusionary discipline (Fisher & Hennessy, 2016; Weisburst, 2019) and arrests (Homer & Fisher, 2020; Theriot, 2009). There is evidence of racially disparate effects, although this dynamic remains underexplored in the empirical literature (Homer & Fisher, 2020; Weisburst, 2019). However, to date, research has not examined the extent to which police in schools are related to the increased punishment of students with disabilities (SWD). This is a particularly pertinent issue and gap in the literature given the overall disproportionate exclusionary discipline rates experienced by SWD and the lack of knowledge police report having about SWD (Lawson & Welfare, 2018). Although prior research points to the involvement of school-based police in discipline processes (Curran et al., 2019; Kupchik, 2010; Na & Gottfredson, 2013) and shows that schools with police tend to have higher rates of exclusionary discipline (Fisher & Hennessy, 2016; Weisburst, 2019), less is known about the impact of the association of police presence with punishment of SWD, particularly as it pertains to further exclusion through school-based arrests. The racial disparities in each of these domains suggest that the intersection of race and ability may be a particularly relevant area of focus given the theoretical frame of DisCrit (Annamma et al., 2016), yet such intersections need further empirical exploration. Therefore, the purpose of this chapter is to link the presence of police in schools to the arrest rates of students with disabilities, with a particular focus on any differences found among specific racial/ethnic student subgroups.

Effects of Police in Schools on Student Punishment

The evidence base on the effects of police in schools on student punishment has generally been considered fairly weak due to data limitations and study designs with poorly matched comparison groups (Petrosino et al., 2012). However, some recent studies have used increasingly rigorous methods to help elucidate the impact of police in schools on student punishment. For instance, a meta analysis of the relationship between police presence in schools and secondary schools' rates of exclusionary discipline found that among schools using longitudinal designs police presence was associated with higher discipline rates, yet there were no significant relationships found using cross-sectional designs with comparison groups (Fisher & Hennessy, 2016). Weisburst's (2019) study based in Texas advanced this literature by examining student outcomes associated with schools who received grants to place police in schools. This study found that middle schools who received these grants experienced a 6% increase in discipline rates largely driven by highly subjective low-level offenses. Moreover, the discipline rate among Black students increased at a significantly higher rate compared with White students. Related research based in California used monthly school-level data to examine changes in discipline rates before and after adding police to schools, finding that, consistent with prior research, adding police increased exclusionary school discipline (Gottfredson et al., 2020).

Population of Focus

To date, only limited empirical research has examined the relationship between police in schools and discipline rates of SWD (see Gottfredson et al., 2020). DisCrit theory suggests that this relationship is worth investigating. DisCrit scholars Adams and Erevelles (2016) contend that, politically, special education is not viewed as a "respectable" setting and thus receives little focus at the policy level, thereby creating an environment conducive to segregation and dislocation of Black students. In this vein, the overrepresentation of Black students in "deviant" disability categories like emotional/behavioral disorder (EBD; Losen et al., 2014) allow for hyper-surveillance of Black SWD, including by police. Given the findings from prior research about increased rates of punishment for low-level, interpretable offenses associated with having police in schools (Na & Gottfredson, 2013; Theriot, 2009; Weisburst, 2019), these findings, along with the theoretical frame of DisCrit, predict that SWD are at higher risk for increased punishment under these conditions.

Disparate Impact

Any negative effects of police in schools among SWD are likely to be compounded by race/ethnicity. Per DisCrit theory, the racialized patterns of assignment to special education are indicative of broader biased conceptualizations of Black students as threatening to the status quo (Annamma et al., 2013; Watts & Erevelles, 2004). This is supported by evidence suggesting that both educators and police view Black students as more threatening and in need of heightened surveillance compared with their White peers (Ferguson, 2001; Gilliam et al., 2016; Goff et al., 2014; Watts & Erevelles, 2004). At the intersection of ability and race, Black SWD are likely to be perceived by adults in the school as particularly problematic and, when they behave in ways considered nonnormative, those behaviors are more likely to be met with punishment rather than treatment and developmental understanding (Moody, 2016). Drawing from DisCrit, this is an example of displacing students who do not follow the status quo. The presence of police in schools may compound these effects.

The role of student gender is underexplored in studies of police in schools and more broadly how it intersects with race and ability. Although the high rates of punishment of Black boys have been examined in some depth (Anyon et al., 2014; Bradshaw et al., 2010; Gregory & Weinstein, 2008; Perry & Morris, 2014), recent research has pointed to Black girls as a population that has been unjustifiably ignored (Blake et al., 2011; Crenshaw et al., 2015; Ferguson, 2001; Morris, 2005; Morris, 2016). Moreover, recent research suggests gendered effects of the impact of police in schools for student arrests, with the impact on boys greater than that for girls (Homer & Fisher, 2020).

However, this line of inquiry has not been extended to examine other forms of school-based exclusionary punishment, nor has it examined the particular dynamics around gender and ability or race.

Study Rationale

In light of the disproportionately high rates of punishment of SWD, the concomitant racial disparities, and the continued expansion of police in schools who may lack training in interacting with SWD, the purpose of this chapter is to report findings from a study that investigates whether police presence in schools is associated with greater rates of punishment for SWD. Moreover, this study examines the extent of disparities in punishment by race and gender.

To date, critical education scholarship has not examined how the presence of police within schools influences the dislocation of Black students within special education, nor has it sufficiently explored differences for SWD from other racial and ethnic groups. There is evidence that Black students and SWD are subjected to increased surveillance and discipline practices in schools relative to White peers with and without disabilities (Annamma, 2017; Shedd, 2015). Therefore, we predict that schools with police presence discipline Black and other minoritized SWD at higher rates than schools without police presence. The current study investigates the relationship between police presence and punishment for SWD students among students with varied racial/ethnic identities and by gender. The researcher seeks to answer the following research questions:

1. What is the relationship between police presence in schools and suspension and expulsion rates among SWD?
2. To what extent do these relationships differ among students with various races/ethnicity and by gender?

METHOD

National Data Set

The data used in this study come from the publicly available 2013–2014 Civil Rights Data Collection (CRDC, 2020) by the U.S. Department of Education's Office for Civil Rights. This biennial school-level data collection includes data from all public schools in the United States ($N = 95,507$) on a variety of topics pertaining to students' civil rights, with a particular focus on differences by race/ethnicity, gender, and disability status. CRDC data include discipline, enrollment in advanced courses, bullying and harassment, and a variety of other topics pertinent to questions of equity. Relevant to the current study, the 2013–2014 CRDC has data about the presence of police in schools. Although a newer version of the CRDC is available (i.e., from 2015–2016), a data collection error on the item about police in schools prevents analyses using those data. As such, the 2013–2014 CRDC is currently the only available nationwide census of schools that includes information about police presence. For the purposes of this study, we removed all schools that were juvenile justice facilities, schools that only served preschool students, and schools with missing data on police presence. This yielded a final analytic sample of 92,863 schools. The CRDC (2020) data were supplemented with data from the Common Core of Data (CCD), an annually collected data repository managed by the National Center for Education Statistics (NCES) that includes information on school characteristics, enrollment, and teachers and staff.

Measures

Suspension

The first set of dependent variables were numbers of the various types of suspensions reported for students. A suspension rate for all students in the data per 1,000 students was calculated, so the findings are comparable across schools. We operationalized suspension in four different ways among students with disabilities broken down by racial/ethnic and gender subgroups. Specifically, we calculated rates for subgroups receiving (a) one out-of-school suspension (OSS) in the academic year; (b) two or more OSSs in the academic year; (c) any number of OSSs in the academic year, combining the number of students who received one OSS with those who had received two or more, and (d) at least one in-school suspension (ISS) in the academic year.

Expulsion

The second set of dependent variables pertained to the rate of expulsions and drew from a series of items tabulating the number of students who received different types of expulsions. We also operationalized expulsion in four different ways, again broken out by all combinations of race/ethnicity and gender among students with disabilities. Specifically, we calculated rates for subgroups receiving (a) expulsions with continued services in the academic year; (b) expulsions without continued services in the academic year; (c) expulsions regardless of whether there were continued services, combining the numbers of students expelled with and without continued services; and (d) expulsions under zero-tolerance policies in the academic year. Federal data collection guidelines define a zero-tolerance policy as

> a policy that results in mandatory expulsion of any student who commits one or more specified offenses (e.g., offenses involving guns, or other

weapons, or violence, or similar factors, or combinations of these factors). A policy is considered 'zero tolerance' even if there are some exceptions to the mandatory aspect of the expulsion, such as allowing the chief administering officer of a local educational agency to modify the expulsion on a case-by-case basis. (CRDC, 2020)

Police Presence

The main independent variable, police presence, was measured by a single-item indicator of whether there were any sworn law enforcement officers in the school.

Balancing Variables

There was also a set of variables used to balance schools with and without police before conducting our main analyses (explained further later). These variables included total school enrollment of the school and whether the school was one of the following: special education school, magnet school, charter school, or alternative school. We also examined the following rates for each school: (a) absences; (b) bullying and harassment based on sex; (c) bullying and harassment based on race; and (d) bullying and harassment based on disability status. Additionally, we used the following school characteristics to balance schools with and without police: (a) the urbanicity of the school's setting (i.e., rural, town, suburban, or urban); (b) whether the school received Title 1 funding, an indicator of poverty; and (c) the student–teacher ratio.

Analytic Strategy

To estimate the relationship between police presence and each of the different dependent variables, we ran a series of ordinary least squares regression models predicting each of the outcomes. However, one of the major threats to internal validity of this approach is that of selection bias. Specifically, schools with police are likely to be systematically different from schools without police. To address this, we used a treatment effects technique called entropy balancing (Hainmueller, 2012). Conceptually, entropy balancing works by balancing treatment and comparison units on a set of baseline characteristics that are likely to explain the process of being selected into treatment. The entropy balancing algorithm then provides weights for the observations in the comparison group that, when applied, equate the two groups on the mean, variance, and skewness of each of the measured baseline variables. This means that we compare schools with police to a group of schools without police that are weighted so that the two groups of schools are as similar as possible on their baseline characteristics.

RESULTS

Descriptive Statistics

The average school in the weighted sample had about 750 students, and relatively few schools were specialty schools, such as the following: (1) special education (1%); (2) magnet (6%), (3) charter (2%), or (4) alternative (4%) schools. On average, 14% of students were chronically absent, and reported rates of bias-based bullying and harassment were rare, with records of 1.89 gender-based incidents, 1.22 race-based incidents, and 0.55 ability-based incidents per 1,000 students. Schools were primarily in urban (40%) and suburban (32%) settings, with substantial proportions also in towns (16%) and rural areas (12%); 73% of schools were eligible for Title 1 funding, and there were on average 22 students per teacher in each school.

Suspensions

Single Out-of-School Suspension

Results of the models predicting single OSS rates are presented in Graph A of Figure 4.1. Single OSS rates of students with disabilities were higher in schools with police than those where police were not present ($b = 17.01$, $p < .001$). In the models combining both male and female students, the highest point estimates of the association between police and single OSSs were for Hispanic ($b = 20.20$, $p < .001$), Black ($b = 17.61$, $p < .001$), and multiracial SWD ($b = 33.35$, $p < .001$). Comparatively, the estimates for Black and multiracial SWD were 6.10 and 21.84 more per 1,000 SWD than White students, respectively. Results by gender were similar across race, with female SWD experiencing an additional 15.84 ($p < .001$) and male SWD an additional 18.60 ($p < .001$) single OSSs per 1000 students. The highest single OSS rates for both male and female SWD were found for multiracial SWD (male: $b = 30.00$, $p < .001$; female: $b = 28.11$, $p < .001$). Additionally, single OSS rates were significantly higher for both male and female Hispanic, Black, and White SWD, with all experiencing at least 11 more single OSSs when police were present. In summary, the single OSS rates for SWD were higher in schools with police and were particularly high for Black, Hispanic, and multiracial SWD.

Multiple Out-of-School Suspensions

Graph B of Figure 4.1 displays results of the models predicting multiple OSSs for SWD. Across all students with disabilities, significantly higher OSS rates were found in schools with police. The largest statistically significant point estimates were found for Hispanic ($b = 16.55$, $p < .001$), Black ($b = 16.43$, $p < .001$), and White SWD ($b = 8.18$, $p < .001$), indicating that the relationship between police presence and multiple OSSs was roughly twice as large for Black

Figure 4.1. Additional Suspensions per 1,000 SWD in Schools With Police

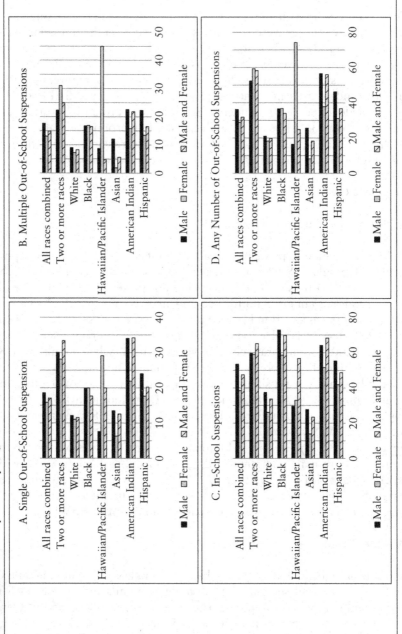

A. Single Out-of-School Suspension

B. Multiple Out-of-School Suspensions

C. In-School Suspensions

D. Any Number of Out-of-School Suspensions

All races combined
Two or more races
White
Black
Hawaiian/Pacific Islander
Asian
American Indian
Hispanic

■ Male ▨ Female ▨ Male and Female

and Hispanic SWD than for White SWD. Among models examining multiple OSSs for males only and females only, results were significant in both models by race for Hispanic, Black, White, and multiracial SWD. The highest rates of multiple OSSs were found for both female and male multiracial SWD (female: $b = 31.04, p < .001$; male: $b = 22.24, p < .001$). These models show that schools with police had especially higher rates of multiple OSSs for Black, Hispanic, and multiracial SWD.

In-School Suspensions

Results for ISS rates are shown in Graph C of Figure 4.1. In the models combining male and female SWD, significant point estimates were found for Hispanic ($b = 48.61, p < .001$), American Indian ($b = 68.30, p < .001$), Asian ($b = 4.36, p < .001$), Black ($b = 69.66, p < .001$), White ($b = 33.70, p < .001$), and multiracial SWD ($b = 65.17, p < .001$). Similar patterns were found by race for female SWD as were found for total OSSs, with the highest point estimate reported for multiracial ($b = 59.09, p < .001$) and Black female SWD ($b = 58.54, p < .001$). However, ISS rates for male SWD revealed the highest point estimates for Black SWD ($b = 72.85, p < .001$), followed by American Indian ($b = 64.17, p < .001$), multiracial, ($b = 59.50, p < .001$) and Hispanic SWD ($b = 55.26, p < .001$). Moreover, male SWD experienced an extra 15.01 ISS per 1,000 SWD ($b = 53.50, p < .001$) than female SWD ($b = 38.49, p < .001$). Altogether, this again shows that police presence was associated with higher rates of suspension of SWD—in this case ISSs—and that multiple groups of minoritized students bore the brunt of this.

Total Out-of-School Suspensions

Graph D of Figure 4.1 represents a combined OSS total, which includes both single and multiple OSS rates. Results for all SWD, regardless of gender and race, showed an additional 31.81 OSSs ($p < .001$) in schools with police. When analyzing the findings by race, the largest point estimates were found for multiracial SWD ($b = 56.21, p < .05$). Comparatively, Black ($b = 34.03, p < .001$), Hispanic ($b = 36.74, p < .001$), and multiracial SWD experienced 14.34, 17.05, and 36.52 total OSSs, more than White students ($b = 19.69, p < .001$). In terms of gender, female SWD experienced 28.85 ($p < .001$) and male SWD 36.18 ($p < .001$) more total OSSs in schools with police. More specifically, female multiracial SWD experienced 59.14 OSSs ($p < .001$), which is 22.43 more OSSs than the second highest significant point estimate found for Black female SWD ($b = 36.71, p < .001$). Similarly, male multiracial SWD had the highest OSS rates ($b = 52.24, p < .001$), followed by Black male SWD ($b = 36.52, p < .001$). These models again show that Black, Hispanic, and multiracial SWD received particularly high rates of OSSs in schools with police.

Expulsions

Expulsions With Services

Graph A of Figure 4.2 displays the results of the models predicting expulsion with services. Note that missing rows in each of the four graphs indicate that not enough cases were present in the data to make valid calculations. In the models with male and female students combined, there were significantly higher expulsion rates of SWD for all races combined, as well as for Hispanic, Asian, Black, and White SWD. Among these, the point estimate for Black students was the largest, indicating an additional 2.64 expulsions rates for Black SWD ($p < .001$). The pattern of findings was somewhat different for female students. Although there was a significantly higher rate of expulsion with services for female SWD of all races combined, the models were only significant for Hispanic and White female SWD. For male students, however, more models attained statistical significance and showed larger effects. The rate of expulsions with services was significantly higher for males of all races combined, as well as for Hispanic, Black, White, and multiracial SWD. Among these models, the largest point estimates were those for multiracial SWD ($b = 3.50$, $p < .001$) and Black students ($b = 3.59$, $p < .001$), indicating that schools with police expelled Black and multiracial SWD at a rate of over 3.5 additional students per 1,000 than schools without police.

Expulsions Without Services

Graph B of Figure 4.2 displays the results of the models predicting expulsions without services. Compared to the models predicting expulsions with services, there were far fewer significant models, and the effect sizes were substantially smaller, and occasionally in the opposite direction (i.e., fewer, rather than more expulsions). In the models with male and female SWD combined, there were significant effects for the model, including SWD of all races and Black SWD, but the effects were small, with less than one additional expulsion per 1,000 students in schools with police compared to those without police. None of the models including only female SWD achieved statistical significance. In the models including only male SWD, the only model that achieved statistical significance was that for American Indian SWD, which showed that schools with police had 1.56 fewer expulsions per 1,000 male American Indian SWD than schools without police.

Expulsions for Zero-Tolerance Offenses

The results for the models predicting expulsions for zero-tolerance offenses are shown in graph C of Figure 4.2. These models generally followed the same pattern as the models predicting expulsions with services, but the effect sizes were somewhat smaller. In the models including both male and female

Figure 4.2. Additional Expulsions per 1,000 SWD in Schools With Police

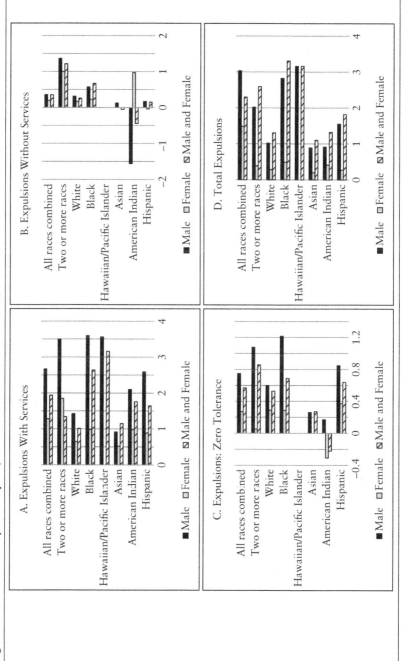

SWD, the models for students of all races, Hispanic, Black, and White SWD, showed that there were higher rates of expulsion for zero-tolerance offenses in schools with police than those without, although the effects were small, with less than one additional expulsion per 1,000 students. In the models including only female SWD, the models for SWD of all races combined, Hispanic SWD, and White SWD achieved statistical significance, although the effect sizes were even smaller than the models including male and female students. In the models including only male students, the models for SWD of all races combined, Hispanic, Black, White, and multiracial SWD were all statistically significant and indicated higher rates of expulsion for zero-tolerance offenses in schools with police than in schools without police. The largest effects—each just above one additional expulsion per 1,000 students—were for Black and multiracial male SWD.

Total Expulsions

Graph D of Figure 4.2 displays the results for the models predicting total expulsions. These models also generally followed the pattern of the models predicting expulsions with services, which is not surprising given that the measures of total expulsions are composites of the other expulsion variables and expulsions with services were the most common type of expulsion. In the models with both male and female students included, the models for SWD of all races, Hispanic, Black, and White SWD achieved statistical significance. The largest point estimate was for Black SWD ($b = 3.30$, $p < .001$), which indicated that Black SWD in schools with police were expelled on average over three additional times per 1,000 students than in schools without police. In the models that included only female students, the models including SWD of all races, Black, and White SWD achieved statistical significance. The model with all races combined indicated an effect of 1.48 additional expulsions per 1,000 female SWD in schools with police, whereas the models for Black and White female SWD indicated increases of less than one expulsion. In the models including only male SWD, the models including all races, Hispanic, Black, and White SWD were all statistically significant. Among these, the highest point estimates were those for all races combined and Black male SWD, with an average of an additional 3.03 and 2.82 expulsions (respectively) per 1,000 students in schools with police.

DISCUSSION

This analysis has two major takeaways: (a) across the board, SWD had higher discipline rates when police were present compared to schools with no police presence, and (b) this was especially true for Black, multiracial, and Hispanic SWD. Given the national discourse on police in schools, these findings are especially important. The relationship between police presence and punishment was consistently high for Black SWD relative to students of other races, particularly White students. The police-punishment relationship was usually about twice as strong for Black SWD as for White SWD. In accordance with DisCrit, this suggests that the school-based processes that sort and exclude students through both racism and ableism—whether through assignment to special education or through punishment—appear to be reinforced by the presence of police. Theoretically, the presence of police adds another layer to the controlling of Black bodies through punishment and special education displacements (Watts & Erevelles, 2004).

The summer of 2020 saw new momentum for removing police from schools, following calls to defund the police after the brutal police killings of George Floyd and Breonna Taylor earlier in the year. Subsequent protests against police brutality sparked several school districts to remove police from schools, including those in Minneapolis, Portland, Denver, and elsewhere (Superville, 2020). Alternatively, many national organizations, like the national associations of School Psychologists, Secondary School Principals, and School Resource Officers, are calling to redefine policy and practices around the role of police in schools (National Association of School Psychologists, 2020). Police brutality and racism, while present for centuries, has been a topic of national sustained media attention, which has fueled national conversation and dialogue across the country and world. School-based mental health professionals (e.g., school psychologists and counselors) and other school personnel who frequently work in advocacy roles for SWD with minoritized racial/ethnic identities, need to combat collective silence about police brutality and violence and the related racial trauma (Proctor et al., 2021). Not only are the results from this study timely, but they have implications for future research, policy, and practice and the advocacy roles of school personnel who work in schools where disparate discipline and school-based arrests originate.

Research Implications

The findings in this study suggest the need for future research to thoughtfully and carefully consider the intersectionality of racism, gender identity, and ableism when addressing the impact of police in schools. Although it is the case that police presence was related to higher rates of punishment for students representing many combinations of race/ethnicity and gender, these rates were consistently high for Black students across the types of exclusionary discipline examined. When further disaggregated by gender, it appears that much of the racial disparities were consistent among Black males with disabilities. Although the punishment rates of Black female and male SWD were higher than those of their White counterparts in schools with police across a variety of punishment outcomes, Black male SWD often experienced high rates of punitive discipline compared with Black female SWD, particularly among the more serious forms of punishment that are particularly life-altering, such as expulsion. This suggests that gender may be an important consideration when examining racially/ethnically disparate patterns of punishment among SWD. For example, Morris (2016) describes the criminalization of Black females and concomitant lack of attention to it among researchers, policymakers, and practitioners. The implications for research suggest the need to examine data at the intersection of race, ability, and gender in order to better understand the inequitable impact of police presence and how careful attention to multiple identities is crucial.

Additionally, this study brought to light the need to further understand and include students who identify as multiracial SWD. While there were excessively high rates of punitive discipline among Black students, those who identify as multiracial SWD were a group that consistently received the harshest punitive treatment. To our knowledge, although there has been ample research and attention on the Black–White gap in school-based punishment and growing attention to the Hispanic–White gap, little research has examined multiracial students. Unfortunately, data limitations in the CRDC (2020) preclude us from knowing which races are represented in this category, so we are unable to test whether combinations of certain races are particularly subject to disproportionate punishment rates. Moreover, there is a lack of consistency in how individuals choose to indicate multiple racial/ ethnic individual identities (Harris et al., 2017), making it difficult to rely on this method of data collection. This is an understudied group in the literature who require the attention of policymakers, researchers, and practitioners. As the population of multiracial students continues to grow in the coming years, those engaged in this work must pay particular attention to how systems and policies affect all minoritized students' experiences and outcomes, particularly those who identify as multiracial, as this racial/ethnic identity is understudied and not well understood in general, specifically as relating to the intersection with ability.

Finally, in the context of widespread calls for removing police from schools that hit a crescendo in 2020, research may benefit from considering the role of student voice and student activism in schools' use of police. Given that the impacts of police in schools are likely to be most acutely felt by students (as opposed to teachers, staff, parents, and other stakeholders), further work centering student voices is critical. It may be particularly worthwhile to seek out the perspectives of students who are already marginalized, including students with disabilities and minoritized students.

Policy Implications

This study's findings also have implications for policies around police in schools. First, if considerations of equity are central to educational policies, this study provides evidence that legislative support for placing police in schools is likely to have detrimental consequences for some SWD relative to others. In particular, these findings show that Black, multiracial, American

Indian, and other racial/ethnic groups that are already traditionally marginalized in educational settings may become further marginalized when police are in schools, at least among SWD. Given that police in schools research does not indicate other beneficial effects for students or schools, removing mandated police in state, local, and school policies would be a step toward educational equity.

Second, in line with calls to defund the police by shifting some of their efforts onto other institutions, any funds diverted from the police should be redirected to services that benefit students and improve educational equity. This might come in the form of mental health services (e.g., school psychologists, school counselors, and school social workers), improved infrastructure for supporting SWD, incorporating antiracist pedagogy, instituting restorative practices throughout the school, or a variety of other initiatives that center equity. Because police in schools play a variety of roles and do not only act as law enforcers, removing them from schools may create vacuums that will need to be filled by other people or systems, and how those vacuums are filled will likely have implications—either positive or negative—for students and educational equity.

Third, at a federal level, it may be useful to increase the frequency of the CRDC from a biennial to an annual data collection effort. The CRDC is currently the nation's leading source of data on a variety of issues of educational equity, including data on not only school discipline, but access to advanced coursework, bullying and harassment, and a variety of other domains. Increasing its frequency would direct substantial federal efforts toward understanding the current state of educational equity nationwide, allowing both researchers and policymakers to more frequently and more effectively understand the country's changing landscape in regard to educational equity, allowing for policies that are better responsive to current shortcomings. Moreover, collecting more information regarding individuals with disabilities would be a beneficial step in better disentangling issues of equity by race and ability. For example, data collection might include identification of specific disability categories and information regarding individual education plans/programming. Moreover, making discipline referrals and outcomes for students with disabilities publicly accessible would not only benefit scholarship but would help with school accountability when it comes to student discipline practices.

Practice Implications

Although the number of schools cutting ties with police is growing and is a good step toward increasing equity in discipline, consideration of equitable school-level discipline practices is imperative. For schools and districts that are unwilling to remove police from schools, this study's findings suggest that school administrators reconsider the role of police in discipline for SWD. It is particularly noteworthy that even when police in schools say they are not involved in discipline, they still may be involved in discipline in a variety of ways (Curran et al., 2019). The reality is that police in schools do interact with SWD, and many feel unprepared to do so well. A statewide survey of school-based police in Virginia found that training on interacting with SWD was one of the officers' most commonly expressed needs (Lawson & Welfare, 2018). This suggests that police in schools may be unequipped to address behaviors of SWD that they consider nonnormative and may yield increased rates of punishment for SWD. Given that school-based police themselves report having little training in how to interact with SWD, more training about SWD for security personnel and general educators may be warranted. However, the problem with racially disproportionate discipline among SWD is not likely to be solved by more training; broader systemic changes are needed that reorient schools to focus less on controlling behavior and more on learning and growth.

Therefore, alternative options to discipline, especially for students with multiple marginalized identities, may be steps toward equitable educational opportunities. Including culturally responsive and/or restorative approaches to discipline are particularly important given this study identified the highest rates of punishment among Black, Hispanic, and multiracial SWD. Given the elevated media attention on police brutality, students of color may be experiencing racial trauma, which can trigger posttraumatic stress responses within the school setting (American Psychological Association, 2016; Comas-Díaz, 2016). In many instances, the mere presence of police likely counteracts safe and supportive environments for students experiencing racial trauma. Therefore, increasing access to mental health and trauma-informed schools is a way to move toward safer and more supportive environments.

Along with calls to defund or reduce police in schools, demands for increasing funding and accessibility to mental health resources within schools are growing. In addition to increased mental health demands, it is important to put resources toward culturally responsive and restorative practices that include a focus on racial trauma and address students with intersectional identities. Validating racial trauma and using de-escalation strategies can help students to manage emotions (Comas-Díaz, 2016). The National Child Traumatic Stress Network (2017) provides resources for educators in addressing race and trauma in the classroom and should be considered as mental health funding increases.

CONCLUSION

The findings from this study that showed increased levels of punitiveness in schools with police are consistent with previous literature showing higher rates of punishment in schools that have police (Fisher & Hennessey, 2016; Gottfredson et al., 2020; Homer & Fisher, 2020; Na & Gottfredson, 2013; Theriot, 2009; Weisburst, 2019). However, no prior studies have specifically

examined the impact of police in schools among SWD with considerations for race/ethnicity. Therefore, this study's findings extend the prior literature and offer further evidence about excessive use of exclusionary punitive discipline in schools that have police. The concern with high rates of SWD punishment remains, and in either case police presence proves problematic, especially for Black, Hispanic, and multiracial SWD. Not only is this study timely, as attention to the inequitable impact of police in schools gains media attention, but it has implications for future research, policy, and practice.

Black Women Teachers' Counternarratives on School Discipline

Ability in Student, Teacher, and Space

Angelina N. Nortey

Studies on Black educators, namely teachers and principals, document a history of personal characteristics and professional practices pre- and post–*Brown v. Board of Education* (1954) that have been effective in the schooling of African American students (Ladson-Billings, 2009; Walker, 2013; Tillman, 2004). Historically, Black educators represented surrogate parent figures, disciplinarians, counselors, role models, and advocates for the academic, social, cultural, psychological, and moral development of African American students (Milner & Howard, 2004). Scholarship suggests that Black educators continue to demonstrate characteristics and professional practices that are both political (Dixson, 2003) and culturally responsive (Gay, 2010) based on culture-centered and race-centered ideologies to develop the academic, psychological, moral, social, cultural, and political insights for Black students (Roberts, 2010); therefore, Black educators are actively combating the bias and stereotypes inherent in exclusionary discipline.

Since the culturally responsive and political nature of Black teachers are in stark contrast with exclusionary discipline, it is imperative to include their voices on the topic of disciplinary disproportionality. In Bass's (2012) exploratory qualitative study on Black women educators, she found that caring for others was a "powerful and effective force toward change" (p. 82) as school leaders made decisions about behavioral issues and the application of zero-tolerance policies. Building on studies that center Black women educators' practices and perspectives on school discipline, this study aimed to understand how Black women educators' notions of race and ability shape the discipline process. The current work centers the counter-storytelling of Black women educators as they have played a significant role in maintaining Black students' position within classrooms by operating from a strengths-based perspective, hence mitigating racial disparities in exclusionary discipline.

SPECIAL EDUCATION, RACE, AND DISABILITY

Blanchett (2009) asserted that a lasting legacy of Western racism is a deep-seated belief about intellectual inferiority. This assertion serves as the basis for how notions about race and ability are co-constructed. Within schools, the Individuals With Disabilities Education Act (IDEA) (2016) and related special education legislation and policy largely influence views about disability as they are "cultural institutions" (Irvine, 2012). According to IDEA, disability is viewed as the inability to perform at a particular level, within a certain range, or with significant difficulty, as measured by approved tools. With evidence, it is acceptable to provide remediation (i.e., special education). While this may seem neutral, several scholars have argued the converse and contest the unchallenged embedded views of disability in the policy (Beratan, 2008; McCall & Skritic, 2009). Scholars argue that deficit ideology constructs disability as an intrinsic problem traceable to individual characteristics (Artiles, 2011; Beratan, 2008) and ignores the social construction aspect of disability (Annamma et al., 2013). The social construction of disability moves toward an understanding about perceived differences, responses to it, and meaning making. Therefore, there is a shift beyond viewing disability as a biological or psychological fact that necessitates remediation and segregation.

Annamma et al. (2013) articulated that disability is determined based on context and time-specific social response to interpretations of deviation from the norm. From a historical perspective, racial/ethnic minority students have been seen as "others" and "outside of the norm" within U.S. public education. This exclusion plays out in several dimensions, including dialect of English, knowledge, and decorum (Reid & Knight, 2006). According to Irvine (2012), students of color who are in special education have multiple context-dependent and evolving identities. Unfortunately, most educators often think of students of color based on one identity—their disability—and not one that is an intersection of multiple oppressed identities, including race/ethnicity. Crenshaw's (1991) seminal work on intersectionality supports the idea that an individual's multiple subordinating identities make a complex whole that cannot be disentangled to any single phenomena and that meaningfulness comes from experiences and realities. While Crenshaw's work was framed around race and gender, DisCrit extends the conversation to examine the intersection of race and disability.

When conceptualizing disability in schools, it is important to simultaneously acknowledge embedded historical and ideological roots. If decontextualized, justice for students identified with disabilities becomes conceptualized as individual rights with disregard for intragroup histories (Artiles, 2011), building a form of systemic oppression into special education practice and policy. Specifically, undermining the historical relevance of *Brown v. Board of Education* (*BOE*) for racial/ethnic minority students can lead to exclusion twice, based on both an acontextual notion of race and disability (Ferri & Connor, 2005). The notion of disability in schools differentially impacts racial/

ethnic minority students as they are more vulnerable for being perceived as inherently deficient individuals without appropriate consideration of identity and context.

SPIRIT MURDERING

Williams (1987) coined the term *spirit murdering* to characterize the impact of racism on the human spirit. She adds that a part of ourselves and our dignity is dependent on others in society; therefore, a sense of caring responsibility should be had for the images of others we carry, as well as the narratives that are told about others. However, care is not afforded equitably to all. From an intersectional perspective, Erevelles & Minear (2010) asserted that for disabled students of color, spirit murder may be the "most significant experience in their educational lives" (p. 143). Hines and Wilmot (2018) argued that Black K–12 children are being spirit murdered within educational settings and that school discipline has been used as an instrument of spirit murdering, "the denial of inclusion, protection, safety, nurturance and acceptance" (p. 2) (see also Love, 2016). They explain that over time, this denial turns into "deeply ingrained psychological trauma" (Hines & Wilmot, 2018, p. 67).

Coles and Powell (2020) found that Black students were aware of the inequitable outcomes of school discipline, which resulted in decreased likelihood of educational careers beyond K–12, unproductive pathways, and in some instances bodily death. In varying ways, exclusionary disciplinary practices are forms of symbolic (and sometimes literal) violence that, if schools are not intentional about making fair, perpetuate the notion that Black students are outside the boundaries of humanity and do not deserve to be protected in ways that other students unquestionably are. While schools are engaging in forms of spirit murdering that are perpetuated by individuals, it is important to highlight the work of individuals, such as Ms. Betty and Ms. Tasha, who are explicitly working against the practice of exclusionary discipline.

BLACK WOMEN EDUCATOR PEDAGOGY

Monique Morris (2016) asserted that Black women have been clear about the "liberative power of education" (p. 5) before the decision of *BOE*. Moreover, Black women teachers are inherently political actors, because they work to dismantle racist beliefs and practices that harm African American children by waging political battles with their colleagues and advocating against racial antagonism in schools (Dixson, 2003). In this sense, teachers serve in the role of cultural conduit, informing others about African American students. Similarly, Black women teachers seek to build their students into beings who understand issues of race, racism, and oppression, and how to overcome societal ills that they will likely encounter (Roberts, 2010).

Beauboeuf-Lafontant (2002) conceptualized the political orientation of Black teacher pedagogy by identifying political clarity as a key aspect of this approach to teaching. According to Beauboeuf-Lafontant (2002), political clarity is a characteristic of womanist caring that describes an individual with a personalized sensitivity to social issues. There is recognition that relationships exist between schools and society that differentially impact groups of children (Beauboeuf-Lafontant, 2002). Therefore, there is an underlying belief that fairness is something that must be created. Political clarity is consistent with what Patricia Hill-Collins (2002) articulated about the ethic of care from a womanist perspective, as she stresses the importance of "history, culture, and experiences with individual uniqueness, expressiveness, emotion and empathy" (p. 77). Moreover, this type of care is often a result of heightened sensitivity to social injustice due to one's personal experiences. Consistent with Roberts (2010), educators who possess political clarity readily discuss the implications of systemic injustices with their students and integrate their understandings into professional practice.

Contemporary researchers, with an emphasis on African American students, contend that care is a culturally responsive action with political ramifications (Beauboeuf-Lafontant, 2002; Wilson, 2016). Care is not conceptualized as an individual action, but one that is connected to collective social realities, interested in racial uplift and contingent on both care and justice (Cooper, 2009; Dixson, 2003; Obidah et al., 2004). These domains of care are practiced by educators, a translation encompassing both educational and political action.

Consistent with political and caring practice, culturally responsive teaching promotes environments that are safe, caring, affirmative, and validating (Dixson, 2003; Gay, 2010). Gay (2010) asserted that culturally responsive teaching acknowledges and affirms the cultural background, experiences, and values of students and families. Moreover, Cholewa et al. (2012) found that teachers who engaged in culturally responsive practices built intentional and culturally driven relationships. In addition, the environments that are created when culturally responsive teaching is present promotes psychological well-being within and among students (Cholewa et al., 2012). Political, caring, and culturally responsive education practices buffer against the negative social and emotional outcomes associated with exclusionary discipline such as disengagement (Gregory et al., 2010), distrust of school adults (Brown, 2007), internalized messages of inferiority (Townsend, 2000), and the internalized notion that schooling is not for or accessible to students of color (Noguera, 2003).

CURRENT STUDY

More research is needed that centralizes Black educator perspectives on school discipline, given their keen understandings and lived experiences that translate to culturally responsive classroom practices. Vincent et al. (2011), theorized about the importance of cultural validity and relevance in moving toward culturally responsive behavior support in schools. Various studies have shown that simple implementation of well-intentioned strategies and interventions such as schoolwide positive behavior supports (Vincent et al., 2011; Skiba et al., 2011), social–emotional learning, and restorative justice (Gregory et al., 2015) are insufficient to alleviate racial disparities in school discipline. Rather, there must be consideration given to the schoolwide context, transactional nature of discipline, and extent to which a school is culturally responsive (Vincent et al., 2011). The current study adds to emerging research, which indicates that adequately addressing student behavior requires culture to be central to the solution, highlighting the processes of Black educators.

Moreover, extant research and nationwide data highlight that exclusionary discipline practices disproportionately impact students with disabilities (Camacho & Krezmien, 2018; Losen, 2011; Sullivan et al., 2013; DOE, OCR, 2018). While several researchers identify that race (Skiba et al., 2011) and disability (Sullivan et al., 2014) play a role in disciplinary disproportionality, few scholars talk about the school discipline process as racialized. Many have not yet connected how ideas about racism and ableism impact the aforementioned outcome (Annamma & Morrison, 2018). The current study intends to contribute to scholarship by identifying notions of ability constructed by Black teachers in their classrooms. Specifically, the current study seeks to emphasize that ideology about both race and ability shape how teachers interact with their students, thus contributing to issues of classroom climate, safety, and discipline.

This chapter will explore notions of racism and ableism in school discipline decisions as informed by two teachers with political clarity, a characteristic of care, which describes individuals with a personalized sensitivity to social issues (Beauboeuf-Lafontant, 2002). The study findings presented in this chapter are drawn from a dissertation study. The current study focuses on answering the key question: How do Black women teachers with political clarity conceptualize ability when addressing student behavior?

THEORETICAL FRAMEWORK

Studies have found that both race—namely identifying as Black—and being labeled with a disability—namely emotional disturbance—impact suspension outcomes (Camacho & Krezmien, 2018; Sullivan et al., 2013). Hence, an intersectional (Crenshaw, 1993) approach to the conceptualization of disciplinary disproportionality is needed. The primary theoretical framework for this study is DisCrit, an integration of disability studies (DS) and critical race theory (CRT). DisCrit explores ways in which race and ability are socially constructed and interdependent, seeking to examine the processes through which students are simultaneously raced and disabled (Annamma et al., 2013). This study asserts that racialized notions of ability and behavior serve as an intersectional explanation for the persistent problem of disciplinary disproportionality for Black boys and girls identified as having disabilities. Relying on DisCrit as the overarching theoretical framework creates the opportunity for scholarship to start unpacking disciplinary disproportionality from the standpoint of racialized notions of ability.

The secondary theoretical framework influencing this chapter is womanist pedagogies of care. A womanist ethic of care impacts student classroom and school behavior, and thus the concept of caring becomes significant when thinking about school discipline (Gay, 2010). Moreover, womanist ideals of care influence the ways in which Black women teachers socially construct the behavior of the students in their classrooms. Given womanist pedagogy, and consistent with CRT, the proposed paper is situated in the spirit of "storytelling resistance" on issues of exclusionary discipline and spirit murdering (Solórzano & Yosso, 2002).

EPISTEMOLOGICAL STANCE

African American Epistemology

Epistemology points to the ways in which power relations shape who is believed and why (Hill- Collins, 2009). This study was guided by an African American epistemology, which is characterized as "the study or theory of knowledge generated out of the African American existential condition, that is, of the knowledge and cultural artifacts produced by African-Americans based on African-American cultural, social, economic, historical, and political experiences" (Gordon, 1990, p. 90). African American epistemology critiques knowledge and deconstructs society from an ideological perspective inclusive of historical and contemporary lived experiences, and it merges self-reflection in a way that authentically captures African American life (Giroux, 1981). African American epistemology is also nonsynchronous because it has neither the same economic and political understanding nor similar needs within it at the same point in time as the dominant culture (Gordon, 1990). Therefore, the theories of knowledge that comprise African American epistemology may or may not be shared with the dominant culture simultaneously. Specific to this study, the knowledge that is possessed and understood through the lens of an African American epistemology provided perspective to generate insight about school discipline from African American women. As such, African American women's lived experiences were deemed a good-enough basis, validating their own known knowledge and professional practice.

Black Feminist Thought

Black feminist thought is consistent with African American epistemology. Black feminist thought reflects the distinctive themes of African American women's experiences, relying on paradigms that emphasize the importance of intersecting oppressions (Hill-Collins, 2009). The incorporation of Black feminist thought was appropriate for this study because the lived experiences of the participants impacted their approach for implementing school discipline as well as how their thoughts about race and disability impacted that process. Specific to Black feminist thought is that knowing is both knowledge and wisdom, as the latter is needed to promote survival for successfully navigating multiple systems of oppression.

Consistent with both African American epistemology and Black feminist thought is lived experience valued as a criterion of meaning. As such, ideas and those who create, validate, and believe them cannot be separated (Hill-Collins, 2009). Those who have lived through the experiences about which they talk are more believable and credible than those who have simply read about the same experiences (Hill-Collins, 2009). Therefore, lived experience adds to credibility. One way lived experience is illuminated is through the sharing of stories, commonly referred to as narratives. For the purposes of this study, the narratives of two Black women teachers were gathered.

METHOD

Setting

In the conveniently selected school district in the state of Florida, 8.9% of all students and 17.4% of all Black/African American students received more than one school suspension (DOE, OCR, 2012). In the county, Black/African American students who were identified as having a disability received at least one suspension at a rate twice that of the general student population. Of the total percentage of students who received multiple suspensions, Black/African American students represented 70% of them (DOE, OCR, 2012). Considering all data taken together, teachers in the research setting worked within a context where the application of exclusionary discipline procedures resulted in a disproportionate number of Black/African American students being suspended from school. Despite the concerning exclusionary data, the county where the study was conducted has a rich history of education for African Americans, documented back to the 1860s.

Participants

The author submitted an institutional review board (IRB) application for the original study, from which these data were extracted. The author recruited all participants during the 2013–2014 academic year. Participants were selected based on a community nomination process, by which a researcher relies on community members and community-oriented vehicles— institutions, organizations, or means through which ideas of a community are conveyed (i.e., churches, social and community organizations)—to suggest the best people to interview for a study (Ladson-Billings, 2009; Roberts, 2010). A community nomination form was disseminated, asking community members to identify an educator who exhibited the following attributes (but not limited to this): understands how race impacts education and recognizes the relationship between schools and society that differentially impacts groups of students. This method allowed the researcher to directly interact with the community, who had the opportunity to validate their own knowledge (Tillman, 2002). An integration of the community's perspective from stakeholders and gatekeepers increased the likelihood that nominated participants would reflect the perspectives, values, and beliefs consistent with the pedagogy of successful Black educators. For the findings reported in the current chapter, two participants were selected using purposive sampling (Merriam, 2009).

Study Participants

Ms. Betty, a high school reading teacher, had been teaching in public schools for 31 years at the time interviews were conducted. She self-identified as an African American woman, born and raised in Florida. Her degrees included a bachelor's degree in special and elementary education and a master's degree in counseling, both from a historically Black university. Ms. Betty listed one of her accomplishments as maintaining employment at one school throughout her career. Her school was racially and economically diverse. Many of the students she taught experienced difficulty meeting statewide standardized testing requirements in reading and qualified for special education under the category of Specific Learning Disabilities (SLD). Ms. Betty was the advisor of two extracurricular activities that focused on service and academics at her school. She was also involved in social organizations within the community.

Ms. Tasha self-identified as an African American woman teacher who had been teaching in the public school system for 30 years. She was from a military family stationed mainly in Virginia and expressed that her experiences traveling helped her to truly embrace diversity. Ms. Tasha held an associate degree from a community college with a certification in special education. She also held a bachelor's degree in education from a large research institution in Florida. Prior to becoming a special education teacher at the middle school level, she taught students with academic and behavioral disabilities at the elementary level. At the time of the interview, Ms. Tasha was teaching middle school students with disabilities in a self-contained classroom. Her school received Title I funding and served predominantly African American students. Ms. Tasha sponsored student organizations and reported engaging in and leading community activities to increase her awareness and appreciation for families and the community.

Data Collection

In-depth, semi-structured interviews were the primary method of data collection for the larger study. Because of the scope and focus of this chapter, only the interviews from the two teacher participants who also work directly with students with disabilities were utilized. Each teacher participated in three in-person interviews with the researcher, across 2 months. The interviews were guided by preestablished questions, with probing questions being used to follow up and explore information provided by each participant (Hatch, 2002). Rapport building was the emphasis for the first interview, decision-making for the second interview, and clarifying gaps in data for the third interview. Interview protocols were reshaped after each round of interviews to gain better cohesion with the initial research interest and emerging data. The series of three interviews allowed the collection of a substantial amount of data, thus reducing the likelihood of the researcher making misleading claims or conducting superficial analysis of the data. These decisions were made to lend credibility. The series of three interviews were done to establish "prolonged engagement" and "persistent observation" (Korstjens & Moser, 2018, p. 121), focusing on the lived experiences of educators who were most germane to the study. All interviews were audiotaped and transcribed verbatim. Ms. Betty's interview data totaled 218 minutes and Ms. Tasha's three interviews totaled 104 minutes.

Field Notes

During the collection of data, field notes were collected to include my reflections and observations (Bogdan & Biklen, 2003). Immediately following each interview, I wrote down my initial thoughts and observations. This practice increased trustworthiness of the data through reflexivity, using field notes to examine my own lived experiences (Korstjens & Moser, 2018). After the audio recorder was off, some participants candidly expanded on ideas expressed during the interview. Therefore, summaries of these conversations were also included in field notes. Afterward, I replayed the recorded interview and noted the participant's overall demeanor, changes in tone of voice, frequently used words/phrases, recurring ideas, and patterns of responding. Also, I listened attentively and developed follow-up questions for each participant to be used in subsequent interviews. Field notes captured my authentic impressions during data collection.

Data Analysis

Critical race methodology in education offers a way to analyze experiences with and responses to racism and ableism (Solórzano & Yosso, 2002). Using data gathered during the research process and existing literature, counternarratives were created. Composite stories or narratives draw on various forms of data that tell about the contextual experience of people of color and place them in social, historical and political situations to discuss forms of subordination (Solórzano & Yosso, 2002). Counternarratives within school discipline can help us to better understand the problem in a way that does not further criminalize Black students and perpetuate ideas of inferiority about Black students with disabilities.

The interview protocols did not explicitly ask participants about ability; however, the educators' notions of ability were revealed as they talked about race and school discipline, which they were explicitly asked about; therefore, a logic of rhetorical analysis (Feldman & Almguist, 2012) was adopted. This type of analysis allows for the exploration of unstated or implicit features of stories since stories are loaded with embedded, sometimes hidden information. This form of narrative analysis provides insights not only into what is being said but also into understandings of participants about why and how the story they are telling is happening. This form of secondary analysis was deemed consistent with the tenets of DisCrit. With an interpretative study such as the current one, describing the coding and analysis facilitates whether one rejects or accepts the findings as valid (Feldman et al., 2004). The approach to the current narrative analysis is political because choices were made to include some things and exclude others in a particular way when other interpretations were possible. As such, the current analysis contends that the implicit understandings exposed are not the only way to interpret the gathered narrative.

All six interviews were coded using the same process with Nvivo qualitative data analysis software program. Initial coding was the first step to exploring the theoretical possibilities the data suggested (Charmaz, 2006). The purpose of initial coding is to stick closely to what the data suggests. Segment-by-segment coding was used during this phase. This method of coding was selected based on the ways the participants in the study used language and communicated. At times, when participants were asked a question, they responded with anecdotes, parables, or analogies or by telling stories. This narrative story pattern of communication is embedded within an African American epistemology where experience is viewed as logic (Hill-Collins, 2002). When transcribed, participant responses occupied several lines or paragraphs. In an effort to maintain the meaning of their response and not distort their meaning, segment-by-segment coding was most appropriate. Through a process of interacting with participants and their statements many times over, a set of action-oriented codes was developed. According to Charmaz (2006), coding with gerunds provides the opportunity to define an event, describe an incident, make apparent implicit processes, and establish connections between codes. At the end of the initial coding process, there were 106 codes. The high number of codes signifies the researcher's attempt to stick closely to the original words used by the participant.

Using rhetorical analysis (Feldman et al., 2004), the researcher sought to make logic of the implicit, about an emerging storyline of ability and race in school discipline. An assumption underlying the next step of analysis was that a story could indeed be identified. After the next round of coding, there were 16 codes that described the emerging storyline versus simply identifying the story using the speech provided by participants. The significant decrease in codes is attributed to identifying larger stories rather than fragmented pieces of data. In this step of coding, codes were based on theme descriptions. Consistent with the selected analytical approach, the researcher identified opposition(s) implicit (and sometimes explicit) in the story. Looking for opposition to the codes allowed the researcher to uncover the meaning of key elements of the discourse by analyzing what the teachers implied their narrative was not. All emerging storylines contained at least one opposition. Building from the emerging story lines and oppositions, the third level of analysis assumed that an argument could be identified and represented in an inferential, logical form. This assumption led to the production of three stories in the form of syllogisms, logical arguments that helped the teachers express their ideas (Feldman & Almguist, 2012). For the current study, presented themes are syllogisms that were created to represent what seemed to be central to the narrative of the teachers but also consistent with the tenants of DisCrit theory.

Memo Writing

Memo writing in qualitative research is used to link, structure, and contextualize concepts (Flick, 2009). The purpose of memo writing is to help the analysis become more explicit and transparent for the researcher and readers. For this study, memo writing specific to data analysis was used in conjunction with field notes. Thus, notes were taken throughout the research process. Overall, memo writing supplemented the codes derived during data analysis.

Trustworthiness

Credibility, dependability, and transferability have been accepted as criteria that ensure trustworthiness in qualitative research (Tracy, 2010). As the current study is a secondary analysis, the initial analysis established credibility through member checking (Hatch, 2002). Study participants reviewed interview protocols for accuracy as well as findings and interpretations. While participants did not engage in member checking for this chapter, the researcher contends a strong understanding of participants and the data. Off-the-record comments were captured in field notes, which provided additional information to enhance meaning of the recorded data. Dependability of the data was established through an audit trail that captured the researcher's reflections on methods and analysis through process notes (Flick, 2009; Merriam, 2009). Transferability was established through field notes and researcher reflexivity, briefly captured in the subjectivity statement of this paper.

Positionality

I am a Black woman whose interests in school discipline were shaped by my high schooling experiences. The racial dynamics in my high school were very clear implicit and explicit messages about belonging and worthiness as well as inclusion and exclusion. As a school psychologist, I have witnessed inappropriate responses to students' behaviors, especially those identified with disabilities. To this current chapter, I bring hope that there are spaces in schools that interact with Black students with disabilities in a way that respects their humanity and identity.

FINDINGS

The findings in this study represent a counternarrative to exclusionary discipline practices and privilege the voices of two Black women teachers, a perspective often underacknowledged in the literature. Findings that elucidate meaning at the intersection of race and ability in the form of a counternarrative are consistent with DisCrit. Presented in this section are three themes that build on each other to reveal how ability is conceptualized when addressing student behavior: (1) seeing ability within Black students with dis/abilities, (2) enacting their ability as teachers of liberation, and (3) the ability to intentionally create enabling classroom spaces. The teachers in this study spoke about identity and how notions of race and ability intertwine to guide their approach for addressing student behavior. They described how Black students with disabilities face consequences outside of their control, such as exclusion and other environmental stressors. Despite this recognition, the teachers still viewed their students as capable human beings, themselves as capable professionals, and their classroom as capable of developing students. Unlike most research on understanding school discipline, Ms. Betty and Ms. Tasha did not provide a narrative about deficits. Their verbatim responses are used to elucidate the themes.

Counternarrative 1: Seeing Ability Within Black Students with Dis/abilities

The first finding is consistent with DisCrit, which states that racism and ableism are normal and interdependent (Annamma et al., 2013). As such, underlying ideologies that co-construct race and ability leave some identities positioned as normal and others as abnormal. In schools, this often results in justifying the exclusion, segregation, or remediation of those who are deemed atypical and undeserving. Ms. Betty and Ms. Tasha anticipated how racism and ableism typically shaped school discipline practices and actively sought ways to disrupt them.

Ms. Betty's and Ms. Tasha's responses suggested that they understood their students' multiple identities. When explicitly asked to describe their students relevant to this study, they used identifiers such as "African American," "Black," "lower quartile," and "students with emotional and behavioral problems." However, when not specifically prompted, they did not use such specifiers. They answered questions as if students' identities were implied and understood. The only exception was in Ms. Tasha's narrative when she connected recognizing "color" with visibility:

> We have color. So if you give us identity that we have color, then you could see more of us. This is how we do this, this is how we do that. You gotta give us our identity. If you make an acknowledgment of that, I think the kids would do better and the teachers would do better.

Ms. Tasha's sentiments indicate that acknowledging race and difference is protective and affirming for Black people, including herself. Based on the aforementioned observations about the teachers' narratives, their ideas about race and ability were indeed co-constructed.

Contrary to racist and ableist ideologies, Ms. Tasha and Ms. Betty critiqued widely held notions of Black inferiority. Simply put, Ms. Betty articulated, "There's nothing inherently wrong with our children's brains. There's nothing wrong with them, at all." She cemented her sentiment by repeating many times throughout the series of interviews that "there's no magic to it." Ms. Betty sought to critique the myth that Black students were so problematic that working with them and getting good outcomes was an anomaly. Juxtaposing this idea, Ms. Tasha identified the negative sentiments held by some White teachers about the same students: "They can't get it. They don't want to work with me. They want to be rebellious. They want to be confrontational. They don't care. They are unruly. They're too loud." These quick, misguided, and uninformed judgments were deemed as problems that led to students to be excluded within schools. Their answers explained that their students were desirable and not lacking, as disability is oftentimes used as a metaphor for inadequacy and limitation.

Ms. Betty and Ms. Tasha articulated the importance of resisting ideas of inferiority. According to Ms. Betty, "You have to believe that they can learn, because a lot of them have been just [been] beat down by test scores, beat down by this, the statistics, and all that other stuff. They just been beat down by it. You can either go with that or take a different approach." Echoing her notion, Ms. Tasha specifically talked about keeping her curriculum consistent with general education: "Regardless of what people think of them, I try to run our system as parallel to what the mainstream is. . . . I really want them to gain as much as possible regardless of what their future is, I want them to know they have the ability to learn." She further illustrated belief in her student's intellectual capacity:

> [Regarding] African-American girls, it was time for them to move into the mainstream out of my resource [room] and they really were pretty smart girls, I thought they were ready, and they were going to another class and the teacher was kind of weary. So they went out and the teacher didn't really celebrate their coming, and the girls were kind of fretful. "Ms. Tasha, we'll just stay in your class." I said, "No, 'cause you're stunting your growth, you're going to go out there and you're going to do well."

In other words, Ms. Tasha did not see these students as unidimensional; she saw both their race and ability in an affirming manner, which did not lead to marginalization and instead created inclusion. Ms. Betty and Ms. Tasha took a strong stance on affirming Black students' identities as different and normal; nevertheless, they recognized the societal consequences that come along with these identities.

Counternarrative 2: Enacting Their Ability as Teachers of Liberation

Black feminist thought supports the idea that lived experience is a criterion of knowing for African American women (Hill-Collins, 2002). Ms. Betty and Ms. Tasha understood the ways they had been marginalized based on race and gender; therefore, they practiced in a way that was liberating for themselves as well as their students. For example, Ms. Tasha shared the following story as a lived experience:

> I always share the story with the kids about the situation I had when I went to cash a check. And the people at the cash-check place, strange, true story, wanted to take my money. I'm like, "Wait a minute! I always cash my check, you all never take my money." I said, "Look, just give me my check." . . . They locked the door and before the thing was over, I had three cops on the scene. I was there for one hour. . . . And so I try to tell the kids, I said, "I knew that I had to be calm, because people expect for us to show out, fuss, cuss or whatever."

Her story recognizes that response to behavior is differential and can be tied to notions of race. It was the teachers' solidarity on experiences of racialized discrimination that laid a foundation for connecting with some of their students.

Although the teachers were asked how they addressed student behavior, their responses centered around what teaching meant to them. Ms. Tasha emphasized, "I'm a true believer of teaching and not babysitting," indicating having expectations of herself. At different points in the interview, both teachers expressed being able to execute the following: "change the message," "change the perception," "encourage students," "look for ways to get them out the situation," "hear the student out," "have hope for them," "give everyone a fair chance," "be a model," "protect their image," "be a tool to develop a student," and "widen their thinking." There were many things that the teachers believed they could do for their students under the auspices of teaching.

Due to their expectations and beliefs of self, the teachers described how they conceptualized their roles when addressing student behavior as well as how they conceptualized discipline. For Ms. Tasha, there was a keen intent on her acting in a way that maintained her student's dignity:

> Discipline . . . that don't mean you have to kill the child, that doesn't mean you have to rip out their heart, but to change that behavior. . . . That don't mean that he's never gonna have another chance. That doesn't mean he can't earn his chance again, but I do wanna change that behavior.

For Ms. Betty, there was an acknowledgment that the students are influenced by many competing forces, but she thought it still necessary to engage in actions that prepared students to navigate life. She explained the motivation for her actions in a manner consistent with a womanist pedagogy of care:

> I'm only one person trying [to] plant that seed on top of all the other seeds that have been planted in there, and I look at it as a field. . . . I know my little seed is only going to grow in fertile ground up in here. . . . Let me plant in you as much as I can because you're in the real world, and you're gonna need these tools to survive. And you don't have to be what statistics say you're going to be. You don't have go that way.

Both educators viewed addressing student behavior as part of their job, not in addition to and not separate from. Moreover, they exuded a level of confidence about their ability to execute what they perceived as their responsibilities. Ms. Tasha noted, "I'm pretty good at dealing with discipline in my room." They also acknowledged that the way they did their job was effective. Ms. Betty stated, "My way works and it keeps the confrontations down." The teachers' confidently articulated their competencies. This aligns with Morris's (2016) work centering the voices of Black girls, which asserted that caring and qualified teachers were a part of a desirable learning environment and that students benefit when teachers shared information about how they overcame obstacles they experienced.

Lastly, not only did the teachers believe in themselves, but they expressed that other school personnel did as well. Ms. Tasha described the necessity of serving as a cultural conduit in her school: "So a lot of times I have to say it takes us African Americans to work with the teacher. . . . So I usually like to work with those teachers. Sometimes I have teachers come to me and say, 'Ms. Tasha, I don't know what to do.' Or sometimes they'll say, 'Can you come to my classroom and talk to my class?'" In Ms. Tasha's narration, she explained how she could work with her colleagues to better understand some things as well as work with students in a way that would yield a desired outcome. Going back to Ms. Tasha's professional practices, she validated herself based on reputation: "The reputation I have in the dean's office is, 'Ms. Tasha never sends kids up.'" Similarly, Ms. Betty talked about not writing referrals for defiance or disrespect. The way their colleagues viewed them and relying minimally on other staff or punitive measures to bring about behavioral change was significant in constructing teacher ability to address student behavior.

Counternarrative 3: The Ability to Intentionally Create Enabling Classroom Spaces

The fifth tenet of DisCrit interrogates the ways in which race and ability shape ideas about belonging. Specific to the classroom, functional spaces allow multiply marginalized students of color access to sociopolitical and interpersonal learning spaces. Ms. Betty and Ms. Tasha described how they dismantle ideas of control and inferiority to create functional classroom spaces.

Ms. Tasha and Ms. Betty each talked about having control over their classroom space, not their student's behavior. When asked about her classroom management style, consistent with a caring and political practice that spaces be safe, affirming, and validating (Dixson, 2003; Gay, 2010), Ms. Betty provided the following analogy about how she conducts her space:

> I am the queen and this is my castle, and whatever you do in there, I'm still the queen. You know I don't scream and all of that but generally, 'cause I know, this is my space and I'm gonna take care of this space. As the queen, I know how to make things either a mess or make them calm. And I decide that every day, when I go into my classroom. Every day.

Ms. Betty identified that she intentionally created a space capable of being productive. While Ms. Betty spoke more symbolically, Ms. Tasha explicitly acknowledges the inherent rules and power differential that exist within the classroom. However, it was not used to create an exploitative or hostile space, but was rather useful: "This is Ms. Tasha's class and this is how we're gonna run things. There are gonna be a set of rules. I am the adult, if we have to keep going over it over and over and over again then that's what we're gonna do." Throughout both teachers' narratives, there was a theme of repeatedly enacting disciplinary actions within the classroom space to produce learning and facilitate development, not to punish. Both Ms. Tasha and Ms. Betty can be described as "unilaterally in charge of the classroom" (Gay, 2010, p. 53). As a result of their decisions and its consequences, they communicated their attitudes and expectations in a manner where students believed them and rose to the occasion.

The teachers structured their spaces to facilitate the social aspects of learning in a way that did not perpetuate social inequity in their classrooms, consistent with the political nature of womanist care (Ladson-Billings, 2009).

Both teachers talked about what worked in the spaces they created, highlighting the importance of context in school discipline practices. The processes they identified were purposely constructed through implicit and explicit actions. For example, Ms. Tasha described the following disciplinary approach: "I want to bring attention to the behavior, 'John, is that really necessary?'" Or indirectly, "'Sally, did you check out John? Is he working like you are?' So, I do a lot of indirect kind of stuff. 'Ms. Tasha, I know what you're trying to say.' 'Well, get with the program!'" Ms. Tasha's approach was understood within its context. Ms. Betty also emphasized the importance of being brief in addressing student discipline:

> The best thing you can do, correct and move on. "Put your phone up, honey." Okay, I gave him one. . . . "Okay, now, turn to page 32." Correct and move on, 'cause that staring. . . . And see, a lot of teachers do that. They correct and then they stare, and they wait on them to do what they just asked. I don't ever wait. If you wait and you stare, that means everybody's looking at them, putting the pressure on them, and then, if they cooperate, it looks like they punked out.

In understanding the ways in which social status is constantly challenged for her students, she tailored her approach accordingly. She also added, "You gotta praise and move on. Even with that. A little humor. And just kind of play with them but play and move on." The teachers believed that they could control the space as well as their interactions. Moreover, within this space it was critical that they not bring undue attention to students' challenges and successes, neither further marginalizing nor romanticizing them.

LIMITATIONS

The current study is based on the narrative of two teachers. Due to the emphasis on narrative of this study, there was no opportunity to collect observational data. While this is not to suggest that the teachers' accounts of their own practice are insufficient, additional data pieces would have added to the trustworthiness of the findings. Future researchers may wish to consider a combined analysis of classroom observations and narratives when theorizing under the framework of DisCrit. These data collection methods would add to the literature about functional classroom ecologies. In addition, the data was extracted from a larger data set, and secondary analysis was utilized to derive meaning for the purposes of the current study. Future data collection and design should seek to explicitly evaluate notions of race and ability in educator narrative and practice.

DISCUSSION

By employing DisCrit and womanist theoretical framings, the findings suggest that corrective actions are influenced by the perceived ability of students, teachers, and classroom spaces. Specifically, the counternarratives revealed that race and ability were the variables that constructed how teachers perceived students' behaviors. In line with the current study, Annamma & Morrison (2018) theorized components of a functional classroom system, which they termed the DisCrit classroom ecology. This type of classroom, based on curriculum, pedagogy, and solidarity, refuses deficit-oriented master narratives about learning and behavior of multiply marginalized students of color (Annamma et al., 2018). This discussion illustrates the parallels between the theorized DisCrit classroom ecology and current study findings.

The teachers described discipline practices used with Black students identified as disabled; however, their narrative was not based on deficits, hopelessness, control, or marginalization. The teachers addressed difference, but not in a pathological manner. While research suggests that educators typically focus on students' ability without mention of race, current study findings indicate that educators are talking about race, whether explicit or implicit, hence either supporting or disrupting racism (Alvarez & Milner, 2018). Moreover, the teachers in the current study did not display color-evasiveness or engage in processes that served to justify and disguise the labeling of Black students (Annamma et al., 2017). The term *color-evasiveness*—as opposed to color-blindness (Bonilla-Silva, 2007)—is intentionally used to stray from the metaphor that disability (e.g., blindness) implies undesirable or weak, as those who are blind have sight, just differently (Annamma et al., 2017). Instead, the research findings, and in concordance with DisCrit pedagogy, reveal that disciplinary disproportionality can be disrupted when teachers recognize their students' political identities and the gifts they bring, thereby enacting discipline practices in a manner that is accessible, equitable, and justice oriented.

The notion that ability lies within these teachers centers the voices of Black educators and their lived experiences. This finding provides additional evidence for the concept of political clarity, central to the framing of this study, which purports that professional practices are in part a result of heightened sensitivity due to personal experiences (Beauboeuf-Lafontant, 2002). In this study, teacher pedagogy was a form of resistance, which sought to bring out students' gifts. Classroom spaces were transformative, even when not congruent with the whole school. Relationship building was essential to creating learning ecologies. The teachers in this study controlled their own responses and did not attempt to "safeguard" their classrooms from a typical type of behavior or "weed out" any type of student. Instead, they asserted control over the space and control over their student–teacher interactions.

CONCLUSIONS AND KEY TAKEAWAYS FOR PRACTICE,
POLICY, AND RESEARCH

Research findings and practice guidance indicating that racial and implicit bias play a role in exclusionary school discipline is a step in the right direction. More importantly, educators of color should rely on their cultural knowledge to create collaboratively sophisticated approaches to address the pervasive nature of disciplinary disproportionality. According to research findings, implications for practice, policy, and research must be culturally specific to achieve an educational reality whereby exclusion based on race and disability is nonexistent.

Practice Considerations

The educators in the current study, who possessed political clarity, are part of a tradition of Black educational excellence. They joined the teaching field for that purpose and have their own schooling and lived experiences to complement their professional practice. If the educator workforce was more racially and culturally diverse, there would be more educators who possessed an understanding about students' home language, social interaction patterns, histories, and cultures due to living it themselves. Additionally, there is a need for educators who acknowledge that racism and ableism are current and real tragedies that must be alleviated. Moreover, there is support for racial/ethnic congruency as a protective factor from exclusionary discipline for students of color (Blake et al., 2016).

Educators who understand that notions of race and ability can be used to include, validate, and heal students are needed within classrooms. These educators should be incentivized for engaging in coaching with other teachers either through role change and/or as a part of an ongoing and embedded professional development process, rather than through isolated workshops. Emerging research on coaching models that emphasize high-level teacher problem solving has shown promise in decreasing discipline referrals (Gregory et al., 2016). These effective models can be enhanced by centralizing knowledge from Black educators, such as those in this study, to create context and culturally specific interventions for schools.

Policy Considerations

Brown v. Board of Education (1954) was used as a basis for the creation of the IDEA, which is the major legislation that shapes the discourse about disability in schools. However, if race-based legislation is utilized as a basis, but the consideration of race is not included in the IDEA, it is likely contributing to the exacerbated exclusion of students of color with disabilities, based on behavior. As such, revision to the IDEA should be pursued and provisions made for students' intersectionality. When IDEA is revised, more intentionality is needed for the conceptualization of disability. The current version of IDEA lists cultural considerations as a rule-out factor for disability identification; however, there is no guidance on what constitutes cultural consideration. Educators in this study acknowledged differences and did not engage in a social construction process that resulted in exclusion. IDEA could provide guidance on how school-based decision teams can discuss students' identities, such as race, when making disability decisions. Such conversations are often avoided because they are uncomfortable; however, this study and research suggests that implicit conversations are already occurring, yet not explicitly. Policymakers should provide specific guidance in this area based on an antiracist and anti-ableist approach.

There are also implications for state education agencies in adopting professional development expectations for instructional personnel such as teachers and related service providers (e.g., school psychologists). These professionals have traditionally participated in the disability identification process of students within historical systems and pedagogies of oppression. As such, it is imperative that states support teachers and school psychologists by providing them with intersectional, evidence-based, and culturally responsive approaches to identification, referral, and assessment procedures within special education. For several states, professional development efforts are only focused on positive behavior intervention support (PBIS), yet the aforementioned changes would enhance and complement the development of antiracist pedagogy and practice schoolwide. Additionally, policymakers and administrators at the state and district level must still be held responsible to all students and eliminate racial or ethnic disparities for special education and general education students as it relates to exclusionary discipline. Lastly, states, districts, and schools must be required to consider the range of factors that contribute to racial discipline disparities. The Every Student Succeeds Act (2015) holds schools accountable and requires continuous data disaggregation. As such, there is the potential for schools to assess their climate and quality.

Specific to school-based policy, McIntosh et al. (2014) found that top-down policies have the potential to moderate the effects of explicit bias found within exclusionary disproportionality. Examples of explicit bias include the endorsement of zero-tolerance policies and exclusionary discipline practices, which are often resistant to change (McIntosh et al., 2014). Strong consideration should be given to eliminating the use of suspension and expulsion for lower level and subjective offenses (Redfield & Nance, 2016). Instead, policies should be revised to consider the individual student and their identities as well as multiple contexts, including school and community, which lead to the behaviors being observed. Similar to research implications, the teachers in this study considered the ecological impact of their decision-making and responded in ways that preserved the individual as well as the context (e.g., classroom, school, community). Moreover, teachers like the ones in this study should be invited to participate in policymaking at the school, district, state, and federal levels.

Lastly, bottom-up approaches are needed to directly support students and the interpersonal relationships that occur on a daily basis. To prevent exclusionary school discipline from being a continual instrument of spirit murdering for Black students identified with disabilities, restorative and holistic mental health practices grounded in history, identity, and culture are needed. It will be insufficient and unacceptable for restorative discipline practices or mental health support to continue to avoid racism and ableism within students' daily lives. Therefore, it is time for policies that guide school-based supports and services to convey that Black students' humanity matters by adopting approaches and encouraging the hiring of professionals who can acknowledge the realities of their lives.

Research Considerations

Understanding disciplinary disproportionality for students with disabilities necessitates an intersectional approach. The study findings highlight that race is a critical factor, but it is certainly not the only identity disproportionately impacting Black students. As such, deriving policy and practice implications means that a shift is needed from the usual "race *or* disability *or* gender" approach for alleviating social justice issues such as racial disparities in school discipline. Study findings and in concordance with color-evasiveness, the hidden norms of ableism must be reexamined in schooling discourses, practices, and policies. The social construction processes inherent to understanding identity at the intersection of race and disability is important and at the intersection of student identity, teacher positionality, and space. Hence, intersectionality can be valuable to understand intrapersonal identities, interpersonal experiences, and their associations with sociopolitical outcomes (Moradi & Grzanka, 2017). Using intersectionality (Crenshaw, 1991) and other critical race theories to study school discipline can shift the focus to promising, culturally responsive practices and away from making Black students responsible for their exclusion from classrooms and schools.

In addition, more educator counternarratives are needed in research on school discipline. However, it is important that such research be situated within a historical context whereas educators are viewed as carrying on a longstanding tradition in educating Black students (Walker, 2013). Moreover, counternarratives should highlight techniques, but also deconstruct "controlling narratives" (Hill-Collins, 2000). Patricia Hill Collins coined the term to highlight the racial myths constructed in society to justify social control of Black people. Schools are important sites where such ideas can be resisted or reproduced, sometimes simultaneously. Counternarratives like this chapter should guide research, policy, and practice.

PROMISING EDUCATIONAL PRACTICES TO ADDRESS DISCIPLINE DISPROPORTIONALITY

CHAPTER 6

Trauma and Discipline Disproportionality

Treating the Underlying Concerns

Kristen Pearson, Laura Marques, Monica Stevens,
and Elizabeth Marcell Williams

In 2014, just 9 years after the city of New Orleans was devastated by the flooding associated with Hurricane Katrina and 9 years into the rebuilding efforts of its public education system, a lawsuit was filed by the Southern Poverty Law Center and the Juvenile Justice Project of Louisiana on behalf of a 6-year-old, 1st-grade student (*J.W. v. Vallas*, 2010). The student was handcuffed and shackled to a chair by an armed security officer at a New Orleans' elementary school following an argument the student had with a peer over a seat in the lunchroom. This case laid bare to the general public the ongoing concerns of racial inequality and disproportionate discipline in a system struggling to rebuild itself (Southern Poverty Law Center, 2010).

This chapter addresses the impact of trauma as it relates to discipline disproportionality in New Orleans, Louisiana, a region of the country that diagnoses posttraumatic stress disorder (PTSD) in children at a rate three times the national average (Ending the Epidemic of Childhood Trauma, 2019). The effect that trauma may have on a child's emotional, social, and behavioral functioning is often misunderstood in the school setting and places children at risk for detrimental educational decisions and outcomes, such as expulsion and involvement in the juvenile justice system. Methods grounded in behavioral theory are widely recommended to improve the behavior of students with disabilities. However, this chapter suggests that these methods are not the most appropriate for students with complex traumatic histories. As an alternative, there is a need for a wider range of services and treatment settings for special education students, which includes a trauma-informed day treatment program along a continuum of supports. With a wider range of educational services and supports, students can access necessary treatment in a broad range of settings and return to general education environments better prepared for emotional, behavioral, social, and academic success. Further, specific trauma-informed interventions and frameworks used in effective trauma-informed programs can be implemented in less restrictive school environments to provide continuity in care, which will benefit many students.

CENTER FOR RESILIENCE

The Center for Resilience (CfR) is a therapeutic day treatment program that serves students with emotional disabilities and disruptive behavior disorders, most of whom have traumatic histories. The program accepts referrals from local school districts, serving students between kindergarten and 10th grade who display symptoms of depression, anxiety, verbal and physical aggression toward others, and elopement from the classroom or school. Students remain enrolled in their home school while attending the program full time to receive all academic, clinical, and related services. This setting is considered more restrictive than a self-contained classroom; therefore, placement is contingent on a number of important factors, including documentation of poor progress with implementation of behavior supports and school counseling services. One of the primary goals for students is to return to a less restrictive setting in the student's home school.

The foundation of the program is centered on building relationships and collaborative problem solving, including the child as a participant, as part of organizational alignment with trauma-informed, culturally affirming, and healing-centered principles. Students leave the program better prepared for behavioral success in a less restrictive environment. Ongoing support for returning to school settings is provided. Consultation is provided by CfR faculty and staff at both the administrative and direct service level, which is guided by academic and behavioral data. Further, support is provided regarding effective evidence-based intervention strategies for the student returning to the school setting.

LITERATURE REVIEW

The City of New Orleans

While the city of New Orleans, Louisiana, is represented by a rich history of culture, music, carnival, spirit, acceptance, and diversity, it is equally impacted by inequity, poverty, crime, and violence. For these reasons, to understand New Orleans is to understand both sides of the paradox, and to appreciate the resilience is to recognize the adversity. Following is a description of New Orleans and a brief history of its education system, including the challenges faced prior to and following Hurricane Katrina.

New Orleans is a metropolitan area with a population of 393,292, with 59.8% of individuals identifying as African American and 34.1% as White. According to the Louisiana Budget Project (2018), 25.4% of the population lives in poverty, a rate that is the highest among the 50 largest metro areas in the United States. Overall, the state of Louisiana has the second highest poverty rate in the United States. Further, *ALICE* (Asset Limited, Income Constrained, Employed) is a term that represents households that earn more than the federal poverty level, but less than the basic cost of living for the parish (the ALICE threshold). According to the United Way (2016) ALICE report, 53% of the population, disproportionately minoritized residents, are considered to be living below the poverty line and ALICE threshold.

Minoritized populations are disproportionately impacted by poverty in a number of historic ways in New Orleans. These vast disparities are rooted in systemic and enduring oppression that have intensified in the past 2 decades following the unequal destruction and recovery following Hurricane Katrina and associated flooding. In a report prepared by the Racial Wealth Divide Initiative, Prosperity Now, in 2016, a decade after Hurricane Katrina in New Orleans the average Asian and African American home was worth half the value of the average White-owned home, the unemployment rate of households of color was three times more than the rate for White households, and families of color were six times more likely to live in poverty than White families. These inequities are tied to longstanding historical oppression surrounding housing, employment, criminal justice, and education (Annamma et al., 2013).

Recent Developments in New Orleans Education

The New Orleans K–12 school system is unique and has undergone a complicated development over several decades. The Cowen Institute (2018) provides an outline of the history of the New Orleans education system; relevant recent events are summarized as follows. The first charter school, established in 1998, opened before Hurricane Katrina. In its 1st year, the Middle School Advocates Charter School received 900 applicants for its 117 available spots. In 2003, Louisiana legislators and voters approved an amendment allowing the Louisiana Board of Elementary and Secondary Education (BESE) to take over habitually underperforming schools or to convert the schools to privately managed charters. In doing so, BESE created the Recovery School District (RSD), and by 2005 BESE converted five public schools into charters.

On August 29, 2005, Hurricane Katrina made landfall. The impact of the hurricane, as well as levee failures, resulted in flooding of 80% of the city, damage to 70% of housing units, the evacuation of more than 65,000 students, and literally hardly a foundation on which to rebuild the education system. By December, most schools remained closed, the Orleans Public School District was effectively bankrupt, and racial tensions were rising throughout the city. Adding to the tension, the Orleans Parish School Board (OPSB) terminated over 7,000 employees without pay. It was believed that most of the teachers fired were African American, and those rehired by RSD and the charter schools were White and from places outside of the city (Cornish & Block, 2014), thus perpetuating systemic racism. At the beginning of the 2006–2007 school year, the city had a total of 58 schools, including 22 RSD direct-runs, 17 RSD charters, 2 BESE charters, 5 OPSB direct-runs, and 12 OPSB charter schools, thus creating a fragmented and complicated system that left students of color and students with disabilities vulnerable, and educational stakeholders began to flag inequities.

In 2010, the Southern Poverty Law Center (SPLC) filed a lawsuit claiming that students with disabilities were denied access to New Orleans public schools and often forced into schools that were failing to provide services as required under the Individuals With Disabilities Education Act (IDEA) (*P.B. v. Pastorek*, 2010). The SPLC documented more than 30 New Orleans schools with violations. The Louisiana Department of Education agreed to settle the case in 2014 by providing training, technical assistance, ongoing monitoring, and additions to the renewal process for charters to ensure readiness to serve students with disabilities. As mentioned in the opening of this chapter, an additional lawsuit filed by the SPLC and the Juvenile Justice Project of Louisiana in 2010 resulted in policy revisions by the RSD to protect New Orleans students from abusive restraints, handcuffing, and shackling (*J.W. v. Vallas*, 2010). The case represents a microcosm of the ongoing concerns of racial inequality and disproportionate discipline in the system.

According to a 2017 report from the Education Research Alliance for New Orleans, Black students are twice as likely as White students to be suspended in the city (Barrett et al., 2017). Low-income students were identified as being 1.75 times more likely to be suspended than non–low-income students. Further, suspensions are longer for students who have intersected identities that include having low income and identifying as Black. For fights involving one White and one African American student, slightly longer suspensions were given to the African American student. During the 2015–2016 school year, 7% of students with disabilities were suspended out of school in Orleans Parish (Louisiana Department of Education, n.d.). According to the Youth Index report of 2016, Black students were suspended at three times the rate for White and other students (The Data Center, 2016).

In the decade following the SPLC lawsuits, New Orleans continued making incremental changes with attempts to improve the education system. The number of Teach for America members was increased to meet the need for more teachers, though this perpetuated the feeling that New Orleans was being run by "outsiders" and people who could not truly understand or relate to the city's diverse culture. This cultural mismatch creates a higher probability of misunderstandings that require remedy, perpetuating feelings for students that they do not belong, and also impacts academic performance (Carothers et al., 2019; Stephens et al., 2019). In 2012, the OneApp was implemented to streamline the application process to charter schools. In 2014, the RSD closed its last conventional schools and created the first complete charter school district in the country. And as recently as June 2018, all charters and schools in the city were reunified under the OPSB, closing the RSD (The Cowen Institute, 2018).

In response to concerns regarding students receiving special education services who were failing to respond to school-based interventions, in 2012 the school district allocated government funds to support the development of a day treatment program to serve students with significant emotional and behavioral needs. This program was intended to address gaps in the continuum of care and provide alternatives to exclusionary practices that were created and perpetuated by structural and racial inequities.

Trauma Exposure in New Orleans

Racial inequities and oppression fuel the experience and symptoms of trauma (Polanco-Roman et al., 2016) that undergirds the New Orleans community. The prevalence of clinically significant posttraumatic stress symptoms in students reaches 60%. According to a study conducted by the Institute of Women and Ethnic Studies (2015), youth ages 10 to 16 in New Orleans display symptoms of PTSD at a rate three times the national average. Of the children surveyed, 40% had witnessed domestic violence, a shooting, a stabbing, or a beating, and 18% witnessed a murder. More than half of the children in the survey reported that someone close to them had been murdered. These traumatic events are connected to violence experienced in communities as well as federally sanctioned practices such as redlining, which contributed to a high percentage of Black people remaining in segregated communities with inequitable resources (Rothstein, 2017). Children in New Orleans also experience symptoms of trauma related to significant weather events and natural disasters, including hurricanes and tornadoes, as well as the effects of chronic stress associated with living in poverty (Falk & Troeh, 2017).

Effects of Trauma

Studies on adverse childhood experiences (ACEs), or experiences of abuse, neglect, and family dysfunction that occur between birth and age 18, have been found to disrupt brain development, often limiting social, emotional, and cognitive functioning (American Academy of Pediatrics, 2014). Traumatized students are at a particularly high risk for learning and mental health problems, including behavior disorders and emotional disabilities. Diagnosis of PTSD is frequently accompanied by risk-taking and destructive behaviors, which are often linked to behaviors associated with juvenile justice involvement (Kerig, 2019). A child may experience symptoms such as social withdrawal, lack of energy and/or anhedonia, decline in school performance, difficulty concentrating, threats of harm to self or others, increased arousal, agitation, aggressiveness, repeated nightmares, or regressive behaviors.

The experience of trauma exposure often impacts a child's functioning in the school setting. Symptoms in schools may include developmental delays; higher dropout rates; lower academic achievement; reduced ability to organize, problem solve, and process information; higher suspension and expulsion rates; higher rates of referral for special education; and impaired concentration and memory (Nickerson & Jimerson, 2015). Symptoms of PTSD that manifest as aggressive language and behaviors, hypervigilance, inability to focus, withdrawal, and/or anxiety may be flagged as behavior problems in schools. These behaviors put students at risk for being disciplined and becoming involved in the juvenile justice system, particularly when trauma symptoms are misconstrued as simply misbehavior. In addition to this chain of events leading to disproportionate discipline for students with traumatic histories, schools' reactions to trauma symptoms in students often create an unfortunate cycle that retraumatizes students.

Research has indicated that students who experience three or more ACEs are 2.5 times more likely to fail a grade (Blodgett & Lanigan, 2018). Further, students who experience multiple traumas are significantly more likely to perform below grade level, be identified for special education, experience suspensions or expulsion, and drop out of school. Contributing to, compounding, and reflecting these detrimental outcomes for students are the systems of racist, ableist, and other forms of oppression that currently and historically operate in New Orleans to maintain White supremacy (Annamma, 2018).

School Response and Resources

The problem of discipline disproportionality is related to many issues, including a lack of mental health and behavioral services in New Orleans, and, more broadly, a lack of equitable services of all types. Schools are inequitable, unprepared, and underresourced to provide the range and quality of services that students of color, particularly Black and Brown students, should receive. Schools in this region continue to rely on punitive and developmentally inappropriate methods of discipline, resulting not only in underserving students with significant mental and behavioral health needs, but also retraumatizing them through school-based actions. These punitive school responses themselves may exacerbate future behavioral infractions and contribute to the high rates of suspensions and expulsions of special education students (Mayer, 1995). Retraumatizing forms of discipline include those that are physical, isolative, demeaning, and implemented without consideration of developmental age. Examples might include inappropriate use of restraints, seclusions, or transports; yelling at or demeaning/humiliating students; and suspending or otherwise isolating students without processing or problem-solving events leading up to school responses.

Currently in New Orleans there exists no true continuum of support for children and adolescents who experience the broad ranges of trauma described here. The only option for children requiring a higher level of care is hospitalization, and local psychiatric hospitals do not accommodate children displaying aggressive behaviors that may be a symptom of trauma and other mental health concerns. The nearest residential options for children are long distances from New Orleans, and for some ages of children the nearest options are outside of the state, thus limiting the ability for caregivers to participate meaningfully in treatment. In addition to the CfR, there is only one other therapeutic program (operating within a school) in New Orleans. There are no partial hospitalization options. This illustrates the dearth of mental health care options tied to larger systems of oppression, with one system impacting the other (i.e., trauma and the school-to-prison pipeline) (Abramovitz & Mingus, 2016).

Reduced Impact of Rewards and Consequences

Schools often rely on systems like positive behavior interventions and supports (PBIS) to prevent and address behavior. While findings are promising for reductions in discipline referrals (Horner et al., 2010), and the use of PBIS systems have proven effective for most children, there are limitations to the use of traditional behavior support with children who have experienced chronic stress and trauma. Recent research has examined differences in the neuroanatomy of reward systems (i.e., the basis for behavior theory-based interventions) in traumatized children. For example, Miu et al. (2017) found that participants with a history of interpersonal trauma reported both reduced levels of motivation for reward and increased levels of sensitivity to punishment. Also, McLaughlin and Sheridan (2016) highlight disruptions in particular learning processes, including fear and reward learning. Problems in such learning processes are associated with later developmental difficulties. Many others have cited the neural and behavioral differences in children who have experienced neglect, maltreatment, and institutionalization (Dillon et al., 2009; Guyer et al. 2006; Hanson et al., 2015).

What then remains is a large population of students for whom the traditional and accepted methods of intervention, often ones that are punitive in nature or not designed with an understanding of the trauma most students have experienced, may not be entirely appropriate or effective. CfR attempts to address this dilemma by first recognizing behavior as communication of a deeper need rather than the result of a motivation deficit, and second by partnering with traditional schools to find sustainable solutions for this vulnerable population. A radically different approach is needed to meet the needs of a chronically underserved population of students with significant exposure to trauma and subsequent mental and behavioral health needs. Following is a description of the ways in which CfR redefines "discipline" and addresses the underlying needs of this special population.

Program Theory and Methodology

A case study method is used to examine one center's approach to mitigating trauma and reframing it from a student deficit perspective (resulting in punitive discipline) to one in which the totality of the student's experiences and stressors are considered. French et al. (2020) recognize the importance of moving beyond teaching persons of color to cope and rather, and more importantly, helping them to heal. Following Robert Stake's qualitative case study methodology, the creation and implementation of the program, along with the data collection and analysis procedures, are described (Yazan, 2015).

CENTER FOR RESILIENCE: DEVELOPMENT AND PROGRAM FOCUS

The CfR began as a joint collaboration between the Orleans Parish School Board and Tulane University's Medical School, Department of Psychiatry. This university partnership helps to address the dearth of mental health services and inequities fueled by the school reorganization, which harms the most minoritized populations in the city—students of color with disabilities. The center is a separate setting serving area students in grades kindergarten through 10th grade with the most severe diagnosed behavioral and/or mental health disabilities. A blend of academic, psychological, and psychiatric support is offered to children and families in order to centralize care into one trauma-informed program. The program serves as an alternative to exclusionary practices and aims to treat the underlying problem of behavioral concerns. A key aim of the center is that students return to their enrolled schools better prepared for behavioral success.

Building Community Consensus

As a part of the preparation for launching CfR in 2012, CEO Liz Marcell-Williams strategically met with over 20 stakeholders in the counseling, medical, and mental health fields, including city government officials, hospital executives, and mental health clinic directors. Together with these efforts, Marcell-Williams leveraged longstanding relationships within the New Orleans educational community to convene a working group of relevant professionals who met once a month to inform program planning and design during the year prior to opening.

A result of these strategic groups was a structured and rigorous referral process that focused on equity and school accountability. Children are referred to CfR in a multistep process that schools initiate once a child has been identified as in need of services beyond the scope of a typical school system. In order to ensure that schools are not unfairly referring high-needs children, CfR requires that each referral be accompanied with thorough documentation of school interventions and child response to intervention prior to the referral. This includes the student's educational evaluation, functional behavioral assessment, behavior intervention plan, accompanying data, outline of services, treatment plan, crisis plan, and responses. Teacher interviews, discipline data, and a CfR observation of the student and setting are also considered.

Description of Children Served

Though there is variability in the profile of children served at CfR, the program is best designed to serve children with the special education diagnoses of "emotional disturbance" or "other health impairment." Children typically present to CfR with explosive or aggressive behavior, disruptive behavior, suicidal or homicidal ideations, inattention, impulsivity, anxiety, and/or depression. Children are only considered for admission to CfR if referring schools adequately demonstrate that the child has not responded to a well-designed and implemented behavior intervention plan and appropriate accommodations. Evaluating this might include examining the school's fidelity measures and associated data. A direct observation of the implementation of the behavior systems by a CfR school psychologist is also helpful. Well-demonstrated efforts to maintain the child in their traditional school setting is necessary to ensure that the child is being placed in the least restrictive environment.

CfR does not serve children whose primary disability is autism or who cannot perform basic life and self-care skills such as feeding and toileting. In order to provide appropriate treatment, children's parents must, at minimum, consent to CfR mental health treatment and participate in an in-person psychosocial evaluation. The psychosocial evaluation serves an important role that aligns with DisCrit tenet 2, which emphasizes the value of multidimensional identities, as opposed to singular forms of identity (i.e., race, social status, gender, or disability) (Annamma et al., 2012). The psychosocial evaluation explores information beyond educational disability boundaries and ensures that the student's and family's many identities are incorporated into treatment decisions and recommendations. This helps guard against the deficit lens of the individual and ensures that the student's and family's multiple intersected identities and lived experiences are considered in the evaluation and treatment process.

CfR Theoretical Approach

Rates of PTSD symptoms in New Orleans children are well above national rates. There is a critical need for programs that are focused on trauma recovery and healing. Trauma recovery is multifaceted, especially for children living in chronically stressful environments. Programming at CfR is therefore intended to address the emotional, biological, cognitive, and interpersonal injuries caused by trauma, which requires the use of practices aligned with healthy child development. Promoting healthy development at CfR centers on intentionally equitable practices, trauma-informed care, and healing-centered engagement to counter the multiple systems of oppression and the marginalization of students of color with disabilities.

Equity at CfR is fostered at multiple levels, including staff, students, families, and the larger community. Many practices and activities have been chosen and developed over time in anticipation of and response to student and staff needs. There is great care and concern to create an accepting and healing environment, an alternative to a system that is retraumatizing or perpetuating inequity. Table 6.1 outlines each level at which equity work is incorporated into CfR programming as well as the work to which the organization commits and its anticipated impact.

Table 6.1. Diversity, Equity, and Inclusion at CfR

	Practice/Activity	Anticipated Impact
Staff development	Overcoming racism workshops Antiracism book clubs Affinity groups Reflective, processing groups Equity audit DEI statement DEI steering committee Racial literacy training Staff PLAAY (preventing long-term anger and aggression in youth) training (evidence-based group therapy intervention) Training for board members and leadership team on equity and bias in hiring Use of and training in therapeutic crisis intervention for schools (TCIS)	Development of staff reflective capacity and racial awareness Protected space for common communities to explore identities and organizational priorities Prioritization of equity strategies and objectives Use of DEI statement to prioritize contracts with minority-owned businesses Development of culturally relevant interventions for program use
Student directed	PLAAY groups (evidence-based group therapy intervention) Culturally sustaining curriculum (learning environment and materials that affirm cultural identity) Restorative practices Nonexclusionary discipline practices	Development of racial literacy among students Promotion of healing and positive racial identity development The fostering of a positive association of the school environment for students
Family and community engagement	Quarterly community engagement events Dedicated staff member who operates as a family liaison Quarterly interdisciplinary team and family meetings for parental input, child progress reporting, and treatment planning	Increase in visibility and transparency within the community Offer of culturally affirming, recreational activities Reduction in barriers to family access and engagement

Description of Program Philosophy and Components

A foundational principle of a trauma-informed environment is promotion of psychological and physical safety for all individuals in the environment (Substance Abuse and Mental Health Services Association [SAMSHA], 2014). Psychological safety is fostered at CfR by selecting and training in practices and policies consistent with culturally responsive and antiracist pedagogy and practices, as well as healthy child development and relationships. At CfR an emphasis is placed on staff being authoritative versus authoritarian in their relationships with children. Authoritative caregiving consists of consistent nurturance, clear communication, and predictable limits on child behavior (Kuppens & Ceulemans, 2019). The authoritative style of relating between adult and child is the style associated with optimal developmental outcomes and secure attachment formation. Each child is assigned a particular home-room staffed by a consistent set of adults, which acts as a secure base for the child at CfR. The child-to-staff ratio is small (typically 3:1) to allow children and staff to form close, positive relationships. Regular staff supervision and feedback is practiced to maintain alignment with the core values at CfR.

Physical safety is maintained using positive behavior management practices and skill-building techniques. Behavioral expectations are clearly outlined and tracked, and when expectations are not met, predictable responses are implemented, ranging from loss of privileges to physical intervention if safety is at risk. The most important aspect of maintaining safety includes leveraging adult–child relationships to facilitate processing and reflection in a healing manner using two approaches: therapeutic crisis intervention for schools (TCIS) (Holden et al., 2001) and restorative justice (Costello et al., 2013). TCIS provides a crisis prevention and intervention model that aims to prevent crises from occurring and reduce the potential for psychological and physical injury to children and staff. Restorative justice offers the opportunity to build skills and repair harm when wrongdoing has occurred.

Responses to behavioral concerns do not include physical punishment, suspension, expulsion, or other harsh discipline practices. Rather, efforts are made to understand underlying reasons behind unmet behavioral expectations using relationship-based techniques such as collaborative and proactive solutions (Greene, 2014). These efforts prioritize the input of students and families, representing an organizational alignment with trauma-informed principles as well as DisCrit tenet 4, which privileges frequently marginalized voices (Annamma et al., 2012). Students and families play a critical role in treatment and planning.

Additional approaches to addressing behavioral problems are necessary to maintain physical safety. Figure 6.1 details the hierarchy of systems used to maintain safety in the program. The bottom of the triangle displays the foundational practices in place at CfR that contribute to trauma-sensitive stabilization. Also critical to this approach is staff professional development and ongoing support. These practices are foundational to promoting

Figure 6.1. Hierarchy of Behavioral Support Interventions

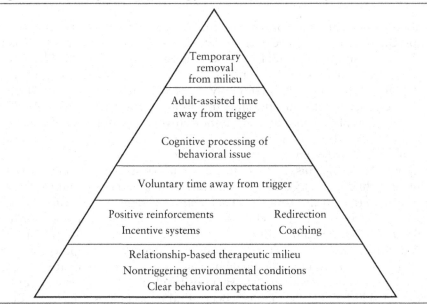

healing-centered engagement for both students and staff, which begins with prioritization of warm and nurturing interactions among children and staff members. The physical layout of the program, scheduled periods of child-led play, and a variety of novel and enriched learning experiences (e.g., creative arts, yoga, martial arts, community-based experiences) are all intentionally designed to provide an overall therapeutic experience for each child. Other professional development practices incorporated as recommended by SAMSHA guidelines include the implementation of self-care days once per month and training on self-care, compassion fatigue, burnout, and vicarious trauma.

Transitioning Students

After a school identifies a student for referral to CfR and the child is determined to be a good fit for CfR programming, schools enter a memorandum of understanding (MOU) with CfR. The MOU outlines the mission of CfR, responsibilities of the referring school and CfR, terms of information sharing with regard to federal privacy and data-sharing laws, and various policies and procedures. School partners are expected to remain involved in their student's progress with CfR throughout the duration of their enrollment so that relationships can be built between the organizations and the child's family and to allow for knowledge and skills sharing.

Determinations about transition back to a sending school are multifaceted and reflect the interdisciplinary priorities of the center. Daily behavior tracking shows trends in the child's ability to consistently meet school-based expectations (e.g., maintaining safety, following the schedule). Clinical progress monitoring reflects the severity of psychiatric symptoms over time, and academic progress monitoring details the child's grade-level performance. Readiness to transition to a home school relies on these three areas of monitoring as well as child, family, and school readiness to support the transition. Once a child returns to the home school, CfR maintains a relationship with the school in that ongoing assessment of the child's adjustment occurs for at least 3 months. Further support is individually determined based on the unique needs of the child and setting. In most cases, the child is referred to community-based treatment providers prior to leaving CfR so that psychiatric and behavioral health care continues without interruption. Depending on the continuing needs, the child's clinician, the program psychologist, the family liaison/social worker, the clinical director, and the academic director remain available for consultation and direct service to ensure a successful transition.

A Separate Setting

Inherent in a setting that is separate from a traditional school is the criticism that students with disabilities and students of color are being further segregated from typically developing peers. This is a valid criticism, and there is much work to be done, including in the city of New Orleans, to address this systemic issue. CfR acknowledges that it provides therapeutic support within a larger context of systems of racialized and ableist oppression, though it is differentiated from other alternative education programs in a number of ways that were highlighted in the preceding sections of this chapter. Namely, CfR provides high-quality treatment often not otherwise available to students who must negotiate the intersection of trauma, race, poverty, and systemic inadequacies and larger systems of oppression. CfR has a thorough referral and intake process that ensures that schools have attempted intervention and that students are truly in need of this special setting and treatment. Schools must demonstrate that interventions have been thoroughly attempted by providing documents, such as the student psychoeducational evaluation, functional behavior analysis, and behavior intervention plan, along with accompanying data and fidelity measures. A psychologist reviews all records, observes the student in the home school setting, and makes a determination with the team regarding fit for the program. Once students are enrolled in CfR, each student's home school remains involved in the treatment and planning. Transitions back to the student's home school are discussed at each quarterly treatment team meeting with CfR, the family, and the home school. The student and family are engaged in the process through frequent communication and empowerment. Throughout the entire stay at CfR, the family voice is ensured and centered, beginning with their required consent to join the program. Also, CfR's dedication to trauma-informed care, diversity, equity, and inclusion (e.g., overcoming racism workshops, implementation of a DEI steering committee and DEI statement, racial literacy training, implementation of culturally sustaining curriculum, restorative practices, etc.) create a safe alternative to segregating programs. CfR is not for students with developmentally appropriate behavioral infractions; rather, it provides treatment to students with the most significant mental health challenges. In the following sections, data are outlined to show the benefit to children who have this option available for their special education.

PROGRAM EVALUATION

As described, a central mission of CfR is to provide intensive academic and mental health interventions that support children in healing from individual, collective, and race-based trauma, as well as gaining and maintaining meaningful participation in family, school, and community/cultural supports that facilitate growth. As a standard practice, copious quantitative and qualitative data are collected from children, families, schools, and staff and reviewed by the leadership team monthly to examine progress toward this mission, inform programming decisions, and inform adjustments to children's individualized plans. This data-based, decision-making process is intended to reduce subjective bias and refine practices to respond to the unique needs of children and families in the New Orleans community. The following section will present program evaluation data, as well as examples of program adaptation in response to data collected. Relevant data include characteristics of children enrolled, rates of referral, admittance, and enrollment, as well as rates of attrition and successful transition. The data demonstrate a reduction in behavior incidents and hospitalizations over time and in academic growth.

Admittance and Enrollment

To ensure an equitable referral process with a critical eye for identifying children who can continue to be reasonably served in the school setting or those who require a higher level of care, a multidisciplinary team including an educator, social worker, psychologist, and psychiatrist are responsible for making admission recommendations to the leadership team. During the first 3 years of operation (2015–2018 school years), 83 children were referred to the program. Of those referred, 52 children were accepted and 45 enrolled, for an acceptance rate of 63% of total referrals. Most rejection decisions were due to the child's needs not being severe enough to warrant a separate setting or the need for additional interventions in the home school (e.g., a referral for a student who just started at a new school and has limited data). However, at times, the evaluation process determined that some children required a more restrictive placement and intensive interventions, such as a residential placement or homebound services with multisystemic therapy services, due to severe behaviors such as sexual aggression or extensive criminal involvement. In most cases, CfR clinical and medical staff (with expertise in referrals to higher levels of care) supported the caregivers, home school personnel, and community service providers in making decisions and obtaining these recommended services. Although gaps in the continuum of care remained, this process supported schools and families in obtaining appropriate existing services for children with the highest need.

Child Demographics

Demographics of the children enrolled, including age, gender, and qualification for free or reduced lunch, were collected during the referral and evaluation process. Across the first 3 years, enrolled children ranged in age from 5 to 15 years (M = 10.67, SD = 2.17) and were 78% male (n = 35). All children were African American and qualified for free or reduced lunch. These rates are only slightly higher than rates of children of minority racial status and qualification for free or reduced lunch seen in open enrollment schools in the Orleans Parish school district from which admitted students are referred (Louisiana Department of Education, n.d.). It is theorized that this rate is reflective of the disproportionate exposure of children of color and those from low socioeconomic backgrounds to trauma and stress that can create or exacerbate mental health challenges. A population that is entirely African American will be exposed to race-based trauma and racist systems of oppression, including structural and systemic racism.

Behavior Incidents

As a trauma-informed organization, CfR leadership and staff are strongly committed to creating a supportive and therapeutic environment that avoids the retraumatization of children through the reduction and elimination of seclusion or restraint. Reduction of seclusion and restraint can also indirectly represent growth among children as they heal and develop coping skills to navigate the school environment effectively. The leadership team reviews rates of seclusion and restraint monthly, discusses data with staff to identify solutions, and uses data to inform professional development and programmatic adjustments. During the first 3 years of operation, program additions or adaptations aimed at reducing use of seclusion and restraint included professional development for staff (e.g., prevention strategies, etc.), individualized tracking and monitoring of student success to inform individualized programming, and model adjustments. As discussed, all staff are trained in therapeutic crisis intervention in schools, trauma-informed and relationship-based crisis intervention strategies, as well as nonphysical interventions to de-escalate children in crisis. Staff are also certified to use safe seclusion and/or restraint techniques when necessary to maintain the physical safety of staff and children.

In the middle of the 1st year of operation, a detailed and individualized system for tracking student success was implemented to inform decisions regarding individualized interventions, progress, and readiness for return to the child's home school. Children were rated on four expectations (safety, staying in assigned spaces, effort to stay on task, and use of appropriate language) regularly throughout the day. These data are primarily intended to provide objective data regarding progress and targets for intervention and not used as tools to motivate children. As previously stated, students of this profile often do not respond well to traditional behavioral supports, such as earning and losing points, and this system might instead create significant emotional and behavioral distress.

In year 3, a series of model adjustments were made in response to data collected on-site and from staff and families. A second program site was opened for the purpose of piloting a modified model intended to serve children with more intensive mental health and behavioral needs, but less severe than would necessitate referral to residential treatment. This model, which has since become the model for all children enrolled, included reduced time but more intensive 1:1 academic instruction, a neutral "home base" recreation space that replaced the classroom as the primary placement during the day, and increased time spent in child-led activities that fostered social skill development and adult-to-child and peer-to-peer relationship building. This new model was intended, in part, to reduce triggers for behavioral crises and to dedicate more time to building skills necessary for children to be successful. Site A continued running programming as originally designed. Monthly data reviews revealed that site B was experiencing significantly less behavior incidents than site A. In fact, site B reported 73% less behavior crises than site A across year 3. Further, children at site B were reported to be more engaged in academic activities, while demonstrating equivalent or better academic growth. Based on this information, the piloted model was adopted uniformly in subsequent years. Further, due to staff observations and caregiver advocacy during year 3, sites were differentiated by elementary and middle school instead of severity of symptoms. Forums for caregiver advocacy included opportunities organic in nature (e.g., conversations with clinicians and administrative staff) as well as direct solicitation via surveys and caregiver events. It should be noted that the success observed at site B was thought to be due to the implementation of school-based practices/a different model rather than internal student deficits or a difference in student profile. In other words, the differences observed were due to school practices changing, and therefore the focus on change should be on adjusting the manner that programs and schools work with and build relationships with students.

CfR continues to evolve each year, and the treatment team continues to evaluate their practices and use data and feedback to identify and explore areas for improvement. With regard to evaluating the progress of the children, the center recognizes the limitations of its current methods. Specifically, the BASC assessments are completed by a single reporter and, at times, due to staff changes, the reporter may change for the child (Reynolds & Kamphaus, 2015). Further, results of the BASC may be impacted by the level of burnout the staff member may be experiencing or whether the child has experienced an acute crisis. There are limits inherent in rating scales completed by adults, including that perception and reality may vary from person to person or context to context. The center plans to expand its assessment and progress monitoring methods of student progress, including adding more parent and child participation in assessment and by adding more narrow-band assessment measures related to stress, trauma, and racial trauma. The center is also exploring ways in which meaningful data can be gathered on student progress following a transition from the program to better inform the ultimate goal of returning students to the home school.

These adaptations made through an iterative process of data analysis and feedback from staff, children, and families contributed to a total reduction of behavior incidents requiring the use of seclusion and/or restraint by 73% from the 1st year to the 2nd. Additional facility changes occurred to further reduce these rates. It was noted that facilities of site A were more easily damaged or destroyed, leading to more concerns about physical safety. Therefore, at the start of the 2019–2020 school year, all programming was relocated to a more secure facility that provided a stronger sense of safety for children. Data analysis of further rate reduction is ongoing.

Hospitalizations

The CfR mission to improve outcomes for youth extended to reducing the need for hospitalizations, which often separated children from their caregivers and other sources of support by long distances. Cumulative data across 3 years of operation indicated that children enrolled in the program experienced a 75% reduction in rates of inpatient care, including both acute care stays and psychiatric residential treatment, pre- and post-enrollment. While 50% of admitted children (n = 23) experienced at least one hospitalization prior to referral, just 20% (n = 9) of children experienced a hospitalization during enrollment. No child experienced their first acute care hospitalization while enrolled in the program. Leadership theorizes that highly trained staff have gained skills necessary to prevent and manage mental health crises on site (e.g., implementation of relationship-based interventions, TCIS, etc.), without necessitating hospitalization. Although this reduction is notable, longitudinal data regarding hospitalizations subsequent for discharge are not currently available, representing an opportunity for further program evaluation.

Discharges and Transitions

Given the goal to support children in building the skills necessary to meaningfully engage in a traditional school setting, successful transitions provide valuable data regarding success of the program. Across the first 3 years of operation, 83% of children who began the transition process, upon recommendation from staff, successfully transitioned back to their home school after being enrolled in the program an average of 15.8 months.

Academic Growth

CfR places an emphasis on providing children access to high-quality academic instruction tailored to their individual strengths and needs. Children enrolled in the program typically arrive from other instructional environments two to five grade levels behind in math and reading. Schools often report children have not been able to meaningfully participate in academic programming or in progress-monitoring activities that help design individualized academic interventions. As part of the skills deficits associated with mental health diagnoses and associated executive functioning and learning problems, children enrolled in the program often present with a history of low tolerance for academic frustration. As with other parts of the model, the academic setting has been adapted in response to qualitative and quantitative data collected over time. Individualized and small group instruction time was reduced in frequency but increased in intensity based on the child's ability to engage and their academic level. Progress monitoring was attempted quarterly. Analysis of academic engagement and progress monitoring suggested that growth varied considerably across grade levels and subjects, with the youngest children showing the highest levels of growth. Academic data in year 3 suggested that children grew .87 years in reading and .75 years in math, with only one student unable to complete any progress-monitoring assessments. It was noted that seven children grew more than 1 year in reading and 11 students grew 1 or more than 1 year in math.

FUTURE DIRECTIONS

This chapter has highlighted the following: the importance of intensive day treatment services to establish a true continuum of care, the assertion that day treatment is cost-effective (e.g., reduction of hospitalizations/crisis services), and the suggestion that access to school-based day treatment be a right for the special education population along a continuum of supports in order to disrupt the school-to-prison pipeline and increase graduation rates. CfR provides services for a population of students with significant mental health concerns and emotional disabilities who are frequently disproportionately disciplined in a community where children are exposed to trauma and systems of racial oppression at a significantly higher rate than the national average and where there currently does not exist a true continuum of supports. While a day treatment program is important along a continuum, it is also important to build services in general education contexts that will allow the city to be more responsive to students who have experienced significant trauma. Discipline disproportionality in New Orleans is certainly a complex and multifaceted problem tied to broader systems of oppression of persons through ableism and racism (Connor et al., 2016), and, as noted, this chapter focused on a specific population of students who experience significant behavioral health concerns that often stem from trauma exposure.

CfR began as a program intended to serve the children in New Orleans with the highest needs. However, CfR has plans to build a continuum of care to eventually address the needs of a wider range of children. The program has grown each year, and future plans include adding a program for children with autism and an early learning center. As the relationships with schools across the city continue to develop, there will be increased opportunities to influence the discipline and support practices. A goal for the center is to have a greater impact in consulting with schools on the use of trauma-informed practices so that they may be more responsive to students who have experienced significant trauma.

While the center works to serve children, it also recognizes the collective responsibility to mitigate the need for a segregated setting, which has resulted from systems of historic and current racial and ableist oppression. These types of therapeutic and restorative supports, as well as professional development in antiracism and culturally relevant pedagogy for teachers and other support staff, should be available in all schools. The following are suggestions to facilitate this process in the realms of research, practice, and policy.

Research Implications

For research, the data offered by CfR could be used to develop a study with more rigorous methodology and in other settings serving students in special education from historically minoritized backgrounds, including both therapeutic day treatment settings and regular school environments in which promising CfR trauma-informed practices could be adapted, implemented, and evaluated. Practices like relationship-based interventions, restorative practices, professional development of team members in racial literacy, culturally affirming practices, DEI-centered policies, culturally sustaining curriculum, and the group PLAAY therapy interventions should be replicated and systematically measured for fidelity, efficacy, and impact. The PLAAY therapy intervention is one of a few that is specifically implemented and targeted for Black youth and is used to teach coping and racial literacy skills through athletics and culture (Stevenson, 2003).

Practice Implications

Elements implemented by CfR should be the basis for other school-based settings, even more broadly in minoritized communities and cities where there are multiple forms of oppression rather than culturally responsive trauma-informed care. Recently, scholars in counseling psychology, such as French et al. (2020), have done important work to help treatment providers change their thinking about historical racist trauma away from pathologizing communities of color. In terms of the model proposed by French et al. (2020), their concept of radical hope fosters radical healing, with a key notion that radical hope is believing that the fight for justice will not be in vain.

Infusing antiracism and DisCrit into mental health, wellness, consultation, and teacher training across the education, mental health, health, legal, and community systems in minoritized communities has profound implications. Programs of this type that are replicable in other localities should consider the unique makeup, local context, and challenges specific to each region and population, including an understanding of historically oppressive systems.

Policy Implications

Though policy revisions will not alone address the issues addressed in this chapter, they are necessary. While CfR serves a mental health need and prevents more restrictive hospital placements, it is still a more restrictive setting than the student's home school setting. Policy and legal approaches can be used to address the dearth of culturally responsive and antiracist mental health practices in communities of color. Advocates can fight to require such policies to be present in systems that have been historically oppressive. Mandating a certain level of training in antiracist and culturally affirming practices is a start, but barriers to accessing training, including funding, must also be addressed. Priorities should elevate and center the voice of minoritized communities. For example, this could be done by training more mental health practitioners of color from the community who would be positioned to provide community-based support. There should also be teacher and educator training in historical racism, legislation to build access to mental health, and educational support in communities of color.

CfR was born from necessity in a unique city with unique local contextual challenges and challenges that permeate nationally, and these efforts could serve as a model for how students should be treated in broader systems that oppress them. CfR was a way of responding to the lack of culturally responsive mental health, academic, and behavior supports found in larger structures in New Orleans. With plans for expansion of services offered, CfR hopes to continue to identify unique solutions to the issue of discipline disproportionality.

KEY TAKEAWAYS

1. The effect that trauma may have on a child's emotional, social, and behavioral functioning is often misunderstood in the school setting

and places children at risk for additional problems (e.g., expulsion, involvement in the juvenile justice system).

2. There is a need for a wider range of services and treatment settings for special education students, including a trauma-informed day treatment program along a continuum of special education supports aligned with IDEA (2016).

3. While the use of PBIS systems have proven effective for most children, there are limitations to the use of traditional behavior support for children who have experienced chronic stress and trauma.

4. The foundation of an effective day treatment program should be centered on building relationships, collaborative problem solving, and an organizational alignment with trauma-informed, culturally affirming, and healing-centered principles.

5. Inherent in a setting that is separate from a traditional school is the criticism that students with disabilities and students of color are being further segregated from typically developing peers. This is a valid criticism, and there is much work to be done to address this systemic issue that is fueled by historical structural racism and led to a lack of community-based mental health and education services. DisCrit is a way of conceptualizing this complex issue.

6. An effective school-based day treatment program should be a right for special education students in order to disrupt the school-to-prison pipeline and increase graduation rates.

Improving Educator Use of Data-Informed Decision-Making to Reduce Disciplinary Infractions for Students With Emotional Disturbance

Sandra M. Chafouleas, Amy M. Briesch, Kathleen Lynne Lane,
and Wendy Oakes

Longitudinal data gathered by the U.S. Department of Education (e.g., National Longitudinal Transition Study, Special Education Longitudinal Study) have painted a consistently troubling picture regarding outcomes for students receiving special education services under the category of emotional disturbance (ED). Findings have revealed that students with ED are less likely to complete high school, pursue postsecondary education, or be employed; are more likely to be involved with the justice system once out of school; and are more likely to be suspended while in school (Bradley et al., 2008; Wagner et al., 2005; Wright et al., 2014). Broadly speaking, students with disabilities of all categories are more likely to be suspended than those without disabilities. Students with ED, however, have the highest rates of suspension relative to other students with disabilities (Achilles et al., 2007; Krezmien et al., 2006; Sullivan et al., 2013). In addition, some research has shown that Black students are overrepresented in ED classification (Morgan & Farkas, 2016) and that Black students designated as having ED are placed in more restrictive placements (Cullinan & Kauffman, 2005). Taken together, the intersectionality of race and disability, particularly among students designated as ED, highlights the critical need for building educator capacity to help change these exclusionary trajectories.

Although many intersecting factors play a role in these deleterious outcomes for students identified as ED, use of prevention science in schools is central to reversing this trajectory. Unlike academic referrals for more intensive supports, which primarily occur in elementary grades, the peak for behavioral referrals occurs in secondary grades (Walker et al., 2000). These findings suggest that what schools consider to be disciplinary problems among students with ED have compounded and escalated to the degree that there is resistance to intervention efforts (Bradley et al., 2008). Within a prevention-oriented model (i.e., tiered systems of support), the goal is to use data to provide appropriate intervention before problems become serious, persistent, and durable. This prevention orientation extends universally to all students, including those already exhibiting the most significant behavioral challenges. In addition, this prevention orientation calls for evaluation of contextual factors in determining intervention response. Attending contextual factors involves engaging in environmental modifications that can benefit not only individual students but also promote conditions that support access, diversity, and inclusion for all.

Calls to accelerate the pace of a shift away from a deficit model view that pathologizes students align with the movement toward more antiracist practices that tackle bias and discrimination (Gorski, 2019). A student deficit approach can be particularly damaging for students of color, given the mismatch between culture and primarily White middle-class norms for behavior (Annamma et al., 2018, 2020). Engaging a prevention lens facilitates changing attitudes from using data to "confirm" that behavioral challenges should be addressed through exclusion and outside services to instead reinforcing educators' role and responsibility to use data to inform within-school decisions and general education supports. For example, data can be used to mitigate deficit models that reinforce the removal of students perceived as having the most intensive behavioral issues from the general education classroom (Trent et al., 1998). Reframing the way educators think about data may change not only how educators view students, but also the responsibility of schools to support an equitable and inclusive environment for every student. In summary, using data to change school practices from reactionary to proactive parallels efforts that question how schools marginalize students, particularly those with multiple oppressed identities, such as having disabilities and identifying as a racial/ethnic minority.

In this chapter, we integrate information from multiple frameworks and from projects conducted by our team to elucidate promising practices for reducing disciplinary infractions for students with ED. Our theory of change begins with acknowledging the systems of oppression and bias that exist for students who have ED, especially those who identify as racial or ethnic minoritized students (Annamma et al., 2018; Migliarini & Annamma, 2020). These systems have contributed to negative life-course outcomes for students identified with ED. Schools have played a complicit role, particularly with regard to behavior, given their historical reliance on reactive and exclusionary disciplinary practices and a deficit-oriented view of students labeled as ED. Schools need positive approaches that rely on data-driven decisions within a problem-solving model. Effective data-driven problem solving requires educators to have requisite knowledge and skills along with attitudes supporting confidence in both their capacity and

expectations about students with ED. Attitudes that modify educator practice away from an internal student deficit lens and increase understanding
of how larger school structures can contribute to oppression are necessary
for change to occur (Annamma et al., 2014, 2018). The intersection of
educator beliefs about students' abilities—particularly those historically minoritized in schools—and their own sense of personal efficacy in equitable
use of data is critical to a social justice lens (Fergus, 2016) that can fuel a
positive trajectory for students with ED.

We acknowledge that individual outcomes are influenced by collective (e.g., organizational characteristics, interpersonal connections) and
systemic factors (e.g., policy, funding), such as the larger policy and historical context of racism and ableism, as conceptualized through theories such as DisCrit (Connor et al., 2016). We intentionally focus this
chapter on intrapersonal factors (i.e., educator knowledge, skills, and
attitudes) because systems change occurs through reciprocal interactions
across collective and individual levels. Thus, one important mechanism
to change negative outcomes for students with ED and engage in more
equitable practices is supporting educators in their capacity for—and
confidence in—effective data-driven problem solving related to addressing students' social, emotional, and behavioral needs. We define equitable
and effective data-driven problem solving as combining elements associated with (a) *knowledge* about the problem-solving process, (b) *skills* in
data use, and (c) *attitudes* that embrace continuous self-reflection about
personal capacity and the ways in which "problem behaviors" are conceptualized, particularly among those with ED and from minoritized
populations.

EQUITABLE AND EFFECTIVE PROBLEM SOLVING FOR SOCIAL, EMOTIONAL, AND BEHAVIORAL CHALLENGES

Our theoretical framework is grounded in the public health model that
has applications to education more commonly known as multitiered system of supports (MTSS). The main components of MTSS include the use
of (a) universal screening to proactively identify students who have been
placed at-risk in key domains; (b) tiered, evidence-informed intervention
supports matched to intensity of student need; and (c) formative assessment data to inform decision-making (Lane et al., 2014). Most commonly,
education has subscribed to a three-tiered model of prevention and intervention in which the universal level (i.e., tier 1) means that all students
have access to an evidence-informed core curriculum designed to teach
those skills believed to be critical to student success. Within the social,
emotional, and behavioral domain, for example, positive behavior supports along with a socioemotional learning curriculum are implemented on
a schoolwide level. Students for whom universal supports are insufficient

are identified using proactive universal screening, which involves conducting a common, brief assessment with all students in the population. Data are reviewed collaboratively, and students identified as needing additional supports are provided with them in the form of tier 2 intervention. Progress monitoring data are collected and analyzed to determine the effectiveness of targeted supports, and for those students who need more support, more intensive and individualized (i.e., tier 3) interventions are provided. In other instances, students exhibiting immediate, intensive intervention needs may be immediately connected with validated tier 3 supports (Lane & Walker, 2015; Walker et al., 2014).

MTSS Systems

MTSS holds promise as a strategy for building equity in schools and has been identified as a promising practice for eliminating disparities in school discipline (Gregory et al., 2017; Welsh & Little, 2018). Enabling systemwide changes that are aligned with full implementation of MTSS, however, necessitates change at many levels, including how educators think, operate, and respond to behavior consistent with a more antiracist lens (Gorski, 2019). This means ensuring that tiered supports are not only evidence-based and readily accessed by all students, but also that supports are developed and delivered in a culturally responsive manner. Additionally, it can be important for educators to consider implicit biases that may not be readily apparent (McIntosh et al., 2014) and commit to mitigating systems of oppression that can be perpetuated through disproportionate exclusionary discipline practices. Although the availability of appropriate tools and system strategies to support MTSS implementation is critical, ensuring that the tiered model produces equitable results for students depends largely on the knowledge, skills, and attitudes of educators and the degree to which they are equipped to self-reflect and question their own beliefs and biases.

In a crosswalk of promising alternative approaches to exclusionary discipline practices (Chafouleas et al., 2020), educator behaviors that are supportive, bias aware, and culturally relevant were prominently identified. Engaging in these behaviors requires that educators use data-driven problem solving with a focus on changing their practices. To solve problems equitably and effectively, educators must be equipped with (a) knowledge of a systematic problem-solving process, (b) skills in data use, and (c) attitudes that facilitate continuous self-reflection (i.e., awareness of expectations, implicit bias, power, and privilege). This self-reflection includes awareness that systems of oppression may be operating within their classrooms, particularly when working with individual students singled out as having behavioral issues (Connor et al., 2016). We provide a brief review of each element, followed by key considerations for social, emotional, and behavioral domains. In addition, a summary of main themes can be found in Figure 7.1.

Figure 7.1. Key Considerations of Equitable and Effective Problem Solving for Social, Emotional, and Behavioral Domains

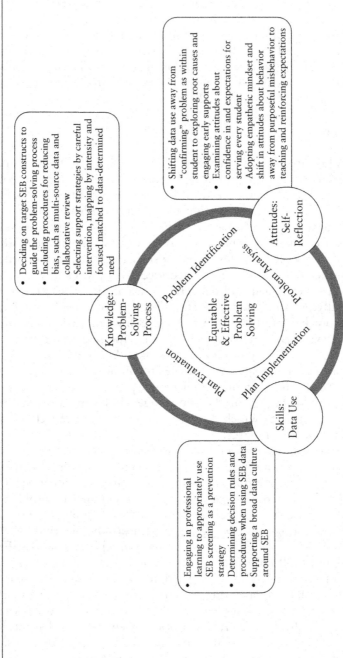

- Deciding on target SEB constructs to guide the problem-solving process
- Including procedures for reducing bias, such as multi-source data and collaborative review
- Selecting support strategies by careful intervention, mapping by intensity and focused matched to data-determined need

- Shifting data use away from "confirming" problem as within student to exploring root causes and engaging early supports
- Examining attitudes about confidence in and expectations for serving every student
- Adopting empathetic mindset and shift in attitudes about behavior away from purposeful misbehavior to teaching and reinforcing expectations

- Engaging in professional learning to appropriately use SEB screening as a prevention strategy
- Determining decision rules and procedures when using SEB data
- Supporting a broad data culture around SEB

Knowledge: Problem-Solving Process

Attitudes: Self-Reflection

Skills: Data Use

Problem Identification

Problem Analysis

Plan Implementation

Plan Evaluation

Equitable & Effective Problem Solving

Note: SEB = social, emotional, and behavioral

© Sandra M. Chafouleas & Amy M. Briesch

Knowledge: Problem-Solving Process

Knowledge of the problem-solving process is a foundational element of an MTSS framework. Problem solving has a long history across both psychology and education (Bergan & Kratochwill, 1990; D'Zurilla & Goldfried, 1971; Lane et al., 2014), and problem-solving approaches to discipline have been identified as a key principle in the Gregory et al. (2017) framework for increasing equity in school discipline. Educators must understand the steps of the problem-solving process in general, as well as the unique considerations when identifying, addressing, and monitoring social, emotional, and behavioral challenges. The first step in the problem-solving process involves identifying and defining the problem. A problem is often defined as the discrepancy between current and desired performance (Bergan & Kratochwill, 1990). Within the academic domain, concrete, universal benchmarks often exist for student performance, such as how many words a student should be able to read or how fluently they should be able to solve math equations. Within the social, emotional, and behavioral domain, however, similar agreed-on benchmarks do not exist. Rather, the question must be raised of how our conceptualizations of "desired performance" are determined and to what extent they may be rooted in our own worldview and unconscious biases. For example, "desired" or "problematic" behavior can be based on White heteronormative and ableist expectations for behavior (Annamma et al., 2020).

Once the problem has been adequately defined, the second step in the problem-solving process involves analyzing the issue. The goal at this stage is to generate and test hypotheses regarding why the issue is occurring. This stage should include steps for reducing bias, such as conducting a root cause analysis. Rather than automatically shifting to focus attention on factors that are either internal to the student or cannot be altered, the goal is to identify malleable factors that may contribute to the problem and are within the control of the school to change (Fenning & Jenkins, 2018). Results from this analysis can then subsequently be used to inform the development of an intervention that targets the suspected root causes. Finally, evaluation of the plan's effectiveness in achieving the intended goal(s) occurs.

Problem solving is a cross-curricular activity that should occur at all levels of the school setting (Orgoványi-Gajdos, 2016). For example, a classroom teacher might meet with a colleague to jointly examine office disciplinary data and consider how to interpret the data that have been collected. Conversation might focus on discussing whether there are any implicit biases or assumptions driving referral decisions before engaging in any action planning (Fenning & Jenkins, 2018), with the goal to be aligned with equitable practices. At the same time, a grade- or building-level team might examine school climate data to identify areas for improvement schoolwide that might help to explain why particular students are struggling, whereas districtwide teams may examine suspension data to determine instructional or environmental modifications that would examine potential biases (e.g., racial/ethnic, disability). It has been argued that problem solving is not an isolated activity but rather an "indispensable high-level skill" that educators should employ in every aspect of their daily lives (Orgoványi-Gajdos, 2016, p. 7). Knowledge about the problem-solving process must be combined with the expectation that it is used in a manner that is student centered and focused on problem-solving needs of individual students identified as ED and/or who have additional minoritized identities. This combination shifts identified "problems" away from blaming the individual student or teacher to an orientation focused on addressing factors within the classroom. Additionally, it puts the responsibility on adults to solve issues that arise. This approach also can increase educators' confidence in their capacity to find an equitable solution to solve the problem and effect the desired outcome.

Considerations in Problem-Solving Knowledge for Social, Emotional, and Behavioral Domains

Although the general problem-solving framework can be applied to all domains of student functioning, there are unique considerations when problem solving is used to address students' social, emotional, and behavioral needs. There are multiple frameworks for considering what constitutes a social, emotional, and behavioral problem (Briesch et al., 2016). A psychopathology (i.e., disease-based) framework, for example, focuses problem identification on identifying students likely to meet diagnostic criteria for a particular disorder (e.g., ED) with the goal of reducing symptomatology. A school-based success framework, however, centers on identifying behavior constructs most relevant to students' capacity to learn and thrive in school (without specific concern for diagnostic status) so that intervention efforts can be directed at improving school functioning (e.g., teacher and peer adjustment). This approach is more aligned with one based on equity because the focus of the data collection is not to identify an internalized pathology. Although there is no right choice regarding a chosen framework, this choice guides the rest of the problem-solving process. Regardless of the chosen framework, collaboration is needed during problem solving so that educators have supports available to ensure confidence and capacity in solving the issue. Comfort in discussing potential biases without being judged must become the rule rather than the exception for educators. Similarly, students and families should be able to participate in conversations about data without being blamed for the challenges shared. Collaborative problem solving among educators, and with families and community supports, can serve to buffer against the potential to blame an individual (e.g., student, family, educator), which can lead to punitive approaches, inequities, racism, and bias.

Another consideration occurs in the problem analysis phase, in which data are used to develop hypotheses regarding what is driving the issue of focus. Researchers have consistently found that educators are much more likely to attribute behavior they observe to internal student factors (e.g., student thoughts, dispositions; Wiley et al., 2012) or home variables (e.g., parental attitudes, parental modeling of behavior; Mavropoulou & Padeliadu, 2002; Soodak & Podell, 1994) than to factors within educators' control (e.g., classroom management practices, environmental variables). When teams automatically attribute behavior to student and family deficit explanations, then these judgments reinforce maintaining current status quo practices (Reed et al., 2020; Valencia, 2010). Therefore, data review without intentionality in exploring internal biases and judgments likely will not lead to new perspectives and ways of thinking. To address this assumption, educators are encouraged to gather data from multiple sources and across instruction (i.e., how content is taught), curriculum (i.e., what content is taught), environment (i.e., external factors that may influence performance), and learner (i.e., student skills and capacities) to unpack educator decisions and practices. Further, educators are encouraged to explore and interrogate their underlying assumptions about what is driving behavior in collaboration and consultation with other team members. Gathering data from a variety of sources and allowing increased opportunity to consider all possible explanations can reduce bias in decisions and lead to the creation of amenable plans for addressing issues arising during teaming and data review.

Yet another consideration occurs in plan implementation, which involves selecting appropriate interventions. For social, emotional, and behavioral needs, matching available interventions may not always be obvious. For example, a recent review of state department of education websites found that although one third suggested social, emotional, and behavioral interventions that might be appropriate at the targeted level, these options were commonly presented in list format without further guidance regarding differential selection or use (Briesch, Chafouleas et al., 2020). Therefore, thoughtful coaching, modeling, and support in data analysis; selection of intervention; and intervention implementation is critical. Unfortunately, without guidance, educators risk selecting social, emotional, and behavioral interventions that are not warranted or matched appropriately to the problem. For example, although ample evidence exists in support of the use of Check-In Check-Out (CICO) program as an evidence-based targeted intervention, research has shown intervention effectiveness may vary depending on the function of the problem behavior, as CICO is more effective for attention-maintained problems (Maggin et al., 2015). Taken together, knowledge about the problem-solving process is critical but likely insufficient in producing equitable and effective practices. Knowledge must be integrated with skills in data use, as well as attitudes of continuous self-reflection.

SKILLS: DATA USE

Engaging in equitable and effective problem solving requires skills in data use, including data literacy. Although the past 2 decades have brought an era of accountability and a decided emphasis on the use of data to inform decisions, this push has not necessarily resulted in intended outcomes of increased educator skill with data use and, ultimately, equity in decision-making. As noted by Jacobs et al. (2009), many directions exist when educators are first presented with data, ranging from believing that data provide useful information to too much information, to dredging up additional issues that the one does not know how to solve.

Although the current data-driven culture pushes educators to use data, one identified barrier is the lack of current mechanisms through which they can be appropriately trained in these skills (Mandinach, 2012). Jimerson and Wayman (2015) found that training in data use often focused on teaching educators how to access data within a technological system yet stopped short of suggesting what to do with the data. Therefore, the conceptualization, problem solving, and support for educators to make any meaningful change is lacking. The underlying message seems to be that the data themselves will provide guidance to educators in terms of what to do next (Spillane, 2012). It is, therefore, unsurprising that studies have repeatedly documented teachers' lack of self-reported efficacy in using data (Dunn et al., 2012; Woolfolk et al., 1990).

Results from studies exploring what happens during data review meetings have identified troublingly consistent themes. That is, even when educators bring data to meetings, these data often are ignored during conversations. Rather, educators tend to focus on noninstructional explanations for performance that are often outside of their control (e.g., parental expectations; Little, 2012), and educators often need to be redirected back to the data several times during a meeting (Earl, 2008; Lasky et al., 2008). These findings run contrary to the principle of data-based inquiry for equity in Gregory et al.'s (2017) framework for eliminating disparities in exclusionary discipline. There is also the potential to continue perpetuating a deficit view of student behavior that maintains the system quo of ableism, racial oppression, and othering of students (Annamma et al., 2020). Instead, skills are needed in data use to identify patterns that could suggest differential treatment of specific groups (e.g., disability, race) and to direct efforts to ensure high-quality implementation of evidence-based strategies for every student and a deep dive to mitigate biases (Staats, 2015–2016). Such a deep dive could include exploring individual, structural, and systemic biases through questioning reasons for existing disparities. This questioning could prompt focus on school-based explanations for what teams are seeing in data patterns.

Considerations in Data Use Skills for Social, Emotional, and Behavioral Domains

To date, studies of educator data literacy have largely focused on academic domains, yet data literacy may be of even greater importance in social, emotional, and behavioral domains given the relative infrequency with which educators have historically interacted with those data as well as the concerns regarding disproportionate use of exclusionary disciplinary practices.

A recent exploratory project, for example, found that school personnel appreciated the information obtained through social, emotional, and behavioral screening, but they were less confident that they understood how to use those data to guide decision-making and document student improvements (Briesch, Cintron et al., 2020). Data collection alone has been shown to be insufficient to influence student academic performance. Instead, educators must make instructional modifications, which are most likely to occur when provided with explicit decision rules for interpreting data such as comparison to a goal line (Stecker et al., 2005). Thus, an added challenge when using social, emotional, and behavioral data is the absence of commonly agreed-on decision rules (Briesch, Cintron et al., 2020). Further, there is limited consideration of how biased policy and practices may be root-cause drivers of what is being observed in data (Fenning & Jenkins, 2018).

Another consideration is broader support for these practices. Hamilton et al. (2009) stressed the need to create a data culture, or a school environment that "includes attitudes, values, goals, norms of behavior and practices, accompanied by an explicit vision for data use by leadership for the importance and power that data can bring to the decision-making process" (p. 46). For social, emotional, and behavioral domains, the national landscape of a prevention-focused data culture (i.e., screening) falls behind that of academic and physical health assessments, with social, emotional, and behavioral screening occurring at much lower rates, with limited guidance provided to schools by state departments of education (Auerbach et al., 2018; Briesch et al., 2017). Collectively, the lower prevalence of social, emotional, and behavioral data use may contribute to challenges in enabling data-based inquiry for equity. Lower prevalence suggests limited opportunity to build capacity and confidence in data use, which can pose barriers to attitudes that reinforce shifts from reactive to proactive problem solving about behavior.

ATTITUDES: CONTINUOUS SELF-REFLECTION

The third element to establishing a strong foundation for equitable and effective problem solving includes attitudes about data use and student behavior. Mandinach and Gummer (2016) argued that data cannot be used effectively without context and should be continuously challenged through self-reflection. That is, educators must "understand what the data mean in reference to the goals and learning objectives of the content domains" (Mandinach & Gummer, 2016, p. 4). Thus, understanding not only the *how* but *why* in data collection and use is necessary in problem solving. Ongoing reflection about the why of data establishes educators as "researchers of their own practice" who are able to understand their school culture and their role within it, identify problems with attention to their individual perceptions, and adjust their professional learning to meet identified gaps and mitigate bias (Orgoványi-Gajdos, 2016, p. 28).

Relatedly, ambiguity or subjectivity in defining problem behavior is a contributing problem to implicit bias in school-based decisions (McIntosh et al., 2014), again highlighting the critical need for problem solving how *and* why in data collection and use. Orgoványi-Gajdos (2016) reiterated the importance of a well-defined statement of the issue to solving the problem, noting the challenge associated with perception as an important influencer of decisions. Incumbent on the involved individuals is embracing understanding of perception, such as through reflection on the many sides to a problem when establishing the problem definition and setting goals. Orgoványi-Gajdos (2016) offers activities and example questions to facilitate engagement in continuous self-reflection. Some examples of questions are "Is this really a problem and, if so, is it my problem?" and "Why is this situation frustrating to me?" Collaborations that consciously question in these ways allow for explicit consideration of how inequities, disparities, and exclusion may be present.

Considerations in Attitudes Embracing Self-Reflection for Social, Emotional, and Behavioral Domains

Attitudes about data use and student behavior play a particularly important role in the social, emotional, and behavioral domain. First, educators may not fully understand the purpose or goals of social, emotional, and behavioral assessment within a prevention-oriented framework such as MTSS. For example, within the academic realm, educators typically think about collecting assessment data as a way to identify what a student knows and consequently how they may need to be either challenged or further supported (Jacobs et al., 2009). When educators find that students are performing below expectations academically, they are encouraged to reflect on how instructional practices could be improved. In contrast, when social, emotional, and behavioral screening data are collected, results may be framed as broad groupings of students according to level of risk. For students already exhibiting the most significant behavioral challenges, this can result in "confirmation" of behavioral challenges that necessitate services beyond the scope of the school setting. For example, a recent nationally representative survey of public school districts found that 12% of district administrators indicated that their primary approach to identifying and supporting students with social, emotional, and behavioral challenges was to refer them to an outside consultant or agency (Dineen et al., 2021). These administrative decisions reinforce pushout and exclusionary practices that drive the inequities and exclusion that are common among students with social, emotional, and behavioral challenges. As described by Annamma et al. (2012, 2014), this control and containment around behavior is particularly relevant for those students who are Black and have disabilities or additional intersected identities. Such an approach clearly contrasts with a prevention-oriented attitude that reinforces the role and responsibility for school-based data use in proactive problem identification to facilitate supports to address the problem before it becomes more significant.

Explicitly tied to attitudes about role and responsibility for school-based social, emotional, and behavioral data use are attitudes about student behavior in general, individually and within a system. Research has shown that positive teacher–student relationships are linked to student outcomes (Zimmer-Gembeck et al., 2006). An important influence on the quality of those relationships is behavior and interpretation of that behavior, meaning that disruptive and challenging behaviors conflict with educator values and are considered problematic (for a review, see Briesch et al., 2016). One aspect of effective school-based solutions to behavior that is perceived as challenging lies in educator attitudes about behavior. This includes shifting from thinking about the problem as stemming from a student who is purposefully misbehaving to adopting an empathetic mindset seeking to understand how a student's lived experiences and resultant emotions may lead to the expression of problem behavior (Okonofua et al., 2016). Within the trauma-informed literature, for example, substantial attention has been directed toward professional learning, facilitating staff knowledge and attitudes about trauma and its impact; the interpretation of behavioral reactions; and use of strategies that de-escalate behavior, avoid re-traumatization, and foster a safe, inclusive, and supportive environment (for a review, see Chafouleas et al., 2016).

In summary, although extension of MTSS problem solving to social, emotional, and behavioral domains is occurring, there is need for attention at multiple levels (grade level, school, district, state) for educator knowledge, skills, bias, and attitudes in problem solving to support all students, particularly those with the most significant behavioral challenges. The identified gaps suggest a need for strengthened professional learning across all elements to enable an equitable and effective problem-solving process. Promising practices do exist yet must be combined in a cohesive way. Next, we provide a brief illustration of this potential using the comprehensive integrated three-tiered (Ci3T) model of prevention (Lane et al., 2014).

DATA-DRIVEN PROBLEM SOLVING: THE CI3T MODEL

The Ci3T model of prevention can be considered as a broadening of MTSS, in that whereas MTSS typically features academic and/or behavior domains, Ci3T integrates both domains with socioemotional learning. The comprehensive and integrated nature of Ci3T may hold promise for all students—particularly those with and at risk for ED—given use of data to problem solve the tailoring of supports. For over 15 years, researchers have worked to support more than 75 schools across four regions in the design, implementation, and initial evaluation of the Ci3T model (Lane & Menzies, 2003, 2005; Lane et al., 2010). Using Ci3T, educators gain knowledge, skills, and attitudes that build their capacity and confidence to address the diverse needs of students through blending evidence-based strategies across academic, socioemotional, and behavioral domains. In effect, Ci3T leadership teams are offered professional learning that builds the knowledge, skills, and attitudes that enable them to serve as social justice allies for students with ED (Melloy & Murry, 2019).

As part of implementing the Ci3T model of prevention, Ci3T building leadership teams collaborate with district leaders to develop a tiered system to make explicit the cascade of evidence-informed supports available across domains and levels of intervention intensity. At tier 1, roles and responsibilities are defined for students, faculty and staff, families, and administrators to make transparent how each stakeholder contributes. General and special educators also learn how to create integrated lesson plans Lane et al. (2022), through which academic and socioemotional objectives are established and behavioral expectations are revisited at the onset and throughout each lesson. Use of low-intensity strategies is woven throughout the various stages of instruction to facilitate engagement for students and to empower teachers with the skills needed to meet students' needs (see www.ci3t.org/imp for sample lesson plans; Lane et al., 2015). In addition to developing a Ci3T intervention blueprint for all intervention tiers, an assessment schedule is constructed to provide an at-a-glance timeline of when screenings will be conducted and when other data collected as part of regular school practices (e.g., attendance, office discipline referrals, suspensions) will be gathered and collaboratively examined.

Data literacy plays a seminal role by empowering educators with the knowledge, skills, and attitudes needed to use student data to inform instructional experiences. Similarly, Ci3T leadership teams use data to inform professional learning plans for faculty and staff. Typically, district leaders host sessions, bringing Ci3T leadership teams together to review data and access professional learning. Teams review multiple sources of data to answer foundational questions in equitable and effective problem solving such as (a) Are procedures for teaching, reinforcing, and monitoring being implemented as planned? (b) What do faculty and staff think about the goals, procedures, and outcomes? and (c) What additional professional learning topics are needed to ensure that faculty and staff can carry out interventions as prescribed (i.e., treatment integrity)?

During one district's 1st year of Ci3T implementation, for example, each Ci3T leadership team received a fall implementation report, which included multiple sources of treatment integrity data as well as social validity data. One source of treatment integrity data was the 38-item "Ci3T Treatment Integrity: Teacher Self-Report" (Ci3T TI: TSR; Lane, 2009), which was completed by all faculty and staff who provided instruction to students. The Ci3T TI: TSR includes three subscales: Procedures for Teaching (e.g., Did I use clear routines for classroom procedures?), Procedures for Reinforcing (e.g., Did I use behavior-specific praise when giving tickets to students?), and Procedures for Monitoring (e.g., Did I use behavior and academic data together... to inform my instruction?). These self-reported data were complemented by direct observation data collected by a trained observer to offer additional feedback. Overall, these sessions are designed to build data literacy through a practice-based professional learning model (Ball & Cohen, 1999; Orgoványi-Gajdos, 2016). These data are used to ensure students have had equitable access to tier 1 practices. Without these data, student performance cannot accurately be interpreted. For example, when looking at a student's "citizenship" scores, educators need to know these answers: Has the student been afforded tier 1 instruction and needs additional supports? *or* Do the scores reflect a need for improved tier 1 efforts? Treatment integrity data will help to answer these questions and plan for instruction accordingly.

This brief illustration provides an example regarding the potential for a Ci3T model to advance equitable and effective problem solving. The Ci3T model engages system change through collective and individual effort that holds promise for reversing the negative trajectory of exclusionary discipline for students with ED. Professional learning coupled with support and feedback from the Ci3T leadership team and coaches builds educator knowledge, skills, and attitudes to effectively engage in solution-focused problem solving that shifts from deficit-focused and reactive thinking. Capacity and confidence to deliver services to effectively meet complex and intense needs are further bolstered through a specified problem-solving process that links data to a range of tiered intervention supports.

CONCLUSION AND IMPLICATIONS FOR DIRECTING FUTURE RESEARCH, POLICY, AND PRACTICE

The purpose of our chapter was to identify promising practices for reducing disciplinary infractions as centered in educator data-driven problem solving, particularly for students with ED. Strengthening educator capacity and confidence to work with students with the most serious behavioral issues occurs through use of data-driven problem solving within a tiered prevention and intervention system. Educators must be equipped with (a) knowledge about the problem-solving process, (b) skills in data use, and (c) attitudes that embrace continuous self-reflection about personal capacity and expectations for all students, especially those with ED. Together, these elements align with three of the recommended principles for reducing exclusionary discipline outlined by Gregory et al. (2017), including MTSS, problem-solving approaches to discipline, and data-based inquiry for equity. The Ci3T model was used to illustrate how these pieces, working together, hold promise to better meet the often-complex needs of students with ED who have historically been removed from class—and consequently instruction. Overall, implications extend the possibility for policy reform that shifts from penalizing schools for "not performing" to focusing on the professional learning supports needed to build requisite knowledge, skills, and attitudes in equitable and effective data-driven problem solving.

Further work is needed to examine the mechanisms behind how guiding questions around data-based problem solving, such as presented in this chapter, can influence outcomes such as reducing pushout practices, strengthening student–teacher relationships, and improving school climate. We briefly highlight suggested directions for research, policy, and practice to support positive trajectories for students historically categorized as ED.

Implications for Future Research

Although we propose that schools can reduce negative outcomes for students with ED by supporting educators' engagement in equitable and effective problem solving, questions remain regarding what these supports should look like. Shifting away from traditional ways of thinking and doing in schools requires schools to explicitly teach adults to engage with data in new ways (e.g., how to consider potential biases or assumptions when analyzing social, emotional, and behavioral data). Future research is therefore needed to understand how administrators and other school leaders should structure professional learning to ensure educators hold the knowledge, skills, and attitudes presented in this chapter. Questions about the necessary dosage, intensity, and frequency of professional learning should be answered, along with how supports at building, district, and state levels interact in strengthening educator capacity. In addition, it is important to understand how these practices help to mitigate systems of bias and oppression in schools across the country, as aligned with a DisCrit theoretical frame. One direction, for example, might focus on identifying the active treatment components to professional learning that can improve not only data use for problem-solving practices but also broader understanding of disability rights and historical racism. In addition, whereas many studies have relied on self-reports (e.g., surveys, interviews) to measure changes in educator behavior, observational studies might be considered, as they "afford a window into the actual practices teachers employ as they collectively examine and interpret student data or the ways in which the contexts of data use come to occupy a central or peripheral part of teachers' ongoing work life" (Little, 2012, p. 144). By observing the dialogue and interactions among data team members, researchers may be able to better understand how educators assign meaning, make inferences, and determine appropriate responses to the data they have.

Implications for Policy

Policy helps to impart a vision for the direction in which practice should be moving and therefore has strong potential to influence day-to-day practice (Cohen & Ball, 2001). Although the 2004 reauthorization of IDEA at the federal level served as a catalyst to implementation of MTSS in U.S. schools, explicit reference was only made in relation to processes for determining whether a child has a specific learning disability, and specific procedural guidance was absent from this legislation. Expanding legislation to include specific reference to the use of an MTSS framework to support students with—or at risk for—ED may help facilitate a shift toward more widespread use of evidence-based interventions to proactively support students with social, emotional, and behavioral needs.

In addition, state departments of education can help to build a shared understanding of equitable and effective problem solving through the development of state-level policy and guidance documents. Prior research has highlighted the desire of educators to be equipped with concrete tools and resources to guide the implementation of both interventions and assessment procedures (Castro-Villareal et al., 2014; Meyer & Behar-Horenstein, 2015). State agencies can provide models and concrete examples of steps that teams might take to engage in more equitable and effective problem solving. For example, providing teams with specific strategies for how to identify patterns suggesting differential treatment of specific groups and self-reflective questions to ask when engaging in problem identification and analysis may help school-based teams to build confidence and self-efficacy. Furthermore, funding of state-level demonstration projects to document the role of professional learning and coaching supports in promoting more equitable outcomes can help illustrate new and innovative ways to address longstanding problems.

Implications for Practice

Finally, although research and policy can be important drivers in influencing educational practice, gaps between recommended and actual practice can nonetheless persist. The importance of leadership in enacting organizational change has repeatedly been identified within the literature (Torres et al., 2018). At the local level, for example, school leaders can either serve as champions for change or can enact barriers toward it. Targeted professional learning may therefore be needed for administrators and other school leaders to support their understanding of the problem-solving process. This type of understanding should be considered a necessary—although not sufficient—first step toward building a school culture that prioritizes the use of data-driven problem solving to promote equitable outcomes. Professional learning might be stimulated through strong relationships such as university–practitioner partnerships that can serve as bridging factors to improved practices.

The Use of the Assessment of Culturally and Contextually Relevant Supports (ACCReS) in High-Need Public School Classrooms

Lindsay M. Fallon and Margarida Veiga

The Individuals With Disabilities Education Act (IDEA, 2016) requires state and local education agencies receiving federal funds to collect and analyze data to determine if any racial and ethnic groups are being disproportionately (a) identified to receive special education services, (b) placed in more restrictive educational settings, and (c) disciplined and excluded from the learning environment (e.g., suspended, expelled). The IDEA specifies that if significant disproportionality is determined, school practices and procedures must be reviewed and revised to focus on prevention and reverse noted trends. Yet federal law provides inadequate guidance about how to do this (Sullivan & Osher, 2019).

Often, inappropriate decisions about identification, placement, and discipline occur after a teacher requests support from a colleague (i.e., refers a student to the school principal for disciplinary action). Therefore, it may be critically important to build educators' capacity to support student behavior and learning within the classroom through a focus on prevention. This is particularly essential for educators of racially and ethnically minoritized (Proctor & Owens, 2019) youth, specifically Black or African American students with or at risk for disabilities, who are most often impacted by exclusionary discipline (Gage et al., 2019). Improving teacher training and professional development to be prevention focused, data analytical, and inclusive of students' culture within school classrooms could change instructional pedagogy and build a more just and equitable classroom ecology. This, in turn, may ultimately reduce the number of inappropriate referrals for disciplinary action and address the vast inequities in the use of exclusionary discipline practices in the United States.

THEORETICAL FRAMEWORK AND ADVANCING SCHOLARSHIP

Reliance on exclusionary discipline can be disrupted by framing the design and implementation of multitiered systems of support (MTSS) frameworks in schools as culturally responsive (e.g., Bal et al., 2012; McCurdy et al., 2003). In such a framework, educators comprehensively support students by implementing empirically validated practices with fidelity, scaling interventions to the appropriate intensity and monitoring students' progress over time (Algozzine et al., 2011; Cook & Odom, 2013; Simonsen et al., 2008). In addition, staff are encouraged to engage in high-quality professional development that focuses on prevention (Gregory et al., 2015) and structuring the classroom ecology (Annamma & Morrison, 2018) to value students' culture (McIntosh et al., 2014) and intersecting identities (Annamma et al., 2018). Given that the use of exclusionary discipline has been systematically applied to Black and Brown students with or at risk for disabilities (i.e., Whitford et al., 2019), this professional development should be rooted in a framework that acknowledges the interdependent constructions of race and dis/ability in education (Annamma et al., 2013). Without an understanding of individual, structural, and systemic racism, as well as other forms of oppression, professional development and subsequent student interventions will not likely be successful toward effecting change in teacher practice (Proctor & Meyers, 2014).

DisCrit provides a critical lens in this work as race and ability are understood as socially constructed, interdependent constructs (Annamma et al., 2013). That is, racism and ableism are seen as enmeshed in the fabric of American culture (Delgado & Stefancic, 2001) and are therefore deeply embedded within educational systems. This is critical to acknowledge when creating a classroom community as it is relevant to the design of the curriculum, instructional pedagogy used, and social/behavioral supports provided to students (Annamma & Morrison, 2018).

CULTURALLY RESPONSIVE BEHAVIOR SUPPORTS

MTSS frameworks can be culturally responsive and integrative of critical tenets of DisCrit through attention to students' intrapersonal identities, interpersonal experiences, and structural/systemic power in the environment to create transformative school spaces (Moradi & Grzanka, 2017). Vincent et al. (2011) conceptualized a culturally responsive schoolwide positive behavioral interventions and supports (PBIS) model, a framework aligned with the core principles of MTSS (Briesch et al., 2020). This model may be useful in designing such a learning environment, ultimately increasing equity in school disciplinary practices (Gregory et al., 2017). This model specifies four interconnected features: (a) *systems* to promote staff members' cultural knowledge and self-awareness and implementation fidelity, (b) *behavioral* and *academic practices* that are culturally relevant and empirically validated for racially and ethnically minoritized learners, (c) *data* that are culturally and contextually valid for decision-making, and (d) student *outcomes* that are culturally equitable and enable maximum and meaningful academic and behavioral success in school.

Systems

Culturally responsive MTSS theory (Vincent et al., 2011) emphasizes systems to support staff, including training educators to first build awareness of their own cultural identity (McAllister & Irvine, 2000). As the majority of educators in the United States are White (Hussar et al., 2020), this might involve learning about predominant White identity development models (Ponterotto & Park-Taylor, 2007) to lay the groundwork for understanding power, privilege and implicit bias. Most White educators have never had to think about their own identity development, which is part of White privilege. This work can then lead to professional development related to understanding and valuing students' culture and designing educational environments that promote stronger racial-ethnic identity. A strong racial-ethnic identity has been linked to students' academic achievement, and parent reports of fewer behavioral concerns (Miller-Cotto & Byrnes, 2016), promoting student success in school. Systems include time and resources for educators to engage in self-reflection, training, and coaching (individually or collectively as a school staff) to promote educators' implementation of practices with adequate levels of fidelity.

Practices

Culturally responsive MTSS theory also posits that academic and behavior support practices (e.g., scaffolding instruction, collaboratively defining and explicitly teaching classroom expectations) should be empirically supported and validate students' identities, therefore increasing cultural relevance. When describing culturally responsive MTSS, Vincent et al. (2011) reference Cartledge and Kleefeld's (2010) guidance to provide social and behavioral support that (a) reflect students' lived experiences, (b) are aligned with family expectations, (c) are modeled by individuals sharing the students' background, and (d) are delivered in students' language. Teachers should be self-reflective (especially those who are White), and instruction should be rigorous and relevant to promote meaningful connection to the curriculum and classroom environment, maximizing student engagement.

Data

Valid data for decision-making is also central to culturally responsive MTSS. As discipline disproportionality permeates the rationale for school-based prevention and intervention frameworks using a multitiered approach, many may not question the validity of behavioral data collected in schools, yet researchers have called into question the subjective nature of many disciplinary incidents that are disproportionately meted out to Black students (Skiba et al., 2014), drawing attention to how problem behavior is defined in the first place and the possibility of implicit bias in decision-making (McIntosh et al., 2018). Vincent et al. (2011) describe that although "objective" operational definitions of problem behaviors are intended to minimize teacher judgment (Horner et al., 2001), it is important to involve educators, families and other community stakeholders from various backgrounds to cultivate these definitions and/or provide specific examples and nonexamples to reduce the prospect of cultural bias.

Outcomes

Vincent et al. (2011) indicate that determining if outcomes are culturally equitable involves disaggregating academic and discipline data to see if biases are evident. Specifically, in a report from the National Education Policy Center (Losen, 2011), school administrators and staff were encouraged to regularly collect, review, reflect on, and publicly report exclusionary discipline data disaggregated by race and ethnicity. These data can be used to conduct analyses to determine root causes of discipline disparities (see Osher et al., 2015, for a step-by-step guide) to guide discipline reform (Fenning & Jenkins, 2018). Cook, Duong et al. (2018) identified common root causes, including historical racial oppression, teacher–student racial mismatch, teachers' implicit bias, teachers' use of reactive classroom management, lack of effective teacher professional development, lack of teachers' multicultural awareness, and poor discipline policy, among others. Identification of root causes could then inform administrator decision-making about revisions to discipline policies, teacher practices, as well as staff training needs (Fenning & Jenkins, 2018).

TEACHER SELF-ASSESSMENT DEVELOPMENT

Results from research indicate in-service teachers (i.e., educators working in K–12 school environments) may not feel prepared to deliver culturally responsive instructional and behavioral supports based on the training they received in their preservice programs (Chu & Garcia, 2014). Many leave the field due to lack of perceived competency in supporting both student instruction and behavior (Gutentag et al., 2018). In addition, there is often limited training and professional development for in-service teachers to support minoritized students effectively (Polat, 2010). To offer opportunities for critical self-reflection and to provide data to support more effective training, validated assessment tools of teachers' culturally responsive practice are needed.

RATIONALE FOR THE CURRENT STUDY

Although there are validated measures that promote teacher self-reflection and assessment of practices, many are centered specifically on teaching or classroom management (Culturally Responsive Teaching Self-Efficacy Scale [CRTSES], Siwatu, 2007; Culturally Responsive Classroom Management Self-Efficacy Scale [CRCMSES], Siwatu et al., 2015) rather than culturally responsive classroom supports more broadly. The Assessment of Culturally and Contextually Relevant Supports (ACCReS) was developed to include items pertaining to teachers' instruction and behavior supports as well as teachers' use of data for equitable decision-making and access to high-quality professional development and resources, aligning with critical features of culturally responsive MTSS (i.e., systems, practices, data, outcomes; Fallon et al., 2021; Vincent et al., 2011). The purpose and promise of the ACCReS are to address the lack of validated instruments and interventions available to support student learning and behavior within a culturally responsive MTSS framework.

DESCRIPTION OF THE ACCRES

ACCReS items were derived from a systematic literature review of culturally and contextually relevant practices (Fallon et al., 2012) to align with Vincent et al.'s (2011) conceptualization of a culturally responsive MTSS model (Fallon et al., 2018), with a specific focus on universal supports with all youth. Specifically, items were derived to align with systems to promote (a) staff members' cultural knowledge, (b) culturally relevant practices empirically validated for racially and ethnically minoritized learners, (c) culturally and contextually valid data for decision-making, and (d) culturally equitable student outcomes to promote meaningful academic and behavioral success in school. Once items were developed, a panel of 20 experts (university researchers and K–12 educators) reviewed and provided qualitative feedback about the instrument (Fallon et al., 2018). Finally, exploratory and confirmatory factor analyses were conducted with data from a national sample of 500 and 400 teachers, respectively. Analyses indicated acceptable fit indices with items loading on to three factors: equitable classroom practices ($\omega^1 = .87$), accessing information and support ($\omega = .86$), and consideration of culture and context ($\omega = .77$). See Appendix A for a copy of the ACCReS.

Description of Factors

Items within the equitable classroom practices factor target teacher practices to promote students' equitable access to high-quality instruction and a safe and supportive classroom environment. Items within the consideration of culture and context factor more explicitly target teachers' consideration of students' culture as it pertains to the design and delivery of teaching and behavioral supports provided in the classroom. Items on the accessing information and support factor target data and systems of support that teachers may access to engage in culturally responsive practices in the classroom. When completing the ACCReS, teachers rate the degree to which they agree with items (strongly disagree [0], disagree [1], somewhat disagree [2], somewhat agree [3], agree [4], and strongly agree [5]) on a 6-point Likert-type scale.

PURPOSE OF STUDY

The current study reports results from a field test of the ACCReS with teachers in two high-need districts in the northeastern part of the United States. Specifically, participating teachers completed the ACCReS and allowed researchers to conduct three classroom visits. Classroom visits involved assessing teachers' implementation of ACCReS items in the equitable classroom practices factor, as well as systematic observation of students' academic engagement and disruptive behavior. Data were collected to answer the following primary research questions:

1. Is there evidence of a relationship between teachers' responses on the ACCReS and student behavior as determined via direct observation? It was hypothesized that teachers with high self-ratings on the self-assessment would also have high rates of student academic engagement and low rates of disruptive behavior.
2. Is there evidence of a relationship between observers' ratings of teachers' implementation of ACCReS items (specifically *equitable classroom practices*) and student behavior as determined via direct observation? It was hypothesized that students with classroom teachers who were observed to implement items in the equitable classroom practices factor at high rates would display high rates of academic engagement and low rates of disruptive behavior.

In addition, data collection targeted the following secondary research question:

1. Is there evidence of a relationship between teachers' responses and observers' ratings of ACCReS items (specifically equitable classroom practices)? We hypothesized that observers' and teachers' ratings in equitable classroom practices would be similar.

METHOD
Participants and Setting

Twenty teachers from two school districts participated in the study. District 1 was large and suburban (NCES, 2020a). Over 75% of students identify as African American or Hispanic, 25% are English learners, and 50% are considered economically disadvantaged. Out-of-school suspensions exceeded the state average, specifically for students who identified as male, African American, Hispanic, multiracial, English learners, or students with disabilities and those designated as economically disadvantaged. District 2 was smaller and sub-urban (NCES, 2020b); however, the majority of students identified as a race or ethnicity other than White and demonstrated similar trends as the district with regard to out-of-school suspensions.

The professional teaching experience of participating teachers ranged in years, and the average class size was 23 students. In addition, two doctoral students in their 1st year of a school psychology PhD program conducted classroom observations. For the purpose of calculating interobserver agreement (IOA), one-third of observations were conducted by both students. Students were trained by the first author to engage in data collection procedures by first receiving explicit instruction on data collection protocols before practicing ratings with video examples until acceptable agreement was met (> 90%).

Procedures

Once a teacher provided informed consent and parents were notified of the study, data collectors scheduled classroom observations. At the end of each of three 30-minute observations, data collectors calculated the percentage of intervals during which all students were academically engaged and disruptive. They also completed a checklist of equitable classroom practices derived from ACCReS items. As data collectors visited teachers' classrooms three times, a grand mean was generated for students' academic engagement and disruptive behavior, as well as teacher practice. After the final observation, teachers were asked to complete the ACCReS and a teacher and student demographic questionnaire.

RESULTS

Average scores calculated across measures for each participant are presented in Table 8.1. In the current study, teachers rated items in equitable classroom practices (mean = 92.74%; SD = 0.05) the highest, followed by consideration of culture and context (mean = 78.40%, SD = 0.09) and accessing information and support (mean = 58.79%, SD = 0.13). Overall, average self-ratings across teachers on the ACCReS were 77.5% (SD = 0.07).

A nonparametric procedure (Spearman's rho) was used to examine the relationships between the ACCReS score and classroom behavior. To address the first research question, there was not a statistically significant relationship between teachers' self-reported ACCReS score and classwide student academic engagement observed ($r(19) = 0.36$, $p = 0.22$). There was, however, a significant negative association between teachers' self-reported ACCReS scores and classwide student disruptive behavior ($r(19) = -0.38$, $p = 0.05$).

Table 8.1. Mean and Range of Classroom Observation Data and Mean of Self-Report ACCReS Scores

Teacher	Mean (%) and Range of Observation Scores			Mean (%) Self-Report Scores			
	Academic Engagement	Disruptive Behavior	Equitable Classroom Practices	Equitable Classroom Practices	Consideration of Culture and Context	Accessing Information and Support	Total
1	67.5 (61.3–73.8)	12.5 (7.5–17.5)	95.5 (90.9–100)	93.1	81.8	65.3	80.1
2	70.4 (68.8–71.3)	18.3 (12.5–23.8)	53.4 (30.0–66.7)	91.7	69.4	56.9	73.3
3	85.4 (77.5–92.5)	2.1 (1.3–2.5)	74.6 (68.2–77.8)	94.4	77.8	62.5	80.0
4	92.5 (90.0–93.8)	9.6 (7.5–11.3)	95.3 (90.0–100)	94.4	81.9	73.6	83.8
5	80.0 (76.3–85.0)	11.7 (8.8–17.5)	58.5 (44.4–72.7)	93.1	68.1	59.7	75.7
6	95.4 (95.0–96.3)	5.8 (3.8–7.5)	73.0 (55.6–83.3)	86.1	75.0	30.1	65.2
7	93.3 (87.5–97.5)	13.3 (3.8–21.3)	61.1 (55.6–66.7)	93.1	68.5	72.2	79.0
8	86.7 (78.8–91.3)	7.1 (3.8–11.3)	79.4 (66.7–93.8)	94.4	73.6	34.7	70.0
9	94.2 (83.8–100)	8.8 (3.8–10)	27.3 (10.0–40.0)	97.4	95.4	66.6	87.1
10	91.7 (85–95)	9.2 (8.8–10)	93.1 (90.0–95.0)	93.6	71.2	62.1	76.6

(Continued)

Table 8.1. (Continued)

Teacher	Mean (%) and Range of Observation Scores			Mean (%) Self-Report Scores			
	Academic Engagement	Disruptive Behavior	Equitable Classroom Practices	Equitable Classroom Practices	Consideration of Culture and Context	Accessing Information and Support	Total
11	85.0 (78–91)	12.0 (8–16)	97.2 (91.7–100.0)	92.3	77.2	40.9	71.4
12	88.0 (81–90)	5.0 (5–6)	94.4 (91.7–95.8)	100.0	71.2	48.4	74.7
13	78.0 (70–86)	16.0 (11–20)	77.1 (62.5–93.8)	94.9	80.3	57.5	78.5
14	94.0 (91–98)	4.0 (1–8)	100.0 (100.0)	97.4	83.3	72.7	85.2
15	81.0 (68–89)	15.0 (8–24)	76.4 (66.7–87.5)	87.2	75.7	66.6	77.1
16	89.0 (85–95)	13.0 (1–20)	91.7 (87.5–93.8)	88.5	80.3	53.0	74.7
17	88.3 (80–96.3)	12.9 (7.5–20)	94.8 (94.4–95.5)	93.1	69.6	40.9	69.0
18	97.1 (93.8–98.3)	1.3 (1.3–1.3)	85.9 (81.3–90.0)	92.3	100.0	77.2	90.0
19	88.3 (81.3–97.5)	6.3 (0.0–12.5)	45.9 (38.9–60.0)	100.0	87.8	68.1	86.1
20	87.5 (83.8–90)	7.9 (6.3–10)	81.9 (79.2–83.3)	77.8	75.7	60.6	71.9

In reference to the second research question, Spearman's rho was again calculated. Results revealed no significant correlation between observers' rating of teachers' equitable classroom practices and rates of student academic engagement (r(19) = 0.093, p = 0.70) or disruptive behavior (r(19) = –0.078, p = 0.74). In response to the final research question, there was also not a significant correlation observed between observers' and teachers' ratings on the equitable classroom practices items (r(19) = –0.025, p = 0.92).

DISCUSSION

Data from the current study support the use of the ACCReS as a promising practice in schools. The purpose of the instrument is to proactively promote teachers' use of empirically supported classroom and instructional management procedures that are considerate of student culture and classroom context. The ACCReS was constructed through a lens of intersectionality, as items encourage teachers to consider students' individual identities, interpersonal experiences, and how power and privilege is distributed in community spaces like schools (Crenshaw, 1989; Moradi & Grzanka, 2017). Furthermore, items and subscales align with Annamma and Morrison's (2018) description of a DisCrit classroom ecology, where curriculum, student behavior, and classroom pedagogy are intentionally constructed with consideration of the intersection of systemic inequities that impact students. If efforts are made to strengthen teachers' skills and promote positive, equitable learning environments, fewer minoritized students may be subject to exclusionary discipline practices or removal from inclusive learning settings through placement in restricted special education settings.

DisCrit theorists have called for targeted research-based practices that approach the problem of over-identification of Black and Brown youth in special education and disciplinary systems from a centered and collaborative perspective (Cavendish et al., 2020). The ACCReS specifically focuses on teachers' beliefs and actions with the distal goal of reducing misidentification and misplacement of students in disciplinary systems and special education. Data from the ACCReS can support educators and school leaders to develop measurable goals to implement culturally relevant practices and monitor progress toward change. As such, this instrument may be useful for state and local education agencies adhering to IDEA (2016) guidelines to revise practices upon determining discipline disproportionality as evidenced in school or district data, guiding support, and policy development to reverse noted trends.

The data set in the current study suggests that there may be a connection between teachers' perceptions of their own cultural responsiveness and levels of disruptive behavior in their classrooms. In this study's sample, teachers tended to provide higher self-ratings for items in equitable classroom practices than items in consideration of culture and climate. For example, teachers' responses indicated their relative comfort with providing explicit instruction and differentiating instruction for learners in their classroom but indicated less confidence in their ability to provide culturally and contextually relevant instruction. Likewise, educators tended to indicate that they teach behavioral expectations explicitly, but they did not necessarily consider that students' behavior may be context specific or gather information from families before defining and teaching the behavior expected in school. Therefore, staff professional development and coaching might specifically target lower-rated items in consideration of culture and climate to support educators to reflect and work toward creating more just and equitable classroom spaces considerate of students' culture.

For instance, if educators provided low ratings for the item, "I consider students' culture and language when I select assessment tools," a target of consultation might involve training staff on culturally responsive assessment practices and how to search and evaluate the evidence for assessment tools (e.g., tools that have been validated with samples reflecting the identity similar to the student with whom the educator is working). It may be valuable to see if items targeted with additional training were more favorably endorsed in future administrations of the ACCReS.

In the current study, teachers rated items on accessing information and support lowest overall. These items inquire about access to the data, resources, and supports needed to engage in culturally and contextually relevant practices. Based on the sample's responses, it may be particularly important for school administrators and leadership teams to consider how to build systems to support educators' access to the financial resources, training, and time needed to fully engage in professional development. Systems-level consultation might be leveraged to identify structural barriers to accessing relevant data, training, and support and working closely with school leadership to remove these barriers (e.g., seek grant funding to support teachers' attendance at relevant conferences, provide training on data literacy skills). This may be critical to promoting change in their practice.

Limitations

Several limitations should be considered when interpreting results of this study. First, this is an exploratory study with a small sample from two school districts. As such, there may be state-level indicators and other contextual variables that may impact teachers' responses on the measure. For instance, the interpretation of federal guidelines (such as IDEA, 2016) in the state in which this study occurred may influence how educational leaders and teachers perceive disproportionate discipline of students who have disabilities and additional intersected identities. Another consideration is the limited availability of professional development, consultation, and technical support that schools within these districts receive, given the availability of funding and resources.

It is important that the ACCReS is used in additional and varied settings to continue its validation. Additionally, as teachers volunteered to participate in this study, it is possible that the sample does not reflect the broader teacher population. For instance, it is possible that participants may implement more equitable classroom practices than teachers who did not volunteer for the study. Second, teachers' self-reported practices may not accurately reflect their daily practices in classrooms. Teachers may believe they are engaging in equitable practices but lack the training, resources, and support to actually implement those practices in their classrooms with fidelity. Third, it is possible that teachers were influenced by social desirability bias when completing the ACCReS, overestimating their overall use of equitable classroom practices in particular.

Furthermore, the study involved three classroom observations, yet this may have provided only a limited view into teachers' practices and students' behavior. It is possible that observers simply did not see the implementation of certain practices due to the timing of observations. In addition, student academic engagement and disruptive behavior may not be the best or only possible dependent variable to measure when considering issues that justify creation of the ACCReS. Future research might target other relevant variables (e.g., classroom climate, student sense of school belongingness, teacher/student relationships, teachers' rates of office discipline referrals, etc.). Finally, teachers participated in this project to assist the researcher in developing the instrument for broader use, and therefore did not receive coaching to improve practice in areas rated lower on the ACCReS. Future research studies and work in the field might include this component to increase the promise of the ACCReS and its impact.

Implications

The study's preliminary findings indicate a need for further examination of the intersection of teachers' perceptions of their own culturally responsive practice, their actual practice, and the lived experience and outcomes of the students within their classrooms. Ultimately, the purpose of the ACCReS is to build teachers' capacity to serve students equitably and dismantle oppressive systems grounded in ableism and racism. Use of the ACCReS can promote critical self-reflection and development of clear action steps to improve practice. Further, the tool can be used to support consultation and professional development efforts mediated by school support personnel by specifically targeting growth areas in the implementation of equitable classroom practices. In this way, the ACCReS has the potential to be a critical part of broader efforts to examine how the systems and individuals within schools are serving students, with a particular focus on disrupting existing structures that harm students with minoritized identities that intersect with disability, race/ethnicity, and additional identities.

Implications for Research

Future research might examine why some hypotheses in the current study were not supported. As the ACCReS involves self-ratings, it may be necessary to provide teachers with more instruction, feedback, and professional development to engage in authentic self-reflection. It could be that as teachers become more aware of the tenets of culturally responsive practice, they may adjust their responses to items on the tool to be a bit lower to reflect that they more accurately identify needed areas for continued professional growth and have a better understanding of culturally responsive practices. Therefore, initial ratings might be more elevated (and perhaps lack validity) because teachers may not have a nuanced understanding of culturally responsive practice prior to ongoing professional development, coaching, and support. This is a hypothesis in need of exploration, and additional research would involve further validation of the tool and use of it in additional educational contexts beyond those reported here.

In addition, future research should explore how ACCReS scores predict student behavior and teachers' perceptions of students' socioemotional behavior and academic risk, as these data (from office discipline referrals, universal screeners) are often used to make decisions about which students will receive additional support (e.g., tier 2 intervention) in an MTSS context. It is problematic if data indicate minoritized students are most in need of additional support and yet they receive low-quality services, are perceived to be nonresponsive to intervention, and are subsequently referred to special education. Indeed, this could perpetuate existing disparities. Instead, researchers might explore using ACCReS data to support interventions for educators. These might include changes to empower teachers to work toward and advocate for discipline policy reform, offer high-quality professional development to alter classroom practice, and provide the resources to assess and promote teachers' cultural responsiveness in the classroom so that students are supported proactively and comprehensively.

In addition, future research might use a qualitative approach to focus on students' perspectives about their experiences in the classroom among teachers who are implementing ACCReS items more consistently. Student voice may be particularly impactful when reflecting on effective and ineffective teacher practices (see Chapter 3 by Leverett in the current volume). Students could be empowered to co-lead this process of data collection and use it to co-facilitate discipline policy and practice reform.

Future studies might also explore comparing ACCReS responses of teachers with different racial identities. For instance, White teachers might benefit from using the tool in the context of exploring their identity and their privilege in the classroom. This could be foundational to understanding their implicit bias in disciplinary interactions with students and making changes to reduce bias and promote equity in classroom interactions. Also, as there is limited research relating to the experience of teachers with minoritized racial identities (see Chapter 5 by Nortey in the current volume), it may be valuable to explore how teachers of color experience using the tool and receiving related professional development opportunities as an additional implication.

Implications for Practice

Based on results of the ACCReS, teachers might work independently or in the context of teacher professional learning communities to generate goals and work toward expanding their practice accordingly. If a teacher notices certain items are rated lower, the teacher may work to target those items to strengthen their overall classroom practice. An example of this might be if item 35 on the accessing information and support domain is an area of relative weakness; the teacher might seek the resources needed to partner with families effectively. This could involve asking for support from community outreach personnel or family liaisons to support meaningful family–school partnership efforts.

The ACCReS might also be used in individual consultation in schools (e.g., multicultural consultation; Ingraham, 2000). For instance, support personnel serving as consultants might observe teachers (consultees) to collect ACCReS data and provide a summary with suggested feedback. The consultant and consultee could then work together in setting goals toward a change in practice to promote desired student outcomes in the classroom. Specifically, if the consultant targets collecting data to track the equity of interactions and disciplinary actions between the teacher and students (referencing item 27), the consultant might then guide the teacher to set a goal to increase the equity of these interactions and help to monitor the teacher's progress over time.

Relatedly, support personnel engaged in systems-level consultation may encourage staff to complete the ACCReS anonymously and use the data produced to determine professional development needs. Specifically, if many staff in the school disagree with items within a certain domain (e.g., consideration of culture and context), training might specifically target these practices with opportunities for direct strategy instruction, opportunity for practice, and feedback. As school psychologists and social workers can act as consultants to lead school- and district-based efforts, leaders might think strategically about investing in additional personnel for the school community. These individuals may have relevant training in systems change and implementation science to drive the work of altering structures in which marginalization, racism, ableism, and other forms of oppression have been maintained.

Finally, the ACCReS may be a beneficial tool to integrate into preparation programs for general and special education teachers, support personnel (e.g., school psychologists), and administrators. It may guide school stakeholders in conceptualizing the types of classroom supports relevant to creating a culturally responsive environment. It may also help to shift the culture of how we prepare educators and staff to support behavior in schools from being more reactionary and centered in Whiteness to more proactive, integrative of students' culture, and considerate of the school and community context.

Implications for Policy

It is imperative that action to address disproportionality in discipline (e.g., out-of-school suspensions) is centered in local, state, and federal efforts. This might include prioritizing root cause analyses in policy guidelines. Policymakers might also work toward aligning law and guidance related to MTSS and special education identification to be consistent across local education agencies and states (as it is currently not consistent; Briesch et al., 2020). Alignment might also occur in how state- and local-level policymakers guide administrators and educators to weave initiatives intended to address culture, race, behavior, and special education. That is, the ACCReS could provide data to support monitoring progress toward a strategic goal to integrate teacher practices, which are often fragmented across initiatives in schools. This could guide state- and/or district-level support and technical assistance to improve teacher practices. There has been a proliferation of states that have engaged in school disciplinary reform to promote proactive interventions instead of suspension and expulsion (Committee for Children, 2018). A tool like ACCReS can facilitate these broad scale efforts.

In addition, individuals in policy positions might also encourage adequate allocation of resources to ensure policy is subsequently linked to practice and that schools have adequate funding, resources, and training to engage in high-quality implementation. This is critical as teachers in the current study indicated a lack of access to supportive and ongoing professional development to promote culturally responsive practices in their schools. This may be indicative of a lack of funding, availability of programming/trainers, or focus on such professional development. Disrupting this trend might require support and resources from local or state governments, state-level or national technical assistance, or external grant funding agencies to increase access to professional development and reduce barriers that may prevent teachers from taking advantage of such opportunities. Professional development that is systematic and supported by evidence-based tools is essential if state-level discipline reform efforts are to be implemented in the realities of classrooms.

CONCLUSION

This chapter describes how a recently developed teacher self-assessment may be a promising practice for use in schools. Specifically, results presented from a field test with the ACCReS endeavored to strengthen the tool's technical properties for use more broadly. Preliminary results show initial evidence of a relationship between teachers' perceptions of their own culturally responsive practice and students' disruptive behavior in the classroom. Ultimately, the ACCReS is intended to be used as a method for producing data to guide teachers to set professional goals and support educational leaders to make relevant decisions about resources, and supports may be beneficial to educators' efforts to create change. The ACCReS may be used as a self-reflection exercise with individual preservice or in-service teachers in the context of one-on-one coaching or consultation or as part of large-scale, systems-level change efforts to address classroom instruction and behavior supports schoolwide. These efforts are needed to create more equitable, supportive, productive learning environments to disrupt discipline disproportionality that has impacted Black and Brown youth with and without disabilities for decades (Gage et al., 2019).

CHAPTER 9

Building Bridges

An Alternative to Suspension Program

Emma Healy, Michelle Rappaport, and Carly Tindall-Biggins

"I don't belong in school," Jess announced during her first meeting with the social worker. Since she was 5 years old, the educational system has reinforced this belief. As a Black female receiving special education services for an emotional disability starting when she was 7 years old, she had consistently received the message that she did not belong. This narrative was amplified when Jess was expelled from her neighborhood school in the 7th grade. School administrators explained to Jess's grandmother, her guardian at the time, that they could not provide the type of support that Jess needed. The principal told Jess's grandmother about an alternative school for students with emotional and behavioral disorders that would be able to provide the intensive, therapeutic approach she required. The school team stated that they would like to initiate the transfer by the end of the day, and Jess's grandmother did not feel like she had a choice but to agree.

At her new school, Jess had a hard time making friends. She again felt like an outsider, and she was frequently sent away from the classroom for disrupting class. Jess earned a reputation for being unafraid to fight with other female students. One day her science teacher sent her to the office for pushing another student. Jess was prepared for a suspension, sure that it would be the first of many in this new school. Instead, a licensed clinical social worker walked in, said, "Let's talk," and waved her into another room.

"I didn't do anything wrong," Jess said, before she sat down. The social worker apologized for the confusion and offered to walk her back to class. "Not back to science," Jess said. The social worker waited and asked Jess to clarify. Jess explained what had happened in the classroom and, after another question from the social worker, Jess said, "Well, then I barely pushed this girl." The social worker listened and then described a program that the school used in place of suspending students. "Sounds like you've already begun going through the steps of the program," the social worker said. "Can you write down what happened too?" With that, Jess began her first experience with the Building Bridges program, the school's alternative to suspension curriculum.

Jess was involved in a fight with another student a few weeks later, and the social worker spent a few more days working with her through the Building Bridges program. The social worker learned that Jess had never had a lasting, positive female friendship, and she had a history of being disconnected from loved ones. The social worker recognized that Jess needed relationships and skills to initiate and maintain friendships.

A few weeks later, Jess was sent out of the classroom again. This time, Jess went to the office and asked the administrative assistant, "Can I have Building Bridges?" During the next sessions, Jess reported feeling over-reliant on relationships with males to help fill a void of female friendships. Over the next 3 years, the time that Jess spent in the Building Bridges program was devoted to building an understanding of healthy relationships and developing skills for establishing and maintaining these relationships. Over time, Jess reported feeling in control of her behaviors, having friends, and enjoying school. The social worker noticed that Jess was utilizing the skills she had learned and that she had created a community for herself. She asked Jess if she would like to join her for a Building Bridges meeting with a younger student.

While explaining the Building Bridges program to the younger student, the social worker asked Jess if she had anything to add. "It's like, when you have Bridges, you go in and you talk about what's going on and you work it out. It's not like the normal 'get-sent-to-the-principal-thing' here," Jess said. Clearly, Jess had not just resolved a situation or a peer conflict. Rather, she had been given the opportunity to feel a sense of belonging and connection, which facilitated more learning and equity than she had previously experienced.

This story did not actually happen, but the fictional story of Jess is based on some of the experiences of the many Black students who are labeled with disabilities and directly or indirectly forced out of American schools. The push-out process perpetuates racist and ableist structures and ultimately maintains White supremacy. This chapter tells the story of one person, a mental health professional working in an alternative day school, who used her position to challenge the exclusionary practices at her school by creating an alternative option.

MECHANISMS TO CONTROL AND CONTAIN

Exclusionary discipline is a powerful tool that has aided in the continued segregation of students of color and students with disabilities. Not only are students of color and students with disabilities more likely to be removed from the general education setting within their home schools, but they are more likely to be suspended, expelled, and sent to schools designed for students at risk of educational failure, known as alternative schools or alternative education placements (AEPs; Fedders, 2018).

Alternative schools were created for students whose needs could not be met in their home schools. Available data on student enrollment in AEPs is outdated (Carver & Tice, 2010); however, in the past 20 years, there has been an increase in AEPs that now serve well over 500,000 students in the United States (Fedders, 2018). The percentage of districts offering AEPs is increasing rapidly across the country, particularly in areas of the southeastern United States and school districts that are urban or serve largely low-income or minoritized students (Fedders, 2018). While AEPs were introduced as a way for students to make up lost credits, they have evolved to include students with behavioral needs that cannot be met in their neighborhood school. AEPs then became a warehouse for students who have been labeled with an emotional or behavioral disability (Johnson & Naughton, 2019; Miller, 2020) or, in some states, simply labeled as "at risk" (ISDE, n.d.). Students at AEPs are "seen as having troubling personal circumstances" or "[exhibiting] behaviors deemed problematic" (Fedders, 2018, p. 898) and are disproportionately African American (Stanard, 2016) and disabled (Lehr et al., 2009).

While alternative schools received federal, state, and local funding, analysis of school district data indicates that certain alternative schools found ways to provide less funding to students in alternative schools as compared to the students at their neighborhood schools (Hill, 2007). The shortage of funding contributed to AEPs employing less-qualified teachers, having insufficient learning materials, and holding classes in less-desirable buildings than neighborhood schools (Fedders, 2018).

Moving a student to an AEP, similar to other breaks in one's education, forces a child to adjust to a completely new environment after losing support and positive relationships that may have existed in their previous school. Moreover, it is not unusual for alternative schools to offer no extracurricular activities that promote school engagement, social opportunities, and relationship building (Johnson & Naughton, 2019). Predictably, moving to an AEP is associated with decreased academic performance, not graduating on time, developing depression, and an increased likelihood of getting arrested later in life (Rumberger, 2015). Thus, instead of offering supports needed to bolster positive development, alternative placements often place students at more risk.

Educators need to reconsider discipline, including transfers to AEPs, through the lens of equity and explore how systems of oppression result in the placement of Black and Brown students with disabilities in the most segregated settings. While educators are working to address the disproportionality and bias embedded in the system, it is crucial that practices are framed with the understanding of how racism and ableism shape the education system and schools, both historically and currently. While students like Jess may benefit from some of the services offered at alternative schools, they are also segregated from their general education peers and face an increased likelihood of not graduating on time, being incarcerated, and experiencing mental health concerns (Rumberger, 2015).

DISCRIT AND THE PRESERVATION OF EDUCATION
AS A SPACE FOR WHITE AND ABLED PEOPLE

Jess's story is an example of how behavior and discipline in schools cannot be divorced from larger ableist and racist systems and structures. U.S. schools were designed for White, abled students and, through direct and indirect means, schools continue to serve those with the most privilege. Suspension, expulsion, and transfers into alternative schools operate as tools used to push students of color and students with disabilities out. A DisCrit lens encourages the exploration of the practices that are created and maintained to promote racist and ablist ideals in Western society. For the purposes of this chapter, DisCrit provides a critical lens to examine how alternative schools are used to sort the type of students who belong or do not belong to ultimately maintain a status quo of White supremacy (Fedders, 2018; Perzigian et al., 2017). More specifically, the following four tenets of DisCrit are particularly relevant to this case study:

1. *"DisCrit focuses on ways that the forces of racism and ableism circulate interdependently, often in neutralized and invisible ways, to uphold notions of normalcy" (Annamma et al., 2016, p. 19).*

Like the authors of DisCrit, the authors assert that racism and ableism are separate, socially constructed concepts that interweave within each other. By interweaving their threads, both forces are strengthened, but they remain separate materials. Racism and ableism are "so enmeshed in the fabric of our social order, [they] appear both normal and natural" (Delgado & Stefancic, 2001, p. 21). Accordingly, the exclusion of students of color and students with disabilities has been so prevalent and commonplace that we, as a society, normalize the continued practice of removing students from classrooms and schools to maintain White supremacy. In doing so, the systems are disconnecting students from their community and access to equitable education. Dean Adams and Nirmala Erevelles (2016) recognize that:

> not all dis-locating practices are readily recognizable by an outraged public, nor are all perpetrators and victims easily identified in these dis-locations. In fact, because some dis-locating practices are so obviously violent, they serve to obscure other normalized everyday practices enacted by seemingly well-intentioned individuals to dis-locate bodies from classrooms, families, and communities and into carceral settings such as alternative schools, prisons, and institutions. (p. 132)

This chapter focuses on one school that challenged dislocations that have been normalized and the necessary components to create sustainable change.

2. *DisCrit emphasizes the "social constructions of race and ability and yet recognizes the material and psychological impacts of being*

labeled as raced or dis/abled, which sets one outside of the western culture norms" (Annamma et al., 2016, p. 19).

The social worker works at a school that serves students who have been identified to have emotional or behavioral disabilities in the education system. These disabilities are known to be the most subjective and culturally loaded (Sullivan et al., 2019). For example, to meet the criteria for eligibility, the federal definition requires that school professionals evaluate for "inappropriate types of feelings under normal circumstances" (34 C.F.R. § 300.8(c)(4)) and evaluate a student's ability to maintain "satisfactory" relationships with peers and teachers (Individuals With Disabilities Education Act [IDEA], 2016). These "inappropriate" feelings, "normal circumstances," and "satisfactory relationships" are subjective and are compared to the experiences of a White, abled person. White supremist norms play out in determining what are considered "acceptable" versus "unacceptable" norms for behavior.

Students labeled to have emotional or behavioral disorders may experience difficulties with academics and social functioning at school. They face increased likelihood of receiving exclusionary discipline, dropping out, facing employment difficulties (Kauffman & Landrum, 2013), and being incarcerated (Hoge & Rubinstein-Avila, 2014). Moreover, students with an emotional disability are the most likely to be placed in restrictive settings, a decision that is often based on subjective criteria (Kaufman & Landrum, 2013). Accordingly, it is not a coincidence that Black students are disproportionately determined to have "unacceptable" behavior and deemed to meet criteria for an emotional disability, which results in their removal from general education spaces. This is just one example of how emotional and behavioral disabilities are socially constructed and used as a way to "other" those who are not White and abled. As Annamma et al. (2016) note, "Specific consequences are associated with labeling" (p. 17). Thus "while ability and racial categories are socially constructed, they continue to have real material outcomes in terms of lived experiences" (Annamma et al., 2013, p. 17). These outcomes include being forced out of "regular" classrooms and schools in ways in which White and abled peers frequently do not experience.

3. *"DisCrit recognizes Whiteness and Ability as Property and that gains for people labeled with dis/abilities have largely been made as the result of interest convergence of White, middle-class citizens" (Annamma et al., 2016, p. 19).*

White, middle- and upper-class families first advocated for more alternative schools in the 1990s as school violence took over the national conversation and parents sought separation from students they perceived to be dangerous (Lehr et al., 2003). Additionally, by pushing out students with low test scores or attendance, traditional high schools are able to increase their achievement scores and graduation rates. Students excluded from their neighborhood schools are disproportionately Black or Latinx and have identified disabilities. In fact, in the 2017–2018 school year, of all students between the ages of 14 to 21 with a disability, Black students were the racial group that received the fewest diplomas from neighborhood schools (65%) but had the highest percentage of graduating with an alternative certificate (12%). Comparatively, 77% of White, disabled students aged 14–21 graduated with a regular diploma, and 9% graduated with an alternative certificate (NCES, 2020c).

4. *"DisCrit considers legal and historical aspects of dis/ability and race and how both have been used separately and together to deny the rights of some citizens" (Annamma et al., 2016, p. 19).*

While legislative efforts have been made to decrease gaps in opportunities for marginalized students, legal remedies alone have not been sufficient in giving students of color and students with disabilities equal or equitable access (Ladson-Billings, 2008). In the 1990s, the Gun Free Schools Act and zero-tolerance policies led schools to adopt punitive, predetermined consequences for certain behaviors regardless of context or situational factors. Those behaviors were ultimately subjective and disproportionately excluded students of color and students with disabilities, often for minor infractions including dress code violations and foul language (Fedders, 2018). In 2001, when No Child Left Behind created new policies to evaluate schools, alternative education became a way for schools to push out underperforming students to boost their school achievement scores. Additionally, while the 2004 reauthorization of the IDEA requires that schools address racial disproportionality in special education, it does not define what constitutes as significant disproportionality nor what would be deemed inappropriate policies, procedures, or practices (Sullivan & Osher, 2019) that contribute to disproportionality. Thus, schools have been left to determine how to address biased referral processes, unequal resource allocation, discriminatory behavior management systems, culturally loaded assessments, and other inequitable practices. Despite policies intended to increase equity for students of color and students with disabilities, the education system continues to promote White supremacy in more nuanced ways. As Sullivan and Osher report in their 2019 synthesis of disproportionality policy, "it is not enough to have sound policies and procedures in place; they must be applied equitably" (p. 408).

Decades of research have proven that exclusionary discipline is ineffective and disproportionately impacts students of color and students with disabilities (Losen, 2011). The creation and use of AEPs appear to be another way to segregate students with disabilities and students of color and uphold White supremacy (Fedders, 2018). Given what is known about the poor outcomes of students transferring to AEPs, it is important to question if alternative schools are intended to meet children's needs or to maintain neighborhood schools as places for White, abled students. There has subsequently been a call for more proactive and equity-based responses in school discipline, including alternatives to suspension programs (Fenning et al., 2012).

ALTERNATIVE TO SUSPENSION PROGRAMS

The social worker at an alternative school created an alternative to suspension program to offer a more proactive approach to behavior and socioemotional concerns. She understood that the education system, and exclusionary discipline in particular, was set up to create "winners and losers in American schools" (Baglieri, 2016, p. 167). Students at her school had received the message that they were not going to be winners at school. The social worker and her alternative school colleagues were dedicated to showing students that their education and their futures mattered but that they were not equipped with sufficient resources. The social worker realized that exclusionary discipline sent students a clear message that they do not belong. By creating an alternative to the suspension program, the social worker aimed to reduce out-of-school suspensions and reinforce students' sense of belonging in school.

In general, alternatives to suspension programs are designed to combat the overuse of suspension and keep students in school to avoid missing needed instruction. Arguably more important, alternatives to suspension programs may promote learning and belonging as well as improve school climate. Additionally, alternatives to suspension programs offer socioemotional supports to students and work toward addressing the cause of challenging behaviors. Indeed, alternatives to suspension programs are components of what many educators and policymakers have called for in order to reform school discipline. It appears that in some places, state and federal legislators and policymakers are listening. By 2015, 22 states had revised laws with the intention of decreasing exclusionary discipline and increasing supportive, inclusionary discipline practices (Steinberg & Lacoe, 2017). However, because these substantial reforms have largely taken place in the last few years, there is little empirical evidence documenting the efficacy of alternatives to suspension with respect to student outcomes (Steinberg & Lacoe, 2017).

Because of the history, current reliance, and biases involved in exclusionary discipline and AEPs, reforming school discipline at the local or school level will require a cultural shift in a school community's values as well as an active approach to dismantling White supremacy. The cultural shift is needed to move from punitive, exclusionary discipline practices that lead to reduced feelings of belonging and poor school climate. On the other hand, discipline strategies rooted in restorative justice can empower individuals to resolve conflicts, maintain relationships, strengthen community, and develop skills. Restorative practices are defined as methods that "include informal and formal processes that precede wrongdoing, [and] those that proactively build relationships and a sense of community to prevent conflict and wrongdoing" (Wachtel, 2013, p. 1).

The continuum of restorative practices includes utilizing affective statements, affective questions, small impromptu conferences, groups or circles, and formal conferences. Restorative justice has roots in ancient and Indigenous practices from various cultures around the world (Graves & Mirsky, 2007). In the 1970s restorative justice emerged in the United States within the legal system. Decades later, it was introduced in education as a more appropriate way to discipline students rather than relying on punitive and exclusionary methods. Through restorative practices, educators can still encourage accountability for students' wrongdoing but with an emphasis on empathy and repairing the harm done (Stutzman et al., 2005). In addition to restorative practices, considering contextual factors and specific circumstances, including race and ability, also promotes equity in discipline procedures. Thus, the alternative to suspension program that the social worker created utilized restorative practices and focused on relationships in an effort to slow down the interchanges that implicitly and overtly push out students of color and students with disabilities due to biased assumptions.

BUILDING BRIDGES OVERVIEW

The School Community

The alternative to suspension program was developed and implemented in a public, alternative day school starting during the 2012–2013 school year. This particular alternative day school is part of a special education cooperative, which serves 10 high school and 21 elementary school districts located in a suburban county near a large, urban city. The alternative school aims to promote the academic, socioemotional, and behavioral health of students with the goal of transferring back to their home school. Utilizing a multidisciplinary team approach, the staff strives to utilize a therapeutic approach in all their offerings. Various therapeutic supports and services, including individual and group counseling, art therapy, and multisensory room access into daily programming, are interwoven throughout the school day.

Classrooms at the school typically consist of 12 or fewer students, with one teacher and one paraprofessional. Additionally, for every two or three classrooms, there is an assigned social worker. Teams meet weekly to discuss student progress and what changes can be made to improve the well-being of the group or certain individuals within it.

When the alternative to suspension program was implemented, the school served 122 students in grades 9–12. The racial makeup of the students was approximately 57% White, 23% Latinx, 18% Black, and 2% multiracial. Students are enrolled in the alternative day school program only if their home school deems them eligible per their individualized education program (IEP). Accordingly, all students at the high school receive special education services. Moreover, while students receive services under a variety of special educational eligibility categories, all students have significant emotional and/ or behavioral needs. Every student enrolled at the alternative school has been disenfranchised based on a socially constructed label; almost half are multi- ply marginalized due to their skin color and ability status.

Once enrolled at the alternative high school, students historically con- tinued to face out-of-school suspensions. During the 2011–2012 school year, 1 year prior to the implementation of the alternative to suspension program, 43 students were suspended, 19 (44%) of which received more than one out-of school suspension that year. In addition, there were 34 re- ferrals to law enforcement and 19 school-related arrests (U.S. Department of Education [DOE], Office for Civil Rights [OCR], 2014a). The discipline strategies at the alternative high school worked to further marginalize those students and sent yet another message of not belonging. A different approach was clearly needed.

The social worker noticed that students at her school were not accus- tomed to having their perspective valued or listened to. She wanted to pro- mote a strong sense of community and talk with students to understand their perspective about incidents that would typically result in a suspension at the alternative school. By making an effort to understand the student's perspec- tive, the social worker hoped to strengthen her relationship with the student, come to an agreement, and reduce the suspension rates at the high school.

Introducing Building Bridges

Although there was a clear need for a new approach to suspendable behav- iors, staff were unable to identify an existing program that would be a good fit for their school's needs and was backed by a strong research base. This made the social worker nervous, as implementing a program or curriculum that did not have some empirical support was perceived as riskier than a program that had proven results. However, the social worker also noted that there was no evidence-based program normed on students who have been marginalized like the students at her school. She convinced other school pro- fessionals that creating a program may be the best path forward, as it could be tailored to their school community. As a result, she created and introduced the Building Bridges program.

Once the social worker developed the curriculum, she needed to get ap- proval to try it out. The social worker began by reviewing the school's cur- rent discipline data to be able to discuss the issue of suspension in a concrete way and gain buy-in from other school-based professionals. Fortunately, the school's principal was fully supportive of an innovative approach to address the concerns about the school's discipline procedures. The principal was un- der pressure from the district to show a decrease in punitive practices, and that motivated him to communicate regularly with the social worker, dedicate time to discuss the Building Bridges program with the entire staff, and address school professionals who expressed hesitation or resistance to change. The support and active help from leadership was instrumental in creating change at the systems level.

Program Description

Building Bridges (Rappaport, 2014) is a curriculum-based program, rooted in restorative practices and a cognitive behavioral approach, that combines prevention and intervention to promote socioemotional skills. Originally created in 2014, the latest installment of the curriculum was published in March of 2018 (Rappaport, 2018). The program focuses on increasing self-awareness, self-regulation, social awareness, decision-making, and relationship building. Rather than pushing out students when they demonstrate challenging behaviors, the Building Bridges program emphasizes belonging, understanding, and learning from one's lived experiences. The program includes common components of restorative justice practices, such as mediation and restitution, that are effectively used as an alternative to punitive and exclusionary discipline (McCold, 2006). In addition, Building Bridges incorporates aspects of cognitive behavioral therapy, which focuses on changing one's harmful thinking patterns and interfering with undesirable learned behavioral responses (American Psychiatric Association, 2017). By integrating aspects of restorative practices and cognitive behavioral therapy, professionals implementing Building Bridges can help students in a way that is meaningful to the student, teaches instead of punishes, and does not remove the student from the school environment. Perhaps most importantly, the Building Bridges program is designed to facilitate a greater connection between an adult at school and the student who is experiencing some difficulty. The time spent one on one with the student allows the staff member to better understand the student's perspective and work collaboratively moving forward.

Core Components of Building Bridges

Choice

In contrast to the usual model of punishment being imposed on a student, Building Bridges gives the student and family a choice in regard to discipline. The Building Bridges program is presented as an option to the student and their family in situations where behaviors within the school setting would typically warrant a suspension based on the school's discipline policy. The social worker or the administrator contacts the student's parent or caregiver and offers an explanation of what has happened and the options moving forward. If the parent and student choose to participate in the Building Bridges program instead of an out-of-school suspension, the student comes directly to the school's main office the next day. Rather than serving a suspension, students who choose to participate in the Building Bridges program will spend an entire day working one on one with the social worker.

Mediation

Mediation, or a process in which two people come together to resolve a conflict, is held between students and staff, or between staff at the alternative school. The Building Bridges curriculum includes guidelines for mediation preparation, how to meet, rules of mediation, and a mediation contract. The mediation contract serves as a formal agreement for the student to do their part in preventing negative interactions with others or objects and makes it clear how the school will respond. Alternatives to the harmful behavior are provided so that a student has options when feeling overwhelmed. For example, one student may be allowed to leave the classroom and go for a walk while another may have the option of listening to music or drawing. A sample sheet used as a part of a mediation contract is included in Appendix A. The sheet provides a list of questions that facilitators can pose when conducting mediation with two students.

Thinking Sheets

Thinking sheets are worksheets that both staff and students complete to begin processing the event and sharing their perspective. The thinking sheets require that individuals describe the following: the behavior or incident that resulted in their Building Bridges program participation; how they feel about what happened; how they think others involved feel; how others are affected; and what might make things better in the future. There are additional worksheets with questions and hypothetical scenarios that are specific to the incident that occurred. Topics that these additional worksheets address include healthy romantic relationships, joking, coping skills, school rules, bullying, and friendships. Through talking and completing the various worksheets, the individual and social worker process the incident together and discuss what can be done to undo the harm that was caused. After all the worksheets and scenarios have been completed and verbally processed, the social worker assisting the student can use the remaining time to help the student complete any schoolwork that was missed during the day.

When appropriate, the student and the adult facilitating Building Bridges also discuss an informal reentry plan that considers how the student suspects they might feel or act when they return to the classroom. This time spent one on one with an adult at school allows for the student to be heard and a staff member to understand the student's perspective. It is intentional, relationship-centered time together, rather than the student being sent from school and being disconnected from school staff and peers. A sample thinking sheet that includes questions for students participating in Building Bridges is included in Appendix B.

Relationship Building

Building Bridges gives students an opportunity to share their perspective. In a system where marginalized students are typically treated as powerless, it is meaningful to have staff listen and validate students' feelings and viewpoints.

The importance of a positive adult relationship at school cannot be understated. By focusing on relationship building, students are more likely to feel connected to the school community. A feeling of belongingness can be transformative for all students, but especially for students at the alternative school who have been told that they are too different or difficult compared to their peers in neighborhood schools.

In addition to Building Bridges allowing for the staff to build a positive relationship with students, staff can also understand where the student may benefit from help. Meeting students where they are and focusing on progress is an important component of Building Bridges. One student who was physically aggressive with other students began to destroy objects instead of acting out against people. This progress was recognized as the social workers continued to show the student other, less destructive, coping mechanisms.

Implementation of the Building Bridges Program

The Building Bridges curriculum was piloted in the 2012–2013 school year. That year, the social worker implemented the curriculum with students, and slowly the other social workers who wanted to be involved began to help. At the end of the pilot year, the social worker reviewed the data on out-of-school suspensions and from the School-Wide Information System (SWIS) (May et al., 2013). Results indicated a 46% reduction in out-of-school suspensions from the previous school year. Moreover, all but one parent that year requested that their child participate in Building Bridges instead of receiving the suspension. This was a promising sign not only reflected in the quantitative data showing that Building Bridges can be effective in reducing out-of-school suspensions, but in that the families being served trusted the school to provide the program and preferred Building Bridges to having their child suspended.

After observing the reduction of out-of-school suspensions and listening to stakeholder feedback, the school officially adopted the Building Bridges curriculum as a school program the following year. During the following school year (2013–2014), three social workers, a paraprofessional, and a few instructional assistants were trained to use the Building Bridges curriculum and were able to process various incidents with students.

As an official program at the high school, Building Bridges continued to increase in frequency of implementation. Slowly, the program became part of the culture at the school, but not without a few obstacles. During the 2013–2014 school year, not all staff were able and willing to prepare and provide academic work for the students to complete during Building Bridges sessions. Preparing the work ahead of time was yet again another responsibility to ask of staff. While some teachers struggled to comply with that component, the social worker insisted that they follow through. By reaching out and helping teachers through the initial struggle, teachers began to see the benefit and value.

There were also staff who questioned whether students who commit certain offenses should be receiving a more punitive response rather than participating in Building Bridges programming. The principal had conversations with staff about restorative discipline and the philosophy behind it. Partially due to the strong opposition to ban all out-of-school suspensions, the school did not completely take away suspension as an option, but all of the staff committed to helping students build necessary skills that would help prevent a similar incident in the future. The expectation for all staff to support the Building Bridges program stayed consistent, the social worker and principal continued to support others as they learned about Building Bridges, and the staff began to fulfill their responsibilities as they saw successful outcomes.

Over the course of the next 2 school years, Building Bridges became increasingly familiar to staff and students and became a seamless part of the school's discipline process. The administrative staff encouraged the social workers to continue utilizing the curriculum, social workers became more skilled in their implementation of the curriculum, and teachers reported a noticeable difference in student behavior. The social worker hoped to see these positive changes reflected in the data.

OUTCOMES

Total Referrals Across Four Years

SWIS and office disciplinary referral (ODR) data were utilized to record all behavioral incidents at the high school. In addition to recording all major disciplinary referrals, the SWIS system (May et al., 2013) allowed for specific demographic information to be recorded, such as gender, race, grade, referral type (e.g., bullying, defiance, out of bounds), location of incident, and referral by educator for ODRs. Hernandez-Melis et al. (2016) conducted a multiyear evaluation of the Bridges program. The findings of that evaluation are summarized here. The reader is directed to the Hernandez-Melis et al. study for more detailed information about the methods and analysis completed. A total of 10,952 referrals were generated between the 2012–2013 and 2015–2016 academic years. Of these referrals, approximately 68% (n = 7455) of ODRs were generated by students who identified as male. Referrals by race were as follows: White 38.5% (n = 4219); Black 45.8% (n = 5023); Latinx 15.5% (n = 1702); Asian 0.05% (n = 5); multiracial 0.02% (n = 2); and Pacific Islander 0.01% (n = 1). The majority of ODRs (38.6%) were generated by students enrolled in the 10th grade (n = 4226), followed by 9th grade (n = 3050), 11th grade (n = 2302), 12th grade (n = 1355), and 8th grade (n = 19).

The SWIS data was further utilized to record subsequent consequences in response to behavioral incidents, including the number of occurrences of Building Bridges sessions. The Building Bridges program was implemented a total of 242 times between the 2012–2013 and 2015–2016 academic years.

During the 2012–2013 academic year, Building Bridges was implemented a total of 69 times. The following year, the program was implemented a total of 55 times. Building Bridges was implemented the fewest times the subsequent school year: 37 times. The 2015–2016 academic year demonstrated the largest number of applications of Building Bridges sessions with 87 total implementations.

Given the nature of the Building Bridges program, one explanation for the inconsistent amount of Building Bridges sessions implemented from year to year could be that students who received it one year were less likely to need it the next year. Alternatively, data could be skewed if one incident involved multiple students and it was recorded as separate Building Bridges sessions. The Building Bridges program appeared to be a success, but more research was needed to determine how it impacted ODRs and school climate.

Effectiveness of the Building Bridges Program

Hernandez-Melis et al. (2016) analyzed discipline referrals collected during the 2012–2013 academic year to evaluate the impact of Bridges. Thirty-one students were referred at least once during the year. Sixteen of these students participated in the program after the major referral, and 15 students did not participate. Analysis of discipline referrals demonstrated that there was no significant association between participation in the Building Bridges program after the first major referral and whether students generated a second major referral. These results suggest that participation in the program after the first major referral did not significantly reduce the likelihood of a second major referral. However, additional analysis revealed that students who participated in the program after their first major referral took significantly more school days to generate a second major referral than students who did not participate after their first major referral. Additionally, for students with two major offenses, there was a significant association between the number of times they participated in the program and whether they generated a third major referral (Hernandez-Melis et al., 2016). Given these analyses, the researchers concluded that there is potential for Building Bridges to reduce behavioral offenses that would be considered a "suspendable offense" in schools. Overall, the outcomes of the Hernandez-Melis et al. study were that Building Bridges reduced out-of-school suspensions at the alternative school and was effective for students; however, more work and replication are needed to understand the role of race and ability in both discipline referrals and program effectiveness.

Lessons Learned

In reviewing data and examining the program through a DisCrit lens, Building Bridges can be seen to challenge some racist and ableist practices in school systems, while in other ways the program may perpetuate them. First is the setting in which Building Bridges is problematic. Alternative schools in the United States generally offer subpar education for children who are not welcome in their neighborhood schools (Fedders, 2018). Students who attend alternative schools have been forced out of their neighborhoods due to socially constructed labels and are disproportionately Black and have disabilities. Ideally, children would not be forced into alternative schools, and they would be able to access programs like Building Bridges in their neighborhood schools. Therefore, Bridges should be replicated in general education settings and embedded in programming for students as they begin to transition to less restrictive settings.

Second, although student choice is a core component to Building Bridges, that choice was only offered when administrators allowed for it. The principal or assistant principal would decide if the student would be assigned an out-of-school suspension or if Building Bridges would be sufficient in addressing the concern without an out-of-school suspension before families were given the choice. Thus, even with the implementation of Building Bridges, allowing for an administrator's discretion to determine whether suspension would also be required reinforces racism and ableism in the process. Future work should consider how the impact of multiple forces, including racism, ableism, and trauma, can be acknowledged in administrative decisions to help mitigate the reinforcement of White supremacy.

Lastly, ODR data suggest that Building Bridges reduced overall suspensions in the alternative school, but due to the limited sample size, no valid conclusions can be made based on race. Future research should utilize an intersectional lens to analyze data disaggregated by race as well as ability status.

IMPLICATIONS FOR FUTURE RESEARCH, PRACTICE, AND POLICY

The implementation of the Building Bridges program is an example of what can be achieved when the school considers the ways that students who are not White and abled are pushed out. While the Building Bridges program is promising, it also needs further study and refinement by future researchers and practitioners specifically interested in promoting equity within school settings through a focus on the intersection of race and ability.

Research Implications

To prevent students from being displaced by their neighborhood schools and forced into AEPs, researchers are encouraged to examine key decision points that result in students being pushed out of their home schools. Understanding the decision-making process that leads to students being forced out of their neighborhood schools provides important information on how to intervene to prevent AEP transfers. Moreover, research is needed to understand how components of the Building Bridges program can be implemented to aid in preventing school pushout.

Future studies should consider systems change in the context of how the systems benefit and perpetuate privileges for White, abled students and the harm done to other students who are outside of that group. As educational research focuses on the efficacy of less punitive disciplinary practices, groups that have historically been most affected by punitive practices should be at the forefront of the research. This means Black and disabled students' voices must be a part of the research process and a beneficiary of the work. Specifically, more research is needed on how alternatives to suspension programs and restorative justice practices are created, adapted, implemented, and received by students with disabilities and students of color. This may be best achieved by framing future research from a DisCrit lens (Connor et al., 2016).

Given the small sample size included in the published study (Hernandez et al., 2016), valid outcomes were not able to be differentiated by race. Future studies are needed with a larger sample size of students in order to better understand whether racial/ethnic disproportionality is impacted. For example, randomized controlled designs could be applied. Further, mixed methodologies, which allow for merging quantitative and qualitative inquiries, would help glean additional information regarding the aspects of the Building Bridges program that help to increase duration of time between disciplinary infractions or eliminate them altogether. These studies should also include input from students and families who participated in or were impacted by the Building Bridges program, as their lives are most impacted by routine disciplinary decisions that are made. Subsequent studies are also needed to better understand how the Building Bridges program can be used in other settings. In particular, it is noteworthy that this study was implemented in an alternative school. The implementation of an alternative to suspension program will likely differ in a school serving general education students in a less restrictive setting. Educators working in neighborhood schools may have very different perspectives about students' behavior, their tolerance of it, and the degree to which they feel responsible for addressing behavior. Therefore, researchers are recommended to use qualitative methodologies to include the insights and perspectives of stakeholders (e.g. students, caregivers, staff, administrators).

Researchers should be encouraged to rethink current conceptualizations of systems change theory. A significant gap in the current literature is the failure of systems change theory to recognize the inherent role racism and ableism play within these systems (Eagle et al., 2015; Fixsen et al., 2005). The influences of racism and ableism are embedded within school systems, helping to uphold and sustain White supremacist and ableist ideals, which further marginalize students of color and students with disabilities. Without addressing these foundational oppressive systems, systems change theory does not meet its potential for implementing change to promote positive outcomes for students. Future conceptualizations of systems change theory must address the influences of racism and ableism if trainers and scholars hope to promote an equitable system instead of continuing to implement programs within an oppressive educational system.

Practice Implications

Practitioners are encouraged to consider how they can implement aspects of the Building Bridges program into their school at the various tiers of support. See Rappaport and Coleman's (2016) book for specific recommendations to adapt the Building Bridges curriculum to other settings. While used as an individualized intervention at the alternative school, Building Bridges can be implemented at the first, second, and third tier in other settings. At the tier 1 level, school staff may utilize the materials in the curriculum to promote self-regulation, self-awareness, and relationship building across the school building, and teachers can use worksheets in class meetings. In classroom settings, facilitators can ask students to write answers down or to discuss the questions as a group. Components of the Building Bridges curriculum can be adapted to use in classrooms to explicitly make expectations known. Specifically, establishing community norms and rules for how to address conflict and restore harm can help build classroom communities. Mediation can also be conducted as a group and incorporated with other aspects of restorative practices. Thinking sheets and restitution can be used when working with students independently. More broadly, the inclusion of staff in the Building Bridges program can promote needed guidance, reflection, and self-evaluation. Components of Building Bridges may encourage school professionals to consider how their own practices may be problematic instead of attributing challenging student behavior to deficits within the students.

While Building Bridges reduces suspensions within the alternative school, reducing transfers to alternative schools would be preferred. Should AEPs become less prevalent, resources that are currently being used on AEPs can be rerouted for additional resources to be used within neighborhood schools. Those resources can help neighborhood schools meet the needs of all their students. Supports should include implementing with fidelity all other available interventions and supports before considering exclusionary discipline, providing specialized supports within the general education classrooms of neighborhood schools, and limiting the amount of time students can be enrolled in alternative school placements.

It is our hope that practitioners will read this chapter and see the power of one determined social worker who was able to make change. Through gaining buy-in and converging with administrators' interest, the practitioner implemented a program, gathered data, and successfully implemented an alternative to suspension. The importance of gaining buy-in and constant evaluation are important considerations for practitioners who hope to implement programs that address an inequity they see in their daily work. Educators are encouraged to conduct a needs assessment to identify the specific problem relating to exclusionary discipline they hope to address in their school (e.g., reduce suspensions, decrease transfers to AEPs, reduce disproportionality within exclusionary discipline). Once the problem is identified, individuals can follow various implementation protocols (Fixsen et al., 2005) to ensure meaningful and sustainable change in their setting.

School-based professionals are also encouraged to think about programs that challenge the structures that maintain racism and ableism in schools. Reviewing disaggregated data to help problem solve and evaluate alternatives to suspension programs will be important as practitioners work toward sustainable implementation. Thorough data collection will allow staff to reflect on the program's success and areas of improvement. Data should include the demographic information for the student and the staff member who facilitates Building Bridges, the behavior that warranted the program, who requested the program be implemented, and the resources required to be successful, as should gathering student and family feedback as consumers of the program. As more alternatives to suspension programs are created, implemented, and evaluated, school-based professionals will have more options for models that have been successful in reducing exclusionary discipline and promoting equity. As schools consider new programs and evaluate their practices, the utilization of equity tools in all decision-making is recommended to explicitly acknowledge and mitigate the ways that decision-making benefits White and able students. Practitioners should also engage in regular implicit bias and cultural competency training that allow staff to reflect on their own beliefs and preconceived notions, particularly with respect to race and ability status (Staats, 2015–2016). With an increase in implementation and data to support alternatives to suspension programs, researchers and practitioners can provide necessary information to policymakers.

Policy Implications

In addition to ensuring federal protections for all students, policymakers are encouraged to consider how protections have historically benefitted White and abled students and marginalized students outside of those groups. More specifically, policies regarding exclusionary practices and reducing the biased practices that have led to disproportionate use of exclusionary practices are needed. Implementing racial and ability equity tools in all decision-making processes is recommended. To reduce the use of exclusionary discipline, policies that provide additional funding and training to support alternatives to suspension programs are needed in neighborhood schools. Moreover, policy should aim to be more preventative, including incentivizing the adoption of specific school-based restorative practices or requiring a continuum of evidence-based support for students who have been labeled as having emotional or behavioral disabilities. Chafouleas, Briesch et al. (2020) offer more specific guidance for supporting students with emotional disabilities through problem-solving models aligned with a multitiered system of supports. A well-developed continuum of support may lead to less suspension and transfers to AEPs, as students would receive incremental increases in support as needed before resorting to exclusionary discipline.

As long as AEPs exist for students who are forced out of their neighborhood schools, policy is needed to improve them and reduce the need. Policy can ensure that all efforts of the neighborhood schools are exhausted before beginning a transfer to an AEP. As other professionals have noted, bringing services to children in their neighborhood schools is preferred to taking students away from schools to receive specialized treatments (see Chapter 6, this volume). This involves documentation of the continuum of support previously mentioned. Additionally, more funding, training, and technical support from state and federal government are needed to improve AEPs and evaluate whether there are positive outcomes for students enrolled in them as well as increase the transition rate back to neighborhood schools and support teachers in their behavioral practices in general education settings.

CONCLUSION

The call for educators to change their punitive approach to behaviors that have perpetuated grave inequities for students of color and students with disabilities is increasing in urgency. Through a creative approach and steadfast leadership, the social worker and other professionals at the alternative school learned to support, not exclude, students after they engaged in harmful behaviors. While more work is needed to implement a sustainable alternative to suspension program that promotes equity for Black and disabled students, Building Bridges provides valuable pieces to further evaluate through rigorous methods in a continuum of educational environments.

LEGAL AND POLICY APPROACHES TO ADDRESS DISCIPLINE DISPROPORTIONALITY

LEGAL AND POLICY APPROACHES TO ADDRESS DISCIPLINE DISPROPORTIONALITY

CHAPTER 10

Changing the Conversation

Moving From Exclusionary Discipline to Trauma-Informed and Culturally Appropriate Practices to Improve Outcomes for Native American Students With Disabilities

Heather A. Hoechst and Donald Chee

This chapter focuses on school discipline of Native American[1] youth with disabilities in San Juan County, New Mexico, and posits that current law and local policies fail to integrate evidence-based and culturally informed practices to address the specific and unique needs affecting these youth. Native American students are disciplined at roughly two times the rate of their White peers and are disproportionately represented in all special education categories (Losen et al., 2015). Further compounding the problem is a lack of awareness or acknowledgement of the high rates of trauma found in Native American populations as compared to other youth and the impact of that trauma on learning and behavior. Utilizing positive behavioral interventions and supports in tandem with culturally appropriate and trauma-informed practices could significantly impact the emotional health and behavior of Native students and change the trajectory of their lives.

REGIONAL CONTEXT

Geography and Demographics

San Juan County is situated in the northwest corner of New Mexico, bordering Arizona to the west and Colorado to the north and touching Utah at a point known as the Four Corners. Spanning over 5,000 square miles, San Juan County incorporates a portion of the Navajo Reservation and a small portion of the Ute Mountain Reservation. In fact, the Navajo Nation comprises just over 60% of the land in San Juan County. Based on the 2010 U.S. Census, the estimated population of San Juan County is 127,000 people, 41% of whom are American Indian or Alaska Native (U.S. Census Bureau, 2010).

The overall poverty rate in San Juan County hovers around 21.5% (U.S. Census Bureau, 2020). The poverty rate jumps to 43% within the boundaries of the Navajo Nation (Navajo Business, 2004).

San Juan County's most populated town is Farmington, a sprawling municipality that is home to about 45,000 residents. The San Juan, Animas, and La Plata Rivers flow into and meet in Farmington, giving it the Navajo name of "Totah" or "Three Waters." Other than a few other lesser populated towns, such as Aztec, Bloomfield, and Shiprock, San Juan County is largely rural and dotted with houses and farms across the desert landscape. On the Navajo Nation, where housing is limited, it is not uncommon to live without electricity or running water, and many students are bussed long distances to attend school. With no major interstates, railways, or bus systems, lack of transportation is a common barrier in accessing employment or resources.

History of Longstanding Racism in Community

An unfortunate component of the area's history involves racial tension between the Native American and White populations. This tension reached a culmination in 1974 when three Farmington High School students were charged with the murders of three Navajo men—acts referred to as "Indian Rolling," wherein White high school students brutally attacked Navajos (Correia, 2015). This incident led the U.S. Commission on Civil Rights to dispatch its New Mexico Advisory Committee to Farmington for a full investigation of race issues in the town. They found widespread inequities spanning employment, the provision of health care, the justice system, and the economy (New Mexico Advisory Council to the U.S. Commission on Civil Rights, 2005).

The advisory council returned to Farmington 30 years later to take inventory of the current climate and published "The Farmington Report: Civil Rights for Native Americans 30 Years Later." In preparation for the report, the advisory council contacted more than 100 community members, "including Native American and Navajo community representatives, local, county, and state officials, law enforcement agencies, members of the local business community, and representatives from schools and health service providers" (New Mexico Advisory Council to the U.S. Commission on Civil Rights, 2005, p. 12). While the report offers some praise to Farmington for its efforts, it also highlights pervasive inequities impacting Native Americans in San Juan County. With respect to education, the report notes the lower test scores of Native Americans as compared to their White counterparts; and community members spoke out about a "lack of bilingual education and cultural instruction as well as resistance from some school board members to obtain input from the community" (New Mexico Advisory Council to the U.S. Commission on Civil Rights, 2005, p. 40). More recently, a 2010 report by the Navajo Nation Human Rights Commission found that, "despite decreasing tensions, the Navajo continue to experience severe economic and health disparities, unequal access to services, benefits, and opportunities, and other examples of institutional racism"

(Robert Wood Johnson Foundation, 2019, para. 2). These inequities follow Native American students through the schoolhouse door and have significant effects on academic achievement and educational success.

CONNECTIONS TO INTERGENERATIONAL RACIAL TRAUMA AMONG NATIVE AMERICAN STUDENTS

Historical Impact of Colonization

Historically, Native Americans have experienced ethnocide and cultural genocide, including forced removal from their homelands, forced removal of children to distant boarding schools and subsequent assimilation, and various forms of physical, mental, and social abuses. These acts of colonization have led to generations of Native youth being historically underserved by our nation's formal education system, experiencing the highest dropout rates and second highest rates of referral to special education of any racial or ethnic group (Powers et al., 2003). DisCrit, which emerged out of disability theory and critical race theory, serves as a useful theoretical framework for explaining how Native American youth "suspected" of having a disability experience multiple forms of oppression (Connor et al., 2016). Relatedly, research suggests that major challenges to a Native American student's school success include cultural discontinuity—or inconsistencies between home- and school-based norms and expectations—and school climate, two critical determinants of learning for Native students (Powers et al., 2003). Federal Indian policy over the past 2 centuries has had the effect of breaking up families, indoctrinating Native American children with non-Native values, and pulling apart the very social fabric that supports a healthy Native community (Seelau, 2012). Therefore, the oppression of Native American students seen today is rooted in centuries of historical racism and White supremacy.

Although steps have been taken to address the impacts of centurieslong colonization, Native American communities still suffer from *historical trauma*, a term used to encompass the cumulative exposure to traumatic events that affect an individual and continue to affect subsequent generations (Brave Heart, 2007). It has been suggested that many Native Americans also experience "historical unresolved grief," which refers to the "profound unsettled bereavement resulting from cumulative devastating losses, compounded by the prohibition and interruption of Indigenous burial practices and ceremonies" (Brave Heart et al., 2011, p. 283). The impact of historical trauma on Native American people can be seen in the prevalence of depression, substance abuse, and youth suicide (Grayshield et al., 2015).

Impact of Trauma on Physical and Mental Health

Experiencing stressful or traumatic events as a child has a direct impact on health and well-being. The landmark Center for Disease Control and

Prevention (CDC)–Kaiser Permanente adverse childhood experiences (ACEs) study looked at the impact of trauma experienced by individuals before the age of 18 on future outcomes as adults. Examples of ACEs include incarceration of a parent, domestic violence in the home, physical or sexual abuse, and problem drinking by a parent. The study found that a high ACEs score correlated with increased levels of substance abuse, poor academic achievement, depression, and even premature death (CDC, 2019). In children, trauma affects the structure and chemistry of a developing brain, making it difficult for children to regulate emotions and reactions (Gunn, 2018).

American Indians and Alaska Natives are disproportionately affected by childhood trauma and have higher rates of behavioral health concerns, mental health disorders, substance abuse, and suicide (Lechner et al., 2016). According to the CDC (2019), American Indians and Alaska Natives have a suicide rate that is double that of the national average. One study on the prevalence of ACEs among Native American youth found them to be two to three times more likely than non-Hispanic White children to have a parent in jail, to have observed domestic violence, to have been a victim of violence/witnessed violence in their neighborhood, and to have lived with substance abuse (Kenney & Singh, 2016). Kenney and Singh further found that Native American children were more likely to have a greater overall accumulation of adverse childhood experiences. These examples demonstrate how multiple systems of oppression have had a devastating impact on the health, wellness, and life outcomes of Native youth.

Kenney and Singh (2016) also surveyed the correlation of high ACEs scores with behavioral concerns. They found that parents reported more behavior concerns in children with more than two or three ACEs, such as "problems in school, arguing too much, difficulty maintaining control in the face of challenges, not caring about school performance, and repeating grades" (p. 9). Given that Native American youth experience greater numbers of ACEs, it follows that a larger number of these children may also experience behavioral concerns at school. While data on the ACEs scores of students in San Juan County is not currently available, at least one study of approximately 1,300 Native Americans in New Mexico found that 29% of those surveyed had experienced four or more ACEs (Paskus & Furlow, 2015).

Linking Trauma to "Disability"

The concept of linking trauma to disability has begun to make its way into educational institutions and courtrooms in at least a few parts of the country. Recent court decisions have opened the door for litigation concerning the relationship of trauma to disability in the educational context. In 2015, a district judge in California acknowledged that "exposure to traumatic events *might* cause physical or mental impairments that *could* be cognizable as disabilities under [Title II of the ADA and Section 504 of the Rehabilitation Act]" (*P.P. v. Compton Unified School District*, 2015, p. 1). Additionally, in a case brought on behalf of Native American students at Havasupai Elementary School located in the Grand Canyon, a federal judge recently recognized the impact complex trauma and ACEs have on a child's ability to learn, to the extent that such children may be disabled and require special education (*Stephen C. v. Bureau of Indian Education*, 2018). Recognizing trauma as a qualifying disability under Section 504 could have a significant impact on Native students viewed as struggling with behavior issues in schools and at risk for being further marginalized through school pushout practices rather than being adequately supported through appropriate behavioral and socioemotional supports. Rather than being subjected to exclusionary discipline, these students would benefit from a well-crafted Section 504 plan that includes accommodations and positive behavior intervention strategies, including culturally informed practices. Despite the implications of historical trauma and the frequency with which Native American youth experience individual trauma and its obvious impact on behavior, the limited use of Section 504 plans to support these youth leads to the conclusion that local schools fail to properly incorporate trauma-informed practices into their policies or curriculum.

LOCAL DISABILITY AND DISCIPLINE DATA

San Juan County is home to four school districts: (a) Central Consolidated Schools, which is located on the western border of the county and includes several schools located on the Navajo Reservation; (b) Farmington Municipal Schools, the largest of the districts; (c) Aztec Municipal Schools, home of the county seat; and (d) Bloomfield Schools, located on the eastern side of the county. The demographics of the school districts vary with their geographic location. Table 10.1 provides an overview of the percentage of Native American students and students with disabilities (as defined by the Individuals With Disabilities Education Act [IDEA], 2016) by district during the 2015–2016 school year.

Table 10.1. Percentage of Native American Students With Disabilities in San Juan County School Districts

School District	Total Student Enrollment	% American Indian/ Alaska Native Students	% Students With Disabilities	% Students With Disabilities Who Are American Indian/Alaska Native
Central Consolidated Schools	6,349	90.1%	15.1%	93.6%
Farmington Municipal Schools	11,699	31.2%	12.2%	46.0%
Aztec Municipal Schools	3,251	13.2%	10.3%	14.8%
Bloomfield Schools	3,047	37.4%	21.7%	47.0%

Source: U.S. Department of Education, Office for Civil Rights (2018)

Among all school districts, Native American students are disproportionately represented in special education based on what would be expected for their overall school enrollment. In Farmington, Native Americans comprise only a third of the student population but make up nearly half of the students identified as eligible for special education under IDEA. These numbers are consistent with findings of racial disproportionality among students identified under IDEA. The U.S. Department of Education Office for Civil Rights (2018) reported that American Indian or Alaska Native, Black or African American, and Native Hawaiian or Other Pacific Islander students ages 6–21 were more likely to be served under the IDEA than were the students of the same age in all other racial or ethnic groups combined.

Nationally, students with disabilities are more likely to be subjected to exclusionary discipline than their nondisabled peers (Skiba, 2002; Zhang et al., 2004). Concerns about disproportionality prompted the DOE to require schools to report data on the race, gender, and disability status of students subject to exclusionary discipline. A review of data from the 2015–2016 school year across school districts in San Juan County revealed trends consistent with those on the national level. Table 10.2 shows the breakdown of students with disabilities subject to in-school suspension, out-of-school suspension, and expulsion as compared with their peers.

As Table 10.2 demonstrates, only 12.5% of students enrolled in Farmington Municipal Schools are eligible for special education services. However, approximately 23% of students subjected to in- or out-of-school suspension receive services under the IDEA. Similarly, students with identified disabilities in the Aztec Municipal School District accounted for a much larger percentage of suspensions and expulsions than would be expected given that they made up only 10% of the overall student enrollment, which shows highly disparate rates of exclusionary discipline among Native

Table 10.2. Percentage of IDEA-Eligible Students Receiving Exclusionary Discipline

School District	Enrollment IDEA	Students Receiving In-School Suspensions Who Are IDEA Eligible		Students Receiving Out-of-School Suspensions Who Are IDEA Eligible		Students Receiving Expulsions Who Are IDEA Eligible	
	%	n	%	n	%	n	%
Central Consolidated	15.1	474	20.3	265	22.6	2	0
Farmington	12.5	565	23.5	589	22.9	10	20
Aztec	10.3	221	17.2	166	22.3	16	25
Bloomfield	21.7	157	22.3	182	19.2	50	100

Source: U.S. Department of Education, Office for Civil Rights (2018)

American students with disabilities. Perhaps the most disturbing finding from the data available through the Civil Rights Data Collection (CRDC) was the Bloomfield School District's expulsion of 50 students in the 2015–2016 school year, all of whom were identified as students with disabilities.[2] Given that expulsion is a low-frequency occurrence in most school districts, this is an alarming number which, by definition, equates with removal of education as a property right.

In general, Native American youth are more likely to be removed from school for nonsubstantive disciplinary reasons and have poorer school outcomes than White students. Across the country, "American Indian and Alaska Native students are more likely to be suspended than any other racial group, with the exception of African Americans. According to a 2015 report by the Center for Civil Rights Remedies, Native American students are disciplined at roughly two times the rate of their white peers" (Clarren, 2017, para. 7). Data collected by the National Congress of American Indians in 2014 revealed that Native American students account for 2% of all school arrests and 3% of all incidents referred by school staff to law enforcement, despite their overall enrollment totaling only 1% of the population (Clarren, 2017). Because these numbers are of low frequency, the disparate rates reported here may not receive the attention they deserve compared to overall discipline rates of other non-White groups.

There has been a significant amount of research on the topic of educational outcomes for Native American youth (e.g., Faircloth & Tippeconnic, 2010; Postsecondary National Policy Institute, 2020; Whitford, 2017). This research is further confirmed by government data sources, such as the U.S. Department of Education's CRDC. For example, "[D]uring the 2013–14 school year, American Indian or Alaska Native students, Native Hawaiian or Other Pacific Islander students, and students of two or more races had a collective enrollment of 5 percent and were 10 percent of students referred to law enforcement or arrested," meaning they were referred or arrested at twice the rate of their enrollment (DOE, OCR, 2019, p. 3). Given the low numbers by comparison with other groups, it is easy to overlook or dismiss these differences, but taken as a whole they tell a story consistent with experiences of Native American families across the country (National Congress of American Indians, 2018). The result is an inequity in the educational experience of Native American children who spend more time out of school and away from instruction than their non-Native peers.

In San Juan County, identification as a student with a disability appears to correlate more strongly with higher rates of discipline than identifying as Native American. Table 10.3 illustrates the percentages of Native Americans (regardless of disability status) in the San Juan County school districts subject to school discipline as compared to their overall percentage of student enrollment. While Native Americans appear to be disproportionately expelled, it is worth noting that the overall expulsion numbers in all school districts, except Bloomfield, were low. For example, the Central Consolidated School District only reported

Table 10.3. Percentage of Native American Students Receiving Exclusionary Discipline

School District	District Enrollment Native American	Students Receiving In-School Suspensions Who Are Native American		Students Receiving Out-of-School Suspensions Who Are Native American		Students Receiving Expulsions Who Are Native American	
	%	n	%	n	%	n	%
Central Consolidated	90.1	474	94.3	265	91.7	2	100
Farmington	31.2	565	33.6	589	32.1	10	40
Aztec	13.2	221	8.1	166	15.7	16	25
Bloomfield	37.4	157	47.1	182	44	50	52

Source: U.S. Department of Education, Office for Civil Rights (2018)

two expulsions during the 2015–2016 school year. However, both of those students were Native American children who were subsequently deprived of an education. At first blush, these may seem like "low numbers" that would not get picked up in reporting systems, but they have life-altering consequences for Native American youth subject to expulsion.

THE STATE OF NEW MEXICO LAW

School discipline policies are developed with guidance from federal and state laws and regulations. All school districts overseen by the New Mexico Public Education Department (NMPED) and located within San Juan County must comply with New Mexico's state statutes.[3] The New Mexico legislature granted authority to the NMPED to promulgate regulations governing school discipline, which are found in the New Mexico Administrative Code. The statutes and regulations also allow individual school districts to develop policies and procedures around school discipline. Because all schools located in San Juan County receive federal funding, they must comply with federal statutes, such as the Individuals With Disabilities Education Act (2016), Title II of the Americans With Disabilities Act of 1990 (2016), and Section 504 of the Rehabilitation Act (2016). Thus, to determine the rules that apply to a school, one must take a deep dive into state and federal statutes and regulations, as well as local school board policies.

New Mexico statutes address school discipline in a very limited context. The laws require local school boards to establish student discipline policies in consultation with parents, school personnel, and students. The discipline policies must "include rules of conduct governing areas of student and school activity, detail specific prohibited acts and activities and enumerate possible disciplinary sanctions" (N.M. Stat. Ann. § 22-5-4.3(B)). The statute and rules delegate substantial responsibility and discretion to local school boards in matters of school discipline.

The primary source of legal guidance regarding school discipline of all students is found in the New Mexico Administrative Code. The regulations quickly establish an authoritative tone, addressing jurisdiction of schools over students such that "public school authorities shall have the right to supervise and *control* the conduct of students, and students shall have the duty to *submit* to the schools' authority" (N.M. Admin. Code § 6.11.2.8(A), 2020, emphasis added). The regulations go on to clarify that "the right to attend public school is not absolute. It is conditioned on each student's acceptance of the obligation to abide by the lawful rules of the school community" (N.M. Admin. Code § 6.11.2.8(C)(2), 2020). They further provide an option for local school boards to "develop rules, regulations, policies, and procedures as they deem *appropriate to local conditions*, including policies which afford students more protection than the minimums established [within the regulations]" (N.M. Admin. Code § 6.11.2.8(D), 2020, emphasis added). In other words, the regulations set the baseline by which schools must provide due process to students, but they do not limit the ability of school boards to develop different and culturally appropriate discipline procedures so long as students maintain these basic protections.

New Mexico regulations differentiate between "temporary suspensions," which encompass out-of-school suspensions up to 10 days, and long-term suspensions, which require the removal of a student for a specified time exceeding 10 days or a lesser period set by a school board. Temporary suspensions require only a "rudimentary" hearing, which "may take place and a temporary suspension imposed *within minutes* after the alleged misconduct occurs" (N.M. Admin. Code § 6.11.2.12(D), 2020, emphasis added). This language grants school authorities nearly unlimited discretion in imposing suspensions up to 10 school days.

Long-term suspensions and expulsions of students require school districts to establish processes governing the imposition of these harsh punishments. The requirements are akin to due process protections afforded to criminal defendants, such as formal hearings, written notice of the "charges," and the right of the student to present evidence and witnesses on their behalf. (N.M. Admin. Code § 6.11.2.12(G), 2020). The regulations prescribe a strict timeline by which schools must make decisions and impose punishment. Students who are suspended or expelled according to this process who are not protected by IDEA or Section 504 of the Rehabilitation Act are not entitled to receive any educational services from the local district during the period of exclusion.

While these regulations apply to all students in New Mexico public schools, students with disabilities are entitled to additional protections in the long-term school discipline process. Within 10 days of proposing long-term suspension, expulsion, or a change of placement, the school must conduct a manifestation determination review (MDR) to determine whether the student's conduct was "caused by, or had a direct and substantial relationship to, the child's disability; or was a direct result of the administrative authority's failure to implement the IEP" (N.M. Admin. Code § 6.11.2.11(C), 2020). If the MDR team determines that the conduct fits the categories described, the student must be returned to their prior educational setting (if they were temporarily suspended), and the school must conduct a functional behavioral assessment (FBA) to determine whether a behavior intervention plan (BIP) would be appropriate. However, a student may still be removed from their placement if the student brought a weapon or drugs to school or caused serious bodily harm to another individual, regardless of whether the behavior was a manifestation of disability.

If the MDR team determines that the student's conduct was not directly related to the disability nor was the result of the school's failure to implement the IEP, the school may proceed with a long-term suspension or expulsion hearing. Finally, if a student with a disability is removed from their current placement because of a disciplinary decision, the student must continue to receive special education and related services, as provided by federal law. Importantly, when an MDR team determines that a behavior was not substantially related to the disability nor the school's failure to implement the IEP, that student is still entitled to a disciplinary hearing to determine whether that student actually committed the rule violation.

While these regulations were promulgated for states to comply with IDEA, students with disabilities are also protected by Section 504 of the Rehabilitation Act (2016), which states in relevant part, "No otherwise qualified individual with a disability . . . shall, solely by reason of his or her disability, be excluded from the participation in, be denied the benefits of, or be subjected to discrimination under any program or activity receiving Federal financial assistance" (29 U.S.C. § 794). Because Section 504 defines disability more broadly than the IDEA, some students may be eligible for its protections even if they do not qualify for special education under the IDEA.[4] While the law and implementing regulations of Section 504 do not provide the detailed guidance of the IDEA, the regulations touch on school discipline in the context of changing a student's placement. Specifically, a school must conduct evaluations of a student protected under Section 504 whenever the school is considering a significant change of placement (Section 504 Regulations, 2017). While not defined in the law, the DOE's Office for Civil Rights (OCR) (2020) suggests that a "significant change of placement" includes suspensions of 10 consecutive days or more. OCR further interprets the regulations to require an MDR for students protected by Section 504 prior to imposition of long-term suspension or expulsion (DOE, OCR, 2016). Thus, all students with disabilities should receive additional protections before being subjected to long-term exclusionary discipline. This becomes particularly important for Native American youth who have experienced trauma and are exhibiting nonconforming behaviors. Section 504 protections could mean the difference between these students receiving supports and services to succeed in school or being expelled.

School district discipline policies largely mimic state laws and regulations—often using identical language. These policies are long, complex, and frequently buried deep within comprehensive school handbooks and busy school district webpages or require a request from the school districts themselves to obtain. As a result, parents are unlikely to know whether the school complied with the statutes and regulations unless they are well versed in state law. These highly legalized and inaccessible documents serve to maintain systematic oppression of students and families by preventing those who are entitled to protections from knowing what those protections are and serve as an example of what critical race theory observes as racism that "has become so deeply ingrained in society's and schooling's consciousness that it is often invisible" (Brayboy, 2006, p. 428).

While the law grants significant discretion to school districts in developing school discipline practices and encourages input from the community, those in San Juan County routinely utilize exclusionary discipline practices, provide only the minimum procedural safeguards as required by law, and fail to invite community input, relying instead on traditional forms of punishment. Further, current law and policy is devoid of any suggestion that a student's behavior should be viewed in the context of that student's individual circumstances or local culture, further erasing the identities and lived experiences of Native American youth and families. Rather, school discipline is doled out methodically and systematically, without consideration of the stark contrasts with traditional cultural practices.

THE ROLE OF CULTURE IN THE LOCAL COMMUNITY

Every Native American tribe has a unique history, culture, language, and story. Native Americans value the wisdom in their history, honoring their ancestral knowledge, ceremony, and traditional practices. Cultural teachings, practiced for centuries, are held sacred and vital to the intertribal survival and resiliency of Native American communities, helping them thrive today. Many Native American communities have turned to traditional practices and sacred knowledge to restore and empower communities, to reclaim tribal identities, and to continue to promote health and wellness for future generations. In describing tribal critical race theory (TribalCrit), Brayboy (2006) suggests that "tribal philosophies, beliefs, customs, traditions, and visions for the future are central to understanding the lived realities of Indigenous peoples, but they also illustrate the differences and adaptability among individuals and groups" (p. 430).

Many students in the San Juan County school districts identify as Navajo, or Diné. The Diné, like many other Native American tribes, possess cultural teachings of connectedness through language, kinship, community, and respect for all living beings. Children are highly valued in Navajo society, occupying a space that is traditionally considered holy or sacred (Eid &

Goldtooth, 2017). According to Navajo custom, "Everyone has a right to be heard at a meaningful time and in a meaningful way," which extends to children if they are of sufficient age and maturity (Austin, 2009, p. 175). Consequently, Navajo children are involved in discussions and have a right to be heard on decisions affecting them.

A key Diné teaching is to maintain *hozhó*—balance and harmony of all aspects of life, including the physical, spiritual, emotional, and mental. When Diné speak of all aspects of life, they are referring to everything, both tangible and intangible, functioning well and being in its proper place (Austin, 2009). This concept also describes the interconnected, interrelated, and interdependent nature of all elements in the universe, including self, immediate and extended family, and the natural world (Eid & Goldtooth, 2017). From this perspective, humans are but one element, and Diné strive to maintain balance among all other elements, including each other (Austin, 2009). Harmony is maintained through *ké*, which is fundamental to relationships and Diné concepts of equality and rights (Austin, 2009). According to Austin (2009), *ké* incorporates the values of respect, kindness, cooperation, and reciprocal relationships that are necessary to maintain *hózhó*.

The impact of *hózhó* manifests itself in the expectation that all can speak and act freely but must do so with respect; a failure to speak or act respectfully causes disharmony (Austin, 2009). If one causes disharmony, then the problem must be identified and addressed so that harmony can be restored. *Ké* is essential to the Navajo concept of due process and is "the force that makes Navajo law and procedure work" (Yazzie, 1996, p. 122). It is key to addressing disharmony and restoring harmony to the individual, relationships, and community (Austin, 2009). One aspect of restoring *ké* involves the "talking out" phase in which a *naat'aani* (leader) is called on to give an opinion on the proper outcome (Yazzie, 1996, p. 122). Unlike a judge, a *naat'aani* acts more like a teacher, relying on traditional values and lore to guide participants (Yazzie, 1996).

Traditionally, the Navajo concept of justice differs significantly from that of the current American legal system. While the American legal system is adversarial and hierarchical, with an individual casting judgment on the accused, the traditional Navajo legal system focuses on "restorative justice which uses equality and the full participation of disputants in a final decision" (Yazzie, 1994, p. 180). The Navajo system relies on relationships and rejects force or coercion (Austin, 2009). In light of these values, modern Navajo courts utilize the concept of peacemaking to resolve some disputes within the community. A key role of a Diné traditional peacemaker is "to guide the whole toward a cathartic understanding of *hózhó* that opens the door to transformative healing" (Navajo Courts, 2012). This process focuses on reaching consensus of all concerned, including the victim; consequently, harmony is restored (Austin, 2009).

In contrast to the cultural values, beliefs, and lived history of Native communities, school discipline policy at the school district level follows the structure of the American legal system, with an authoritarian figure dispensing discipline on a nonconforming student. There are many ways that the dismissal of Native culture appears in disciplinary policy. The disciplinary process rarely includes the other students or staff who are involved and focuses on excluding the student from the community. In direct contrast to the concepts of *hózhó* and restoring *ké*, the New Mexico Administrative Code sets up a clear hierarchy of an authoritarian figure controlling students, who are expected to submit to that authority (N.M. Admin. Code § 6.11.2., 2020). This system leaves Native American students and their families feeling cast out, unwanted, and powerless. Instead of incorporating principles of restorative justice and traditional teachings, schools focus solely on punishing students for their wrongdoings. In the existing systems and under existing law, little is done to build the relationships and restore harmony to the educational environment.

SCHOOL DISCIPLINE IN SAN JUAN COUNTY: VIEWPOINT OF STUDENT ADVOCATES

The Native American Disability Law Center is a nonprofit organization with offices in Farmington, New Mexico, and Flagstaff, Arizona. As a member of the protection and advocacy network, the center's mission is to advocate so that the rights of Native Americans with disabilities in the Four Corners area are enforced, strengthened, and brought in harmony with their communities. As part of its education advocacy work, the center receives referrals from the San Juan County Juvenile Probation Office and other community health providers to assist Native students who are experiencing disciplinary issues at school. Additionally, parents and guardians often contact the law center with questions relating to special education and school discipline. As such, the center is uniquely positioned to understand how parents and students experience the school discipline process.

The cases in which the center has become involved demonstrate the complexities of the school disciplinary system, particularly as it becomes intertwined with special education law. Families are often contending with court appearances due to their child's simultaneous involvement with the juvenile justice system. Additionally, as demonstrated by the Census data, many families live in poverty, and often without reliable transportation or cell service. Without the assistance of an attorney or advocate, many families face significant barriers in exercising their due process rights and accessing the services to which they are entitled by law. Families frequently express feelings of being pushed out of the school, of being helplessness, and of feeling a lack of understanding of the process. Parents and guardians feel that the schools target their children and grandchildren, refuse to listen to their side of the story, and make decisions prior to holding meetings and hearings. On some occasions, the schools appear to be following internal processes that technically comply with the law. However, these processes do a poor job of accommodating the needs of these students and fail to incorporate culturally informed or trauma-informed practices that could have a significant impact on Native students with disabilities.

INCORPORATING CULTURALLY AND TRAUMA-INFORMED PRACTICES IN SCHOOL DISCIPLINE

Native American youth face obstacles to academic success both inside and outside of the classroom. These obstacles are often so overwhelming for students, parents, school leadership, and their communities that the result is a system that fails Native students. The incorporation of culturally informed and trauma-informed practices in the school setting can emphasize keeping students in the school community and increase their chances of educational success. There are efforts underway in some Native American communities that can serve as examples of the effectiveness of incorporating culturally informed and trauma-informed practices in school discipline.

For example, the Menominee Indian School District (MISD) in Keshena, Wisconsin, features a strong educational program for its youth that incorporates the Menominee Indian language and culture into their daily activities. The district found that using culturally relevant and trauma-informed approaches in all aspects of life was much more effective than exclusionary discipline. (Robert Wood Johnson Foundation, 2015). Utilizing the Trauma Smart curriculum in the community, school, and other health care providers increased awareness of students' emotional and mental health needs. This awareness resulted in the decision to build a clinic on campus, such that counseling services and mental health care providers are available on-site during the school week. According to Wendell Wakau, a member of the Menominee tribe spearheading the trauma-informed efforts (personal communication, February 6, 2019), suspensions and expulsions have declined tremendously since their implementation.

Rather than removing students from the educational setting, the school initiated an alternative treatment plan with restorative practices that address the whole student's emotional, physical, mental, and spiritual being. Students are given the opportunity to unpack the underlying issues of personal trauma stemming from domestic violence; family incarceration; and longstanding historical racism, discrimination, and oppression of Native American youth and their families. With guidance from traditional and Western practitioners, the school has integrated trauma-informed care into the classrooms. For example, teachers perform morning check-ins with students to know whether a child is feeling troubled on a particular day, and students have the opportunity to retreat to a Sakom (peace) room when they need time to decompress (Robert Wood Johnson Foundation, 2015). Transition from a traditional Western disciplinary approach to a more culturally appropriate accountability approach of student behaviors has also been implemented, which serves to re-inforce the Menominee tribal Seven Grandfather Teachings of wisdom, love, respect, bravery, honesty, humility, and truth (Wendell Wakau, Menominee, personal communication, February 6, 2019).

The MISD approach reflects values similar to Diné values and can be altered to reflect the culture and norms of different communities, while hopefully achieving similar results. Drawing on cultural teachings that em-phasize strength and resiliency, schools could implement positive behavior approaches to better serve their Native American students, which would also benefit all students. By first clearly recognizing the value of all students and establishing the norms of respect and accountability before there is conflict, schools can develop a different and more positive environment. Using a sys-tem that focuses on including all voices, treating others with respect, address-ing all issues, and reaching a consensus, the school can hold nonconforming students accountable, address conflict, and keep students within the school community, while also honoring and respecting the culture and heritage of Native American youth and their families.

By virtue of its proximity to the Navajo Nation, San Juan County school districts enroll a large number of Navajo students who would benefit from a shift in school discipline policy to a culturally appropriate and trauma-informed Indigenous justice model. Utilizing traditional teachings and edu-cating teachers, parents, and community members on the impact of trauma on students, schools could tap into the strength and resiliency of its students to improve both their behavior and the overall school climate. The experts on culturally appropriate intervention include tribal members living and working within the same vicinity as the school districts; involving them in changes to discipline policy could reap rewards for the districts and, more importantly, the students they serve. Together, the school districts, students, juvenile jus-tice systems, and community members could work together to restore *hozhó*.

Specific recommendations for school districts working with Native American youth across the country include accessing restorative practice training, either through local tribes or professionals experienced in this work. In the school setting, restorative practices focus on relationship building and problem solving by bringing those involved together to resolve conflict. In the neighboring state of Colorado, using restorative practices in schools has resulted in a large decrease in suspension rates, as well as drops in absentee-ism and tardiness (Restorative Justice Colorado, 2021).[5] Further, by involv-ing families and tribal leaders in the drafting of school discipline policies, the marginalized voices of those most often affected by these policies would be heard and the policies would more accurately reflect local cultural values and norms.

On a larger level, the DOE and state public education departments should pay close attention to school discipline data to ensure that neither race nor disability status correlates with higher rates of exclusionary discipline. Because Native American youth constitute a small percentage of the overall population of school-age children, it is easy to overlook the data that shows they are often subject to exclusionary discipline. Awareness of the impact of just one expulsion on a Native American student and their community should drive state and federal agencies to watch this data closely and intervene when there is any suggestion of a disparate impact of exclusionary discipline. Research in this area should incorporate TribalCrit and its tenet that "stories are not separate from theory; they make up theory and are, therefore, real and legitimate sources of data and ways of being" (Brayboy, 2006, p. 429). A TribalCrit approach would require the collection of qualitative data in the form of stories from those affected by these policies that would shed light on the lived experiences of Native American youth and allow their voices to shape future policies and practices.

Further, state law amendments requiring schools to incorporate culturally appropriate and trauma-informed practices into their school discipline policies, and providing funding to do so, would hasten the shift in a more positive direction. By using a tiered approach, schools would have to show evidence that they utilized restorative practices or similar techniques prior to resorting to exclusionary discipline, which should only be used when necessary to protect the safety of students or staff. Closer monitoring of data and the act of legislating away suspensions and expulsions would force schools to rethink school discipline policies in light of local cultural considerations benefiting all students and the communities. The first step, of course, is to simply change the conversation.

Disproportionate Encounters of School Security Personnel and Students With Disabilities

An Update of the Case Law

Thomas A. Mayes and Perry A. Zirkel

When deploying security personnel such as school resource officers (SROs) in schools, school districts and law enforcement authorities must be cautious and deliberate. Otherwise, they might confront circumstances like those posed in *Wordlow v. Chicago Board of Education* (2018). The Chicago Board of Education (CPS) employed Divelle Yarbrough as a security guard. Yarbrough had no prior experience working in a school; his most recent employment was as a bouncer at a strip club. When he was hired as a school security guard, his building principal failed to inform the CPS central office that Yarbrough needed security officer training, which provided training on de-escalation; for that reason, Yarbrough never received training required of security guards who were not off-duty Chicago police officers. Yarbrough and CPS disagreed on whether he could discipline students and whether he could carry and use handcuffs.

In 2016, Yarbrough handcuffed M.M., a 6-year-old female 1st-grade student with a disability, in the presence of M.M.'s homeroom teacher and her special educator, after the special educator "informed Yarbrough that M.M. had taken candy from a teacher and thrown up on herself" (*Wordlow*, 2018, p. *5). M.M. was not a threat due to her small stature, was compliant, and did not attempt to resist. Yarbrough stated he handcuffed M.M. as "'kind of an isolated time out' and as a 'teaching moment'" (*Wordlow*, 2018, p. *5). He took M.M. to his desk, where she spent anywhere between 3 to 20 minutes in handcuffs. After the incident, M.M. was diagnosed with posttraumatic stress disorder, and CPS fired Yarbrough. The plaintiff, M.M.'s mother, sued CPS and Yarbrough in federal court.

The events recounted in the *Wordlow v. Chicago Board of Education* case raise a number of important questions, such as the following: Is taking candy from a teacher's candy dish worthy of handcuffing? Is the use of handcuffs a "teachable moment" and, if so, what does it teach? How compatible are education's and law enforcement's missions and views of the world? The use of SROs and other similar law enforcement and security personnel is a matter of broad public concern (King, 2016; Zirkel, 2019a). At its core, the use of security personnel such as SROs, whether directly employed by the schools or employed by local law enforcement agencies, represents a tension between broad competing public policy concerns: the value of school security versus the values of access, equity, and excellence (DeMitchell & Cobb, 2003). SROs and similar personnel are common (National Center for Education Statistics, 2017) and publicly popular (Phi Delta Kappa, 2018), especially in reaction to school shootings (Ahranaji, 2017), but are also controversial in education (Normore, et al., 2015; Ryan et al., 2018; Sawchuk, 2020), legal (Merkwae, 2015; Shaver & Decker, 2017; Zirkel, 2019a), and law enforcement (National Association of State Boards of Education [NASBE], 2019; National Association of School Resource Officers [NASRO], 2012) circles. A common SRO model has three components: law enforcement, educator, and counselor (Canady, 2018; Meade, 2019; Zirkel, 2019b). In the right circumstances and if these three components are in proper balance, SROs may contribute to a safe and supportive school climate (NASBE, 2019); however, SROs may also "cause harm to the students whom they are charged with protecting" (Zirkel, 2019b, p. 1) and undermine the broad public policy concerns they are intended to address. Given these concerns and disputes, there is a continuing public discussion about whether SROs and similar personnel should be used (Ali, 2021; Sawchuk, 2020).

One area of continuing concern and research is the relationship between SROs and students with disabilities (Fox et al., 2021; Meade, 2019; Shaver & Decker, 2017; Zirkel, 2019a and b). This interaction is complex because some children with disabilities, based on the nature of their disability, may be at greater risk to commit acts that violate criminal law or disrupt the school environment, may be more likely to be victims of crime or violence, may be less able to express their concerns to law enforcement, or may react in unexpected ways to generally accepted law enforcement techniques (Hill, 2017; Mayes, 2003; Stanford & Muhammad, 2018). Further, individuals may falsely assume that all children with disabilities always act in a certain manner (e.g., Mayes, 2018).

Considering these concerns, Zirkel (2019a and b) reviewed case law and determined that SRO litigation about children with disabilities was disproportionately high in relation to SRO litigation and children without disabilities. Further, while schools prevailed in the large portion of the cases based on legal grounds, the SRO conduct at issue was frequently questionable when viewed from professional grounds, such as the use of handcuffs and other aversive measures (i.e., tasers, pepper spray). The purpose of this study is to apply the same analysis to litigation occurring after the coverage period of Zirkel's 2019 studies.

LITERATURE ON EFFICACY OF SROS

The most recent professional literature on the presence of SROs in schools is consistent in evidentiary support, recommendations, and conclusions with that reviewed by Zirkel (2019a and b): uncertain (at best) efficacy of SROs in controlling violence and improving school culture (e.g., Kupchik, 2019; Nance, 2019); deep concern about the negative consequences of misuse of SROs to enforce student codes of conduct—as opposed to responding to and preventing criminal offenses—especially for students of color and students with disabilities (see Chapter 4, this volume); and suggestions for more defined SRO roles and increased SRO training (Canady, 2018; Malcolm, 2018).

LEGAL AND LAW ENFORCEMENT LITERATURE

Recent legal commentators have largely restated previously expressed concerns. As the number of SROs increased, so did arrests of students (Gupta-Kagan, 2019; Henning, 2018; Malcolm, 2018). Many of these arrests are for relatively minor infractions, which have historically been addressed by the school's disciplinary process (Ahranaji, 2017; Edelman, 2019; Gupta-Kagan, 2019; Hill, 2017). This increased number of arrests has had a disproportionate effect on students of color, students with disabilities, students of low income, and LGBTQ+ students (Edelman, 2019; Henning, 2018; Hill, 2017; see also Chapter 4, this volume). The increased use of SROs has come at a cost (Malcolm, 2018) and has not yielded measurable success (Nance, 2019) but does harm school climate and student achievement and increases the likelihood of poor post-school outcomes for children arrested by SROs (Ahranaji, 2017; Gupta-Kagan, 2019; Hill, 2017).

Some recent commentators addressed the proper role of SROs. Canady (2018), president of NASRO, indicated that the traditional three-pronged role of SROs (peace officers, educators, and counselors) may require some revision in light of research concerning childhood trauma, risk, and adverse childhood experiences. Specifically, Canady noted that to maximize the role of trust SROs have in an ideal school community (leading to students' ability to candidly confide in SROs, who may then act to prevent criminal activity), schools and SROs may need to revisit application of traditional law enforcement techniques to the school setting. Other commentators observed the need for detailed interagency agreements between school districts and law enforcement or other state and local policies to limit SROs' ability to arrest for minor infractions (Gupta-Kagan, 2019). Commentators also focused on the need to provide training for SROs on their proper roles, as well as eliminating roles that might be counterproductive (Canady, 2018; Fox et al., 2021; Malcolm, 2018).

Law enforcement literature contains similar concerns. The Congressional Research Service (CRS) (2018) reviewed the available research on SROs, noting a "limited" "body of research on SRO programs to reduce school crime" (p. 7), paired with a positive perception among students and teachers about the efficacy of SRO programs. CRS also noted the concern that any benefits of SRO programs "might be offset by the social costs that might arise by potentially having more children suspended or expelled from school or entering the juvenile justice system for relatively minor offenses" (p. 8), a concern that the CRS found in part to be warranted. CRS recommended that an SRO program be part of a school's "comprehensive school safety program" (p. 12), only if warranted by the school's data. If a school's plan includes an SRO program, the program must have clear goals and guidelines and be staffed by strategically selected and trained SROs.

Taking a practical focus, NASBE (2019) interviewed Tom Manger, the chief of police in Montgomery County, Maryland, about his experience leading SRO programs there and in Fairfax County, Virginia. He advised that SRO programs should focus on prevention and have clear lines of authority described in interagency agreements and noted the importance of hiring, placement, and training decisions, including training on brain development, behavior, and relationship building. He suggested that SRO programs have a "lean and unambiguous" goal: "We want students to feel safe in school" (NASBE, 2019, p. 46). Manger's focus for SROs is two-pronged: building relationships with students while focusing on law enforcement issues, not school discipline matters. "I tell SROs not to get involved with minor stuff like hats. I say to them, 'If you tell a kid to turn his hat around and he doesn't, then what are you going to do?'" (NASBE, 2019, p. 46). In Manger's practice-informed opinion, SROs who develop trusting relationships with students and staff are able to prevent and deescalate crisis situations, such as by learning from students that a peer has brought a weapon to school.

Two separate commentaries advocated increased use of SROs, both in response to school shootings (McQuiller, 2019; Terrades & Khan, 2018). In doing so, McQuiller (2019) acknowledges he does not endorse the use of SROs to address minor disciplinary infractions; however, he states that political reality may require such continued use to secure the funding he recommends. Likewise, Terrades and Khan (2018) cite studies purporting to show that SROs have a "positive impact in schools" due to a "non-confrontational, non-enforcement" (p. 529) approach; however, they appear to acknowledge the risks inherent to an SRO assuming a more confrontational posture.

EDUCATION LITERATURE

The education literature also raises similar concerns about SROs. Summarizing previous research, Stanford and Muhammad (2018) note that SROs frequently act for nonviolent offenses, with a disproportionate effect on students of color and leading to the interruption of special education services. Using a case study approach, Meade (2019) provides narrative of an SRO's interaction with a child with a disability, including teaching notes that summarize research on SROs in general and their interactions with students with disabilities, as well as providing two federal district court cases for discussion (although not noting further 6th Circuit opinions affirming each decision). Meade (2019) briefly discusses how the "general public assumes that SROs should be trained in not only the legal and tactical aspects of law enforcement but also how to work with children, including those with disabilities" (p. 79); however, such training is not universally required or provided.

Reviewing prior research and case law on excessive force claims against SROs, Brady (2018) concluded the case law does not contain clear outcome patterns or standards. His case law review is not as methodologically rigorous as prior research (Zirkel, 2019a); however, he reaches similar conclusions and offers similar recommendations as other literature reviewed: an increased number of SROs, an increased number of arrests (which has a disproportionate effect on students with disabilities), and a need for additional training and clearer agreements between law enforcement and schools regarding the use of SROs.

In a brief review of the conclusion of published studies, Kupchik (2019) observes no clear evidence that SROs make schools safer or prevent mass casualties. In contrast, the available research shows that SROs make arrests for minor offenses and have a disproportionate effect on students of color. Kupchik also notes that "SRO programs are very expensive" (para. 16) and may divert resources from evidence-based programs that improve school climate and safety.

Studying the relationship between student outcomes and SROs in a single state, Anderson (2018) studied whether a 2013 North Carolina statute providing matching state funds had any relationship to the rate of 16 disciplinary acts that North Carolina schools must report. He found no relationship between whether a school received matching funds and incidence of disciplinary acts. He also found no relationship between the amount of matching funds and incidence of disciplinary acts. Examining other variables in relation to reported instances of disciplinary acts, he found that race/ethnicity was a poor predictor of disciplinary incidents but that "grade level proficiency is a reliable predictor of reported acts. The model predicts that a 5% increase in grade level proficiency could reduce reported disciplinary acts by approximately 20%" (Anderson, 2018, p. 17). He recommended that school safety be broadly conceptualized rather than narrowly confined to mass casualty events. He further recommended that SROs focus on law enforcement and that any education or counseling happen in the community, as opposed to the school. (Anderson [2018] noted 85% of the variance in reported acts was unexplained by school- and district-related variables.) He observed that resources invested in improving student achievement improve student safety.

Zirkel (2019a and b) provided the most thorough review of SROs and litigation. In a comprehensive review of all 208 cases in Westlaw, from January 1, 2008, to August 31, 2018, in which the SRO was a party or important to the decision, Zirkel (2019a) found that government authorities prevailed on 72% of issue rulings, individuals prevailed in 9% of issue rulings, and results were inconclusive in 19%. The U.S. Constitution formed the basis of most claims (72%), with government authorities prevailing in 73% of claims. The most common constitutional claim was a violation of the 4th Amendment (62%), with government authorities prevailing in 73% of 4th Amendment claims.

Narrowing the 208 identified cases to instances where a parent sought civil liability against an SRO or their employer, Zirkel (2019b) identified 79 decisions in which the student was an individual with a disability in 22 (28%). Zirkel identified 46 separate claims, with the most frequently asserted being the 4th Amendment and Section 504/ADA (16 each). Of the claims, the defendants conclusively prevailed in 30 (65%), the parents prevailed in only one claim, and 15 were inconclusive. A large proportion of claims involved severe SRO actions (handcuffs in 15 of 22 cases), which in many cases appeared to escalate the child's behavior and was disproportionately applied with children without disabilities. Pertinently, Zirkel (2019b) observed that "in almost every case the child's conduct that precipitated the SRO's actions was connected to the child's individual disability profile" (p. 4), such as conduct related to a child's autism or attention deficit hyperactivity disorder.

METHOD

Similar to prior research (Zirkel, 2019a and b), the authors searched all state and federal cases in the Westlaw computer-aided legal research database from September 1, 2018 (the day following the end of Zirkel's 2019 coverage), to October 15, 2020, using the following queries: "school resource officer," "student resource officer," "school security officer," "school liaison officer," "school safety officer," and "school police." This study is not confined to cases involving SROs who meet the federal definition of "school resource officer," (34 U.S.C. § 10389, 2017), and includes individuals who are not sworn peace officers or who are on temporary assignment in schools. This is because the experience of the end user does not depend on whether the official meets the federal definition of an SRO. Further, the legal claims and legal defenses, such as qualified immunity, are similar. This study uses SRO in this broader, more colloquial usage, unless the context specifically requires the use of the federal definition.

From the cases retrieved by those queries, the authors eliminated criminal appeals, postconviction relief proceedings, juvenile justice and child welfare cases, family law cases, and actions filed by SROs (as opposed to against

SROs). The authors also eliminated cases where the SRO tangentially, as opposed to directly, participated, such as being a witness to an altercation rather than an active participant.

The cases that remained met the following inclusionary criteria: a parent on behalf of a child sought civil liability against the SRO's employer, the SRO personally, or both (Zirkel, 2019b). These remaining cases were also reviewed to determine whether the child was a child with a disability. For cases identifying the child as having a disability, the authors recorded additional information (Zirkel, 2019b), shown in Table 11.1.

This analysis did not include rulings that did not concern the SRO's action or inaction, and also did not include discretionary rulings (e.g., federal court rulings remanding state law claims to state court after no federal claims remained), rulings disposing of a claim on jurisdictional matters, such as a failure to exhaust IDEA administrative remedies, or claims the plaintiff abandoned or waived.

Table 11.1. Data Elements

Element	Description
Disability status	• Whether the child had an individualized education program (IEP), a Section 504 plan, or coverage under the Americans With Disabilities Act (ADA) • The category of disability or diagnosis, if listed
SRO action	The SRO's primary conduct, such as use of handcuffs, restraint, or weapons, or inaction
Claim category (legal theory or cause of action)	• 4th Amendment (claims of unlawful searches or seizures) • 14th Amendment (claims of violations of the 14th Amendment's Due Process clause or Equal Protection clause) • IDEA (claims of IDEA violations) • Section 504 and/or ADA (claims of discrimination under Section 504, the ADA, or both) • Claims under state law, such as assault/battery, false imprisonment, intentional infliction of emotional distress, or negligence
Claim category ruling	Claim category ruling: Based on a long line of research (e.g., Zirkel, 2019a and b; Zirkel & Fossey, 2018), the outcome of each claim in each case according to this scale: 1. Conclusively in favor of the plaintiff (student) 2. Inconclusive (e.g., denial of a motion for summary judgment) 3. Conclusively in favor of the defendants
Comments	Underlying reason for the ruling, as well as additional significant features

RESULTS

Of the cases decided in the period at issue, 78 met the criteria for inclusion (civil cases seeking to impose liability based on SRO conduct). Of those 78 cases, 25 (32%) were based on claims asserted by or for students with disabilities—two of those cases involved the same student and fact pattern. Table 11.2 contains a summary of key results.

Of the 25 cases reviewed, 20 students were identified as eligible under the IDEA, and one was eligible under the broader coverage of Section 504; coverage for four was unclear from context. Four cases did not contain diagnosis information. Of the 21 that did, the predominant diagnoses were autism (11 cases), attention deficit hyperactivity disorder (ADHD) (6), and oppositional defiant disorder (ODD) (3). Similar to Zirkel's (2019a and b) prior studies, the alleged SRO action appeared severe in the majority of cases: use of handcuffs in 13 cases and of tasers in 5.

Plaintiffs raised claims under the U.S. Constitution in 19 cases, federal statutory claims in 11, and state law claims (state constitution, state statute, tort) in 15. Of the constitutional claims, 14 alleged 4th Amendment violations, and 11 alleged 14th Amendment violations. Section 504 and the ADA formed the basis of all but two of the statutory claims; there was an IDEA case and a federal civil rights conspiracy case. Predominant state law claims were negligence (7), intentional infliction of emotional distress, and assault and battery (4 each).

As to the claim category results, the plaintiff prevailed in only one claim. Outcomes in 26 claims (38%) were inconclusive, largely because the plaintiff

Table 11.2. Summary of Results

Topic	Key Finding
Prevalence of SRO litigation concerning students with disabilities	32% (25/78) of cases concerned children with disabilities
Frequency	Nearly five-fold increase between time periods (0.62 case/month to 3.06 cases/month)
Basis of eligibility	• 80% were eligible under the IDEA • 44% (11/25) were children with autism
Legal claims	• 76% of cases (19/25) had claims under the U.S. Constitution • 44% of cases (11/25) had claims under federal statute • 60% of cases (15/25) had claims under state law
Claim results	• Defendants prevailed in 60% of claims • 38% of claims were inconclusive • Plaintiffs prevailed on only one claim
Qualified Immunity	Granted in 64% of cases (7/11) in which it was sought

alleged a violation sufficient to withstand a motion to dismiss for "failure to state a claim upon which relief could be granted" (Federal Rule of Civil Procedure 12(b)(6)), or the defendant failed to prove "no genuine issues of material fact" such that the defendant is entitled to summary judgment (Federal Rule of Civil Procedure 56). Defendants completely prevailed in 41 claims (60%), largely because plaintiffs failed, under the undisputed facts, to show the defendants' conduct violated the applicable legal standard (such as "deliberate indifference" or conduct that "shocks the conscience" (Bon & Zirkel, 2014)), because plaintiffs failed to allege or establish a "policy or custom" required to impose municipal liability (absent a "policy or custom," a municipality is not responsible for the actions of its officers or employees (*Monell v. Department of Social Services*, 1978)), because plaintiffs failed to file their action within the applicable limitations period, or because the defendants were entitled to qualified immunity—immunity granted when the right alleged to have been violated was not "clearly established" (*Pearson v. Callahan*, 2009). Of claims in which a defendant raised a qualified immunity defense, the defendant prevailed 64% of the time (7 out of 11).

The one issue where the plaintiff conclusively prevailed involved one of the starkest circumstances: handcuffing a compliant, nonviolent child for taking a piece of candy from a candy dish (*Wordlaw*, 2018). There, the plaintiff asserted the official's conduct constituted excessive force and an unlawful seizure under the 4th Amendment, while he asserted qualified immunity. On cross motions for summary judgment, the court granted the plaintiff's motion and denied the official's motion.

As to the excessive force claim, the court concluded that official's actions were unreasonable, applying a nonexhaustive list of factors to determine whether an officer used excessive force in accomplishing a seizure: "'the severity of the crime at issue, whether the suspect poses an immediate threat to the safety of the officers or others, and whether he is actively resisting arrest or attempting to evade arrest by flight.'" (*Wordlow*, 2018, p. *7, quoting *Graham v. Connor*, 490 U.S. 386, 396 [1989]). When applying these factors to the undisputed facts of M.M.'s handcuffing, the court concluded:

> Yarbrough handcuffed a six-year-old student who committed no crime, posed no threat, and did not resist in any way. Thus, this Court finds as a matter of law that Yarbrough's handcuffing constituted excessive force in violation of the Fourth Amendment. (*Wordlow*, 2018, p. *8)

Claims of unlawful seizures of students are viewed from an objective standard of reasonableness (*Wordlow*, 2018, p. *8). When viewed through that lens, the court concluded Yarbrough's actions were unreasonable:

> Yarbrough argues that his seizure was reasonable because "[w]ere it not for the use of handcuffs, [his] decision to take M.M. to his desk at the front door of the school would not raise any eyebrows." But the handcuffs are precisely what makes Yarbrough's seizure unreasonable. As discussed above in relation

to Plaintiff's excessive force claim, Yarbrough had no security-related reason to handcuff M.M.—he knew he could not arrest her for taking candy from a teacher, she posed no physical threat given her small size, and the record does not indicate that she exhibited aggressive or resistant behavior. And surely, taking from a teacher is not sufficiently disruptive or provocative under the objective [] standard to justify handcuffing a six-year-old child (and Yarbrough admitted as much, albeit subjectively, when he stated that he handcuffed her solely to teach her a lesson). (*Wordlow*, 2018, p. *8, internal case names and citations omitted)

Having found a violation of the 4th Amendment for excessive force and unlawful seizure, the court rejected Yarbrough's assertion that he was entitled to qualified immunity because his actions did not violate "'clearly established statutory or constitutional rights of which a reasonable person would have known'" (*Wordlow*, 2018, p. *9, quoting *Pearson v. Callahan*, 555 U.S. 223, 231 [2009]). The court concluded that the rights he violated were clearly established and his actions were unreasonable in the circumstances. The court stated: "Therefore, because Yarbrough had fair warning that hand-cuffing M.M. to teach her a lesson was an obvious violation of her Fourth Amendment rights, he is not entitled to qualified immunity" (*Wordlow*, 2018, p. 11). The court granted Wordlow's motion for summary judgment on her 4th Amendment claims and denied Yarbrough's motion for summary judgment based on his defense of qualified immunity.

DISCUSSION

While acknowledging issues in classifying case law "within selection criteria that are inevitably not precise, bright lines" (Zirkel, 2019b, p. 9), this analysis of publicly available case law and the inferences that may be drawn from it are important for many reasons. First, while this analysis is limited to publicly available case law, the available research suggests that this case law is "representative of the larger body of decisions" (Zirkel & Clark, 2008, p. 361). Second, litigation's relationship to society as a whole is complex and multidimensional. Litigation simultaneously reflects and has the capacity to reform society (Cummings, 2013). Therefore, understanding litigation issues and trends will help practitioners and policymakers make prudent, forward-looking, equitable decisions about SROs and similar personnel. Third, litigation data are useful to parties in analyzing the likelihood of success in specific disputes, including whether to take the risk of litigating or whether to pursue mediation or other options (Newcomer & Zirkel, 1999).

Overall Disproportionality

SRO litigation on behalf of students with disabilities represented roughly one-third (32%) of the SRO litigation during the relevant period, only slightly higher and still in line with Zirkel's (2019b) prior research, as well as overall arrest data for students with and without disabilities. "Even though they represent just twelve percent of the student population, [students with disabilities] represent a quarter of the students referred to law enforcement or subject to arrest" (Hill, 2017, p. 215). This convergence of data within and across empirical methods adds weight to the implications drawn from these data.

This disproportionality is explained by both child and adult attributes. The nature of certain disabilities may place children at a higher risk of interaction with law enforcement, such as difficulty controlling impulses and responding to stimuli, difficulty reading and responding to social cues, difficulty adjusting when routines are changed or interrupted, difficulty in communicating effectively with law enforcement personnel, or maladaptive responses to stress or confrontation (Hill, 2017; Mayes, 2003; Stanford & Muhammad, 2018). Although considering alternative hypotheses, which focus on the child and not the adults charged with educating the child (e.g., children with disabilities are more likely to be violent or unsafe as children without disabilities and the parents of children with disabilities are more likely to be litigious), Zirkel (2019b) suggested that the "most likely interpretation" was "that SROs and the school systems that use them are not sufficiently prudent and proactive in addressing the behavior of students with disabilities" (pp. 10–11). These proactive responses include schoolwide approaches, such as multitiered supports (Benner et al., 2013) and alternatives to punitive discipline (Canady, 2018; Lynn-Whaley & Gard, 2012; Schiff & Bazemore, 2012; Teske et al., 2012), as well as student-specific supports, such as behavior intervention plans (Collins & Zirkel, 2017) and special education goals that address challenging behaviors (IDEA Regulations, 2017, 34 C.F.R. § 300.324(a)(2)(i)). Providing these supports will improve outcomes (Teske et al., 2012). Not providing them and relying on punitive discipline strategies, such as handcuffing a child for taking a piece of candy (*Wordlow*, 2018) will not, to the detriment of the school community and individual children (Lynn-Whaley & Gard, 2012; Mayes, 2003). Not providing these supports also runs the risk of escalating student challenging behaviors to and beyond the point of crisis (Fox et al., 2021; Zirkel, 2019b). If school systems using SROs have an interest in improving school safety, they will use these proactive, preventative measures as a first resort and use SROs' investigatory and arrest power as a last-resort intervention.

Additional Considerations

The data builds on and reinforces other findings from Zirkel's 2019 studies. First, the rate of SRO-related litigation has increased. From January 1, 2008, to August 31, 2018, Zirkel (2019b) found 79 cases of civil litigation concerning SROs, a rate of 0.62 cases per month. In contrast, from September 1, 2018, to October 15, 2020, there were 78 cases of civil litigation concerning SROs, a rate of 3.06 per month, a nearly five-fold frequency increase. This increase could be related to the increased number of SROs during the relevant time period (which would increase the opportunity for contact between students and SROs); an increased awareness among parents, educators, and litigators of SROs; and the school-to-prison pipeline (Zirkel, 2019a), or all. This trend of increased SRO-related litigation bears future monitoring and research.

Similar to Zirkel's (2019a and b) findings, the cases reviewed (to the extent a diagnosis is disclosed) skew toward diagnoses associated with challenging behaviors, such as autism and ADHD, reinforcing the need to build a structure of supports around students with challenging behaviors and SROs to reduce the likelihood that both students and SROs are harmed by uninformed and untrained interactions. For students, this includes the macro-level and micro-level supports discussed. For SROs, this would include training and access to information about specific children (e.g., health plans, IEPs) to better support their interactions with those children.

To the extent that privacy law is a barrier to providing that information, student privacy law is misunderstood (Fox et al., 2021; Mayes & Zirkel, 2000). If SROs are school employees, the Family Educational Rights and Privacy Act (FERPA) regulations permit sharing personally identifiable information from student records with school officials with "legitimate educational interests" in that information (34 C.F.R. § 99.31(a)(1)(i)(A)). If an SRO is a contractor of a school district (as opposed to an employee), FERPA regulations allow an SRO with a similar legitimate educational interest to have access to personally identifiable information in student records (34 C.F.R. § 99.31(a)(1)(i)(B)). Finally, schools may release personally identifiable information from student records in response to "an articulable and significant threat to the health or safety of a student or other individuals" (34 C.F.R. §§ 99.31(a)(10), 99.36). The U.S. Department of Education's longstanding interpretation is that on-campus criminal activity may constitute a health or safety emergency (Medaris et al., 1997). Finally, the IDEA regulations (2017) require that IEPs be accessible to all school officials or other service providers who may be responsible for their implementation (34 C.F.R. § 300.323(d)) and that school officials, when making a criminal referral of a child with a disability, provide the child's special education and discipline records to law enforcement to the extent permitted by FERPA (34 C.F.R. § 300.535; Mayes & Zirkel, 2000), although an on-campus crime would be an exception to FERPA's consent requirement (Mayes & Zirkel, 2000). This data sharing will provide vital information to SROs on what may be expected of particular students with disabilities and how to respond in a way that supports school safety (Zirkel, 2019b).

Parents predominately brought constitutional claims, claims under Section 504 and the ADA, and state law claims. Only one case during this period was based on the IDEA, likely for reasons stated by Zirkel (2019b): the lack of centrality of SRO actions to IDEA claims and the unavailability of personal injury damages under the IDEA.

As in Zirkel's (2019b) study, conclusive claims tilted in favor of the defendants, which is largely due to the high substantive bars that plaintiffs face (Bon & Zirkel, 2014; Zirkel, 2019b). Those high hurdles include the requirement of an official policy or procedure for municipal liability under *Monell v. Department of Social Services* (1978), conduct amounting to "deliberate indifference" under Section 504 or the ADA (*K.C. v. Marshall County Bd. of Educ.*, 2019), conduct that "shocks the conscience" under the 14th Amendment (*McCadden v. City of Flint*, 2019), the defense of qualified immunity (*Pearson v. Callahan*, 2009), and the general outcome skew in favor of schools in personal injury actions (Zirkel & Clark, 2008). The one conclusive outcome in favor of the parent shows how outrageous conduct must typically be: handcuffing a nonthreatening, compliant child with a disability—as a teaching opportunity—for taking a piece of candy (*Wordlow*, 2018).

These barriers to plaintiffs obtaining relief except in the most extreme cases call to mind the work of Freeman (1978). Freeman noted that court decisions implementing antidiscrimination statutes—statutes based on race, in his analysis—have the effect of preserving existing social structures and entrenching the discrimination the statutes were designed to redress. Freeman's critique would appear to be applicable to disability law as well—civil rights laws intended to benefit individuals with disabilities that are narrowly interpreted to benefit the status quo.

As to inconclusive claims, these illustrate the high standard for granting a motion for summary judgment or a motion to dismiss, where the record or the pleadings, respectively, are viewed in light most favorable to the nonmoving party. Just because a plaintiff's case survives a defendant's dispositive pretrial motion does not guarantee that the plaintiff will prevail on the merits (Zirkel, 2019b).

The pattern of outcomes illuminates a gap in available remedies to individuals with disabilities and their families. The IDEA provides remedies for denials of a free appropriate public education; however, those remedies do not include monetary damages for personal injury claims (Zirkel, 2011). In contrast, when money damages are available under other laws, those laws require proof of "deliberate indifference," an intentional act, or an act that shocks the conscience" (e.g., Bon & Zirkel, 2014). Students with disabilities and their families are left in situations where they obtain legally available but practically insufficient or insignificant relief under the IDEA.

Even in cases where the defendant prevails on a claim, it comes at a financial and emotional cost, and with a loss of time and talent and trust (Mayes, 2019). "Resources spent on litigation are resources unavailable for education" (Newcomer & Zirkel, 1999, p. 479). This favors a preventative law approach: Rather than hoping to "win" a case about an SRO's action or inaction, a district's time and talent may be more profitably focused on building SRO capacity and reducing risk conditions that make a claim about or against an SRO more likely to occur. The easiest dispute to resolve is the one that never occurs.

IMPLICATIONS FOR PRACTITIONERS AND POLICYMAKERS

This study, like Zirkel's initial 2019 study, uses case law to illuminate central themes concerning SRO practices and students with disabilities: lack of training or clarity of purpose, a disproportionate effect on students with disabilities, and concerns for harms caused by SRO actions. Given the low likelihood of parents prevailing on the merits in SRO litigation, as well as the financial, temporal, and emotional costs for all parties to litigation (Mayes, 2019; Newcomer & Zirkel, 1999), these implications and suggestions for improvement are directed toward policymakers and practitioners who view this issue through a preventative and proactive lens.

Whether SROs Should Be Used

School leaders must no longer assume that SROs and similar personnel are unquestioned assets to the school community. The evidence to the contrary is too strong, and the risks are too high.

First, leaders ought to consider whether SROs are a wise investment. With a limited pool of resources and multiple demands on those resources, should schools be spending those scarce resources on SROs? Given the mixed data supporting the efficacy of SRO programs (Ahranaji, 2017; Anderson, 2018; CRS, 2018; Kupchik, 2019; Nance, 2019), as well as concerns about implementation costs (Ahranaji, 2017; Kupchik, 2019; Malcolm, 2018) and broader social and economic loss, such as increased court caseload, incarceration, school failure, and recidivism (Ahranaji, 2017; CRS, 2018; Hill, 2017; Schiff & Bazemore, 2012), leaders must interrogate claims that an increased SRO presence will improve climate and safety. Such an increased presence will do so, if it is defined and part of an integrated approach to school safety (CRS, 2018). If an SRO program diverts resources from effective practices that support school safety (e.g., Benner et al., 2013), this diversion will be penny-wise, pound foolish (Ahranaji, 2017; Anderson, 2018; Kupchik, 2019). When faced with a battle for scarce resources (DeMitchell & Cobb, 2003), the prudent choice would be the proven over the uncertain or the disproven.

Second, and as a related matter, leaders ought to consider whether their communities have consensus on the proper role of SROs in the school community. This will require addressing a perception–reality gap. SROs are publicly popular (Phi Delta Kappa, 2018), and students and teachers believe them to be effective in promoting safety and discipline (CRS, 2018). More broadly, many teachers believe that punitive discipline improves classroom behavior (Coggshall et al., 2012; Teske et al., 2012). However, these beliefs are not supported by evidence (Ahranaji, 2017; Anderson, 2018; CRS, 2018; Lynn-Whaley & Gard, 2012; Nance, 2019; Schiff & Bazemore, 2012; Teske, et al., 2012). Given this misalignment between perception and evidence (and the potential to exploit this perception–evidence gap for political gain [McQuiller, 2019]), leaders may wish to consult research on implementing policies and programs with evidentiary support, including building consensus that such policies and programs are the right work. Pursuing an unproven course of action based on a belief that it will work is legally and practically problematic (e.g., Mayes, 1999).

Third, given academic achievement as a strong predictor of school safety (Anderson, 2018), leaders must closely scrutinize any diversion of resources from instruction to SRO programs. Anderson (2018) notes that "education enhances school safety, not policing" (p. 19). Ahranaji (2017) is more pointed, observing that a coercive law enforcement presence in schools "sabotages students' educational experience and may lead to long-term negative consequences such as . . . widening of the achievement gap" (p. 1116). This is especially true for the instruction of children with disabilities, who already have a gap in achievement when compared to children without disabilities (Schulte et al., 2016). Any investment in an SRO program must be structured to catalyze academic achievement, not divert resources from academic services and supports. Otherwise, academic achievement and school safety will suffer, to the greater detriment of students with disabilities

Fourth, leaders must be aware of how other ways of difference intersect and interconnect with disability. This study did not explore intersections between race and disability, because that data is not often available from the court decisions; however, that intersection has been explored by other scholars using other methods (e.g., Glennon, 1995). Glennon (1995) powerfully observed how special education classification has been used to sustain racism and how racism and ableism interact and amplify each other in special education practices. SRO use of the coercive power of the state risks further enhancing those interlocking systems of oppression. In addition to SRO interactions with students with disabilities, commenters have expressed concern about the use of SROs and a disproportionate effect on students of color, students with low income, and LGBTQ+ students (Ali, 2021; Anderson, 2018; Edelman, 2019; Henning, 2018; Hill, 2017; Kupchik, 2019; Lynn-Whaley & Gard, 2012; Stanford & Muhammad, 2018; see also Chapter 4, this volume). Black children are more likely to be viewed by teachers as less innocent than White children and are more likely to be viewed as older than their chronological age (e.g., Goff et al., 2014). Ahranaji (2017) noted that students of color and students of low income are more likely to be aggressively policed in the name of school safety, when the typical mass school shooting is perpetrated by an affluent White male in an affluent community. This concern is particularly borne out by data for students with disabilities who are also students of color (Hill, 2017; Stanford & Muhammad, 2018; see also Chapter 4, this volume). If school leaders decide to use SROs and similar personnel, leaders must implement strategies and structures in SRO programs to support students with disabilities who also have one or more additional "marker[s]" (Hill, 2017, p. 208) of difference, such as a periodic review of data and an interrogation of practices and beliefs that may result in disproportionate interaction between SROs and students with disabilities, including students of color.

How SROs Should Be Used

If school leaders determine that SROs are a necessary, if not necessarily wise, investment, they should act with prudence to maximize benefits and reduce the risk of harms of SROs' presence in schools.

First, the cases and literature demonstrate that schools and SROs must have clarity about SROs' proper role (CRS, 2018; Fox, et al., 2021; NASBE, 2019). Are SROs serving a crime control and public safety function (whether preventing or responding to criminal activity) (Anderson, 2018; *K.C. v. Marshall County Bd. of Educ.*, 2019), or are they using the coercive power of the state to assume responsibility from educators for enforcing classroom codes of conduct (Ahranaji, 2017; Canady, 2018; Edelman, 2019; Gupta-Kagan, 2019; Hill, 2017; NASBE, 2019)? Is a school's SRO investigating criminal activity, such as abuse of students by teachers (*K.C.*), or is the SRO's time and talent being used to stop children from being children, such as hand-cuffing a child for taking a piece of candy (*Wordlow*, 2018) or enforcing a school's dress code (NASBE, 2019)? Even SRO actions that appear to be ordinary law enforcement techniques (e.g., handcuffing, use of a taser) and are legal can appear disproportionate to the student conduct at issue, such as handcuffing a child in an after-school program (*McCadden v. City of Flint*, 2019) or handcuffing a child for taking a piece of candy (*Wordlow*). The professional consensus is that SROs' power of coercion needs to be reserved for matters of consequence, not for minor code of conduct infractions (Feierman et al., 2012; Gupta-Kagan, 2019; Malcolm, 2018; NASBE, 2019; Stanford & Muhammad, 2018), the perceived severity of which may be influenced based on bias toward individuals with disabilities, individuals of color, or individuals with low income. Having a clear vision of SROs' proper role, including their role in implementing behavioral supports and interventions for children with disabilities, will allow all members of a school community to properly situate SROs in the community's broader goal of a safe and supportive school climate (Anderson, 2018; CRS, 2018; NASBE, 2019).

Second, leaders must consider whether SROs are properly trained. Five of the 25 cases in this study contain at least one cause of action premised on failure to train SROs. Moreover, the professional literature includes recommendations for training (Brady, 2018; Canady, 2018; CRS, 2018; Fox et al., 2021; Meade, 2019; NASBE, 2019), including training on childhood trauma, loss, and risk (Canady, 2018) and the needs of children with disabilities (Meade, 2019). Proactive leaders and policymakers will keep abreast of available training for SROs, including training about interacting with students with disabilities. This is important given the large number of cases where the SRO action escalated the behavior of the child (Zirkel, 2019b). The effectiveness of SRO training on improving school climate and culture is a possible avenue for further empirical research.

Third, leaders must be aware of potential changes in the doctrine of qualified immunity, including legislation or litigation to limit or eliminate its scope inspired by recent concerns about abusive or racist policing practices (Stecklow, 2021). Commentators have expressed frustration with the judicial expansion of qualified immunity from a doctrine designed to protect public officials who make good-faith errors in judgment to one that provides blanket protection for all but the most egregious rights violations, to the point that civil rights protections are nearly evaporated (Stecklow, 2021). Leaders must stay abreast of any judicial or legislative changes to the judge-made doctrine of qualified immunity, as well as take opportunities to contribute to the public discourse on qualified immunity at the federal and state levels.

CONCLUSION

This study shows that SRO use remains a matter of broad public concern, albeit with no broad public consensus, with successful recourse to courts only in cases of the most clearly questionable SRO conduct. The individual and social harms that motivate litigation are real, as shown by the evidence, even if courts are unable to grant relief. This situation calls for the "professional proactivity" recommended by Zirkel (2019b). It requires alignment of the value of school safety (DeMitchell & Cobb, 2003) with activities that have been proven to support and advance that value. School leaders should recognize that child attributes are not the prime driver of SRO interactions with children with disabilities; rather, the prime drivers are the decisions adults make (or do not make). By focusing the attention on the child, the adults can absolve themselves of the harms their decisions caused (Mayes, 2018).

A preventative law approach to SRO use will accomplish two things: reducing the risk of costly litigation and, more importantly, improving school climate and safety for students with disabilities and other students at risk of harm from imprudent and ill-informed SRO actions. Moreover, this prudent approach to SRO use will advance more global policy goods, such as improved academic outcomes and a safer society.

CHAPTER 12

Rethinking Discipline of Students With Disabilities

A Path Forward for Research, Policy, and Practice

Miranda Johnson and Pamela Fenning

Reforming school discipline must start with an acknowledgement that school systems intended to support children with disabilities are causing harm. High rates of suspension, expulsion, seclusion and restraint, and arrests of students with disabilities are symptoms of this larger truth. When children are excluded, pushed out, and fail to graduate, schools are failing children. Removing children from their school environments runs directly contrary to what they need, which is support, instruction, and a sense of belonging.

As Chapter 10 by Hoechst and Chee urges, the reform process must start by "changing the conversation." We must change the lens by which we view student behavior. School discipline practices that exclude students from the classroom are premised on the mistaken idea that the student is the problem. Rather, high rates of exclusionary discipline and disproportionate impact on certain groups of students—particularly Native American students, Black students, students with disabilities, and students at the intersections of these identities (see Chapter 1)—reveal structural problems that require transformation of educator mindsets (Okonofua et al., 2016) and school practices (see Chapter 2).

The premise of the Individuals With Disabilities Education Act (IDEA, 2016) is that school districts should have an individualized school program for each student with a disability. And yet the continuum of available school services, rather than the supports students require, often drives decision-making regarding placement and services. The chapter authors call to flip the script—to deeply examine what students needed to thrive and question school-based practices that interfere with that goal. We must take a close look at the impact of structural racism and ableism in schools, resulting in segregation rather than integration of students with disabilities (Annamma et al., 2016). The time is ripe to focus on proactive, positive, and relationship-centered systemic solutions that center equity and empathy (Kaufman, 2020). These solutions will look different for each school and district and, to be effective, must engage and involve the students, families, and communities most impacted by exclusionary discipline.

OVERARCHING THEMES

During the June 2019 conference, participants arrived at three key themes for school discipline reform:

- **Using data and creating accountability mechanisms:** How do we use data to reduce the disproportionate discipline of students with disabilities and other intersected identities?
- **Soliciting and centralizing marginalized voices:** How do we centralize the voices of students with disabilities and other intersected identities vulnerable to disproportionate discipline?
- **Deploying effective, equitable, and relationship-centered practices:** How do we deploy effective and equitable practices to reduce the disproportionate discipline of students who have disabilities and other intersected identities? How can we build meaningful relationships with parents, students, and community members?

We encourage others seeking to address discipline disproportionality to ask these overarching questions as a starting or continuation point for change processes.

RECOMMENDATIONS

The following recommendations aim to support a culturally responsive and holistic response to student behavior at the local, state, and federal levels.

Research Recommendations

1. Increase use of counternarratives and participatory action research.

Because racism and ableism have been normalized throughout school ecosystems (Annamma et al., 2016), learning from counternarratives is an essential component of transformative policy and practice reform (see Chapter 2). Research should be conducted from an intersectional lens recognizing multiple layers of identity, including race/ethnicity, dis/ability, and gender. Leverett in Chapter 3 and Nortey in Chapter 5 illustrate the value of qualitative research by centering voices of Black students and the wisdom of experienced Black women educators. Participatory action research can also be used to foster collaborations with students and families from the outset in defining research questions and identifying promising interventions. Grant funders and peer reviewers need to understand the importance of these re-search perspectives.

2. Develop interdisciplinary research and enhance accessibility.

School discipline reform is inherently interdisciplinary, and bringing to-gether professionals from diverse backgrounds enhances the quality, scope, and potential reach of research as well as the nature and specificity of the recom-mendations. Translating research to policy and practice reform also requires dissemination to policymakers and the general public. Broader circulation of re-search can mobilize community movements by supporting their reform agenda.

3. Increase research focused on solutions.

Decades of research have shown the harm caused by zero-tolerance, exclusionary discipline, and school policing (Skiba et al., 2016; see also Chapter 1, this volume). Of critical importance is additional research on effective practices to replace exclusionary discipline and reduce dispropor-tionality. As Chafouleas et al. observe in Chapter 7, more research is needed on how data-based problem solving impacts pushout practices, student–teacher relationships, and school climate. Also relevant is research on how professional development should be structured to ensure that educators contextualize problem solving within the context of disability rights and his-torical racism. Further, there is a need for long-term studies (a minimum of 3–5 years) examining the implementation and outcomes of restorative justice in schools (Gregory & Evans, 2020).

School Practice Recommendations

1. Adopt a trauma-informed, culturally responsive, and relationship-centered approach.

Schools should move away from exclusionary practices toward an ap-proach recognizing their responsibility to prepare students to graduate and successfully transition to meaningful postsecondary paths. This requires reck-oning with racism and ableism in school environments, reshaping schools to meet the needs of all students, and prioritizing students with the greatest need for the highest investment of school resources. Schools' entrenched pu-nitive responses to student conduct are premised on a flawed model relying on coercion to deter student misbehavior (Kaufman, 2020). This approach is particularly concerning when applied to students with disabilities who are receiving individualized services because they require additional supports. Given the linkage between racism and carceral systems (Adams & Erevelles, 2016), educational systems relying on models of control reproduce racialized outcomes wholly contrary to their educational mission.

Schools should reimagine school frameworks based on relationships, collaborative problem solving, and culturally affirming and trauma-informed practices (Gregory et al., 2017; Kaufman, 2020; see also Chapters 3, 6, and 10, this volume). Restorative justice, a model drawn from Indigenous justice systems, incorporates these principles and has shown promise in reducing the use of exclusionary discipline in schools (Fronius et al., 2019; Gregory & Evans, 2020; see also Chapter 10, this volume). For example, an alternative school using the Building Bridges program, a blend of cognitive behavioral and restorative practices, was able to reduce disciplinary referrals of students with significant emotional and behavioral needs (see Chapter 9, this volume). Restorative justice should be implemented with a 4- to 6-year implementation plan (González, 2015) and an intentional focus on racial justice (Davis, 2019).

2. Promote parent, student, and community voice.

Education decision-making often centers the voices of the most privileged, educated, and well-connected parents (Joffe-Walt, 2020), with limited ability of minoritized families and communities to effectuate change (Ewing, 2018). Schools should consider how they can bring student, parent, and community voices into the forefront of reform processes. School leaders and problem-solving teams should intentionally solicit parent and student feedback to see if change processes are effective in accomplishing collectively identified goals. Leverett (Chapter 3, this volume) recommends a "culturally grounded treatment acceptability protocol" driven by student input.

School leaders should also consider how to empower students and parents to meaningfully participate in special education and school discipline processes. The individualized education program (IEP) process is highly specialized, filled with legal jargon and acronyms, and meetings are often too short and filled with paperwork to allow for real conversation about students' needs. Administrators should revisit every aspect of this process to ensure it is inclusive, user-friendly, and accessible to parents, particularly those who have limited formal education or whose primary language is not English. School staff should be equipped to appropriately respond to parental concerns regarding the potential stigma of special education eligibility, particularly from Black families, given the nation's long history of segregating Black students into separate classrooms. In addition, it is vital to promote student voice in IEP decision-making appropriate to the student's developmental level.

Similarly, school disciplinary processes should be revamped to ensure meaningful student and parent voice. Rather than approaching student behavior through a legal model designed to punish student code of conduct violations, approaches should center on problem solving aimed at addressing the underlying causes of the student's behavior (Greene & Winkler, 2019; see also Chapter 7, this volume). Supportive and nondirective student interviews modeled in Chapter 9 by Healy et al. help elicit greater understanding of the circumstances preceding a student's behavior, self-reflective learning, and an agreed-on way to move forward. Similarly, when parents are approached by schools before—rather than after—disciplinary determinations are made, they can be engaged as partners in providing information about root causes of behaviors (Fenning & Jenkins, 2018, 2019).

In partnership with the community, a protocol could also be developed for a community member to serve as a cultural intermediary in a restorative process with the parent, student, and school personnel following a disagreement about a disciplinary situation. Such a protocol, which would require parent and student consent to participate, could help to build positive relationships between families and the school, create a thoughtful plan to move forward, and support the cultural congruity of school practices.

3. Create a meaningful and culturally responsive tiered continuum of supports.

The foundation of any school-based work to reduce the use of exclusionary discipline should be multitiered systems of support (MTSS) (see Chapter 7). Relationship building, socioemotional learning, and cultural responsiveness should be integrated into all aspects of the MTSS framework (Jackson & Wolforth, 2021; Leverson et al., 2021; see also Chapters 7 and 8, this volume). Implementing a culturally responsive framework requires creating respectful partnerships between schools and local communities. Community members serve as keepers of culture, and cultural discontinuity between schools and communities can have profound impacts on students and families (see Chapter 10, this volume). School practices should affirm students' multiple identities, recognize their unique strengths, and expressly counteract discriminatory notions of inferiority based on race and disability (see Chapter 5). Students' acceptance of behavioral interventions is facilitated by trust in staff, connection to cultural identities, and caring adults (see Chapter 3).

MTSS systems, which should include delivery of research-based instruction for all students along a continuum of support, do not supersede students' rights under the IDEA (Musgrove, 2011). Indeed, tiered systems of supports that fueled MTSS (previously coined "response to intervention") were developed, in part, to address limitations in a "refer-test-place" model criticized for looking to internal student deficits and failing to meet the academic needs of students, particularly in the area of reading (Prasse, n.d.; Sailor et al., 2021). When implemented with fidelity, an MTSS framework ensures that general and special educators intervene early and effectively based on universal screening data (see Chapter 7, this volume). All students with disabilities experiencing academic delays—not just students with learning disabilities— should have access to settings offering scientifically based instruction and academic supports at their instructional level, with particular attention paid to students' reading skills. Frontloading these instructional supports can prevent widening gaps, unnecessary special education referrals, behaviors, disengagement from school, and contact with the juvenile justice system (Brunner, 1993; Morgan et al., 2008). More recent models of MTSS integrate tiered supports in the behavioral, academic, and socioemotional domains (McIntosh & Goodman, 2016; National Association of School Psychologists [NASP], 2016). Sailor et al. (2021) point to the exponential rise in the scaling up of MTSS systems across the country, stressing the importance of university training programs being equipped to train the next generation of teachers and administrators to implement MTSS systems as they were intended.

All districts and schools, including charter schools, need to have sufficiently trained educational personnel to deliver, implement, and evaluate the full continuum of educational supports and services required under the IDEA (2016; Sailor et al., 2021). Critical to this end is addressing students' lack of access to appropriate services. An example is the limited services available for students experiencing trauma in New Orleans, a gap that the Center for Resilience helps to fill, albeit in a restrictive educational placement (see Chapter 6). In Chapter 6, Pearson et al. call for districts to offer an expanded range of services for students experiencing trauma, including a trauma-informed day treatment program.

4. Equip educators to meet students' needs.

The school discipline reform process should prioritize ongoing professional development with educators to support them in creating positive, calm, and culturally affirming classrooms (see Chapter 5, this volume), thereby fostering "more just and equitable classroom ecology" (see Chapter 8). Leverett (Chapter 3) calls for teachers at all experience levels to be trained in equity-forward classroom management. Professional development should be focused on enabling teachers to control the classroom environment, rather than the students, by providing consistent classroom routines, clear communication, and high expectations that motivate students (Chapter 5). Educators should also be supported to implement effective data-driven problem solving, as described by Chafouleas et al. in Chapter 7.

Educators require more skills to engage in ongoing self-reflection by asking questions such as the following: What classroom environments am I creating? What educational needs of the student are being unmet? What are my own biases, and how might they be impacting students or my classroom environment? The Assessment of Culturally and Contextually Relevant Supports (ACCReS) (see Chapter 8 & Appendix A) is an example of a tool that fosters critical educator self-reflection on their classroom environments. Districts should also offer teacher consultation and coaching as part of comprehensive reform initiatives aimed at creating equitable practices (Gregory et al., 2017, 2019). Given the need for educators to become more culturally responsive in how they are addressing discipline, experienced Black educators with low discipline referrals should be viewed as a resource potentially able to support their colleagues to implement alternatives to exclusionary discipline. They should be valued, compensated, and supported for this work and have it incorporated into their responsibilities rather than having it be an add-on to an already full load (see Chapter 5, this volume).

In addition to offering professional development for teachers, there should be coherent and equity-oriented professional development for all personnel in the school or district, regardless of whether they are employed by the school. Otherwise, students may experience a positive and cultural affirming environment in the classroom and biased interactions in other settings, such as the bus, cafeteria, school hallways, and school entryways, that interfere with their educational experience and result in disciplinary referrals. All personnel should be trained in child and adolescent development, deescalation strategies, trauma-informed practices, cultural responsiveness, and interacting with students with disabilities.

5. Reexamine discipline referral processes.

A key entry point to school policy change is to reduce subjectivity and bias in decision-making in discipline referral processes (Skiba et al., 2002, 2011). School codes of conduct and disciplinary procedures should eliminate suspension and expulsion for lower level and subjective offenses (Redfield & Nance, 2016; see also Chapter 5, this volume), which can be appropriately addressed through school-based interventions. Out-of-school discipline for young children, including toddlers, preschoolers, and students in kindergarten to 3rd grade, should also be prohibited (Transforming School Discipline Collaborative [TSDC], 2016). School policies would also benefit from the use of a structured tool to guide disciplinary decisions and mitigate the impact of racism (Fenning & Johnson, 2019; TSDC, 2016; see also Chapter 3, this volume).

Instructional, corrective, and restorative responses to student behavior should be embedded in school policies (Chicago Public Schools [CPS], 2021; Fenning & Johnson, 2016; Fenning & Sharkey, 2012). An *instructional* approach teaches students directly and indirectly the expectations and how to comply with classroom rules (see Chapter 5, this volume). A *corrective* approach recognizes that not every behavior requires a consequence. As Ms. Betty explains in Chapter 5, "The best thing you can do, correct and move on." A *restorative* approach centers relationships in every response and focuses on addressing harm and healing any ruptures when it has occurred (see Chapter 9). This is consistent with the importance of educators demonstrating they care about students, understanding the reasons behind their behavior, and working with them to improve (see Chapter 3).

School officials should be required to consider available and appropriate alternatives to school exclusion and segregation of students with disabilities in separate settings or schools. Segregating students with disabilities, particularly in settings where the majority are Black, raises concerns about replicating the segregation existing prior to *Brown v. Board of Education* (1954;

Fedders, 2018). Some settings designed for students with disabilities may be positioned to provide specialized support, such as the Center for Resilience program for students significantly impacted by trauma (see Chapter 6, this volume) and the Building Bridges cognitive behavioral/restorative justice program implemented at an alternative school (see Chapter 9). At the same time, school leaders need to understand how racism and ableism operate to displace youth of color, particularly those with disabilities, from classrooms and school environments (Adams & Erevelles, 2016; Fedders, 2018). Students are often placed in alternative schools on the grounds that their needs will be better met, but such schools usually lack the full range of curricular and extracurricular opportunities in neighborhood schools and have lower funding, accountability, and student outcomes (Fedders, 2018; Johnson & Naughton, 2019). Accordingly, school officials should strictly limit and require strong justification for removing students with disabilities from the classroom or dislocating them into a segregated setting. School practices should promote inclusion of students with disabilities in general education settings to the maximum extent (Kaufman, 2020). In the limited circumstances when students with disabilities are segregated from their peers, there should be a clear plan for a return to the general education environment.

6. Revise student's IEPs in response to their behaviors.

Because the procedural safeguards in the IDEA (2016) are tied to 10 days of suspension, school personnel may mistakenly assume that they have relatively free license to suspend students with disabilities for less than 10 days. U.S. Department of Education (DOE) guidance clarifies that students exhibiting a pattern of behavior that interferes with their learning or receiving a series of disciplinary removals may not be receiving a free appropriate public education (FAPE) (Swenson & Ryder, 2016). Classroom disruptions and code of conduct violations may demonstrate a need to conduct or revise a student's functional behavioral assessment and behavior intervention plan (BIP) (Black, 2016) and to revise the student's IEP to provide positive behavioral interventions and supplementary aids and services, such as meeting with a behavioral coach or school counselor (Swenson & Ryder, 2016). Districts can include teacher training, coaching, or tools to appropriately implement behavioral supports as part of students' IEPs (Swenson & Ryder, 2016).

7. Eliminate police in schools.

Many of the contested encounters involving police use of force in schools involve students with disabilities (see Chapter 11, this volume). Even when police in schools say they are not involved in school discipline, they in fact often continue to play a role (Curran, 2019; see also Chapter 4, this volume). Police remain ill-equipped to address the behaviors of students with disabilities, and their presence contributes to racial trauma, problems not likely to be remediated by increased training (see Chapter 4). Given the well-documented harms from police presence, the limited evidence showing that police presence contributes positively to school safety, and the significant investment required to maintain an SRO program (see Chapter 11), school districts should phase out and eliminate school police from their buildings. When school districts remove school police, they should not simply substitute other personnel who play a similar function but should partner with community organizations, mental health professionals, parents, students, and teachers to develop a comprehensive and research-based school safety plan (Babisak, 2020; CPS et al., 2021).

8. Enhance data reporting.

School districts should regularly report discipline data for students with disabilities, disaggregating further by race and disability classification (see Chapters 3 and 4, this volume), wherever possible while protecting student privacy. Data analysis showing the student populations most impacted by exclusionary school discipline practices and common types of disciplinary infractions should be used for school-based problem solving and educator self-reflection. Additionally, data should be publicly reported in a digestible manner accessible to community members to ensure that school districts are accountable and transparent in their practices and outcomes (see Chapter 3).

9. Build the diversity of the educator workforce and the pipeline of school mental health professionals.

The cultural mismatch between the predominately White educator workforce and the minoritized students most vulnerable to school discipline is an impediment to schools becoming culturally responsive teaching and learning communities. Increased diversity of the teacher workforce would help to ensure that more educators can relate to the lived experience of minoritized students (see Chapter 5), and promote cultural esteem in the classroom (see Chapter 3). In addition, schools and districts throughout the country lack sufficient school-based mental health professionals, particularly school psychologists and school social workers, available to meet students' needs and to support and consult with teachers (Jackson, 2019; NASP, 2021; Whitaker et al., 2019). Districts should work with local higher education institutions and state agencies to find creative ways to train, support, and nurture more diverse educators, school-based mental health professionals, and other specialists (e.g., board-certified behavior analysts [BCBAs]) to fill the workforce gap.

10. Enhance teacher and administrator education programs.

As described in Chapter 8 by Fallon and Veiga, many in-service teachers feel they are not prepared to deliver culturally responsive instructional and behavioral supports, which contributes to teachers leaving the profession. Future generations of teachers and administrators should receive more in-depth education in trauma-informed practices, cultural responsiveness, evidence-based reading techniques, restorative practices, and other relational models to build classroom communities. Higher education programs should also equip educators and administrators with a full understanding of the history of colonization, slavery, ethnocide, and discrimination in the United States so that they can ensure this history is accurately conveyed to students and that school practices expressly counteract the wrongs of the past.

Law and Policy Recommendations

1. Centralize parent, student, and community voice.

A starting point for long-term change related to the discipline of students with disabilities is to actively engage students, families, and communities most impacted by these practices in decision-making. State and federal agencies, along with legislatures, can convene student and parent advisory committees, with a goal of ensuring robust participation by students with disabilities and their parents, particularly those from minoritized backgrounds. Policymakers can also collaborate with community-based organizations to facilitate participatory dialogues in local communities and schools.

2. Invest resources in a comprehensive and prevention-oriented approach.

A comprehensive approach to transforming school discipline and achieving educational equity requires significant investments of federal and state resources. Some of these funds will be new allocations, while others should be resources redirected from punitive practices, such as school policing, school security, and disciplinary referrals. These practices not only have high costs in terms of their lived human impact, but they are also fiscally costly. The national cost of school suspensions to the school dropout rate was estimated at $35 billion annually in lost tax revenue, health care, and crime (Rumberger & Losen, 2016).

A key starting place is to fully fund the IDEA (2016). The IDEA has never been funded at the level required to provide students with disabilities the services and protections to which they are entitled, thus ensuring that some students, particularly minoritized students, are denied FAPE (Losen et al., 2021). While Congress initially promised to fund the education of students with disabilities at 40% of state annual average per-pupil expenditure, it provided only 13% of these costs in fiscal year 2021 (Losen et al., 2021). Funding should be increased by 3%–5% over the next 8 years, with an annual adjustment to reflect rising costs (Losen et al., 2021). Increased federal funding should be targeted at improving instructional quality, enhancing specialized educational supports, and diversifying the pipeline of teachers and school-based mental health professionals into the profession (Losen et al., 2021). Also important is allocating federal funds to support Section 504 students, including young people who have experienced trauma (Losen et al., 2021).

Resources should be devoted to providing high-quality, universal early childhood education, which could help prevent the need for later referrals to special education (Kaufman, 2020). Early childhood is a critical time for cognitive development, making it an important time to invest in high-quality education and to address early disadvantages (as cited in Kaufman, 2020). Executive branch proposals as of the writing of this book call for funding universal preschool for 3- and 4-year-olds (The White House, 2021), a critical and cost-effective investment that would pay long-term dividends (as cited in Kaufman, 2020).

Additionally, federal and state funding should be directed to technical support and grants to encourage the adoption of restorative practices and other disciplinary alternatives. In particular, the adoption of restorative practices would benefit from the development and implementation of a consistent model that can be adapted to different settings (Gregory & Evans, 2020). Through grant funding and technical support, federal and state agencies can spur widespread adoption of restorative practices and other evidence-supported practices, supporting fidelity of implementation and funding research to document outcomes and lessons learned.

Eliminating federal funding for school policing would provide a source of funding for some of these priorities. The continued use of federal resources for police in schools should be reexamined in light of the significant evidence showing harm to students (see Chapters 4 and 11, this volume). Given that research has not found that police in schools benefit students or schools, there is ample support for community demands to redirect funding to school-based mental health, restorative justice, and trauma-informed practices (see Chapter 4).

3. Reauthorize the IDEA.

Students with disabilities are entitled to disciplinary procedural protections under the IDEA and yet are disciplined more than their general education peers. This contradiction illustrates the importance of revamping the IDEA, last reauthorized in 2004, to align with research and state law trends limiting suspensions and expulsions (Rafa, 2019). Reauthorization should be a collaborative process involving key stakeholders, including protection and advocacy organizations serving students with disabilities. Consideration should be given to the following recommended changes:

a. Require exhaustion of positive behavioral responses prior to school or classroom exclusion and mandate that any school exclusion take place in the least restrictive environment needed to respond to the student's behavior.

b. Reduce the required days of suspension prompting a manifestation determination review (MDR) to 5 days, cumulatively or consecutively, and require a functional behavioral assessment (FBA) to be conducted or updated after 5 days of suspension.

c. Require students to receive educational services if they are suspended more than 5 days cumulatively.

d. As part of the MDR process, require the school team to show that it implemented with fidelity appropriate interventions to address the student's academic and behavioral needs; otherwise, the incident should be deemed a manifestation of the student's disability and appropriate supports and services offered.

e. Impose stricter limitations on 45-school day transfers to interim alternative educational settings (IAES), allowing them to be used only for exceptional circumstances on a case-by-case basis.

f. Require school districts to regularly review all student suspensions and expulsions, including for students not yet identified with a disability, to determine whether a student should be referred for an evaluation or if another response is needed, such as classroom-based consultation with teachers to implement effective behavioral, social-emotional, and academic supports.

4. Increase oversight and technical support.

Limited federal oversight of IDEA's implementation has contributed to over-reliance on parent complaints to enforce the statute's requirements, thereby reinforcing inequities (Losen et al., 2021). Moreover, sizeable disciplinary disparities have been allowed to continue for decades due to inadequate oversight of school districts at the state and federal levels. The DOE and U.S. Department of Justice (DOJ) should be funded at levels sufficient to dramatically increase civil rights and special education oversight of school districts. To this end, the Civil Rights Data Collection (CRDC) should take place annually rather than biannually (Losen et al., 2021; see also Chapter 4, this volume).

Federal guidance is needed to clarify that the DOE and DOJ can find discrimination as a result of disparate impact of discipline based on race and/or disability, pursuant to Title VI of the Civil Rights Act of 1964 and the regulations implementing Section 504 of the Rehabilitation Act (Kim et al., 2010; Losen et al., 2021). Agency staff should be empowered to review data available through the CRDC and Office of Special Education Programs (OSEP) to launch systemic investigations based on both data and individual complaints (Losen et al., 2021). Agencies should closely monitor data relating to disproportionate discipline of Native American students to ensure this population of students is not overlooked (see Chapter 10, this volume) and should launch compliance investigations based on data suggesting a failure of districts to appropriately identify students under Section 504 (Losen et al., 2021).

A strengthened role for the DOE in ensuring robust monitoring and oversight of IDEA implementation is also critical. Particularly noteworthy are the regulations regarding significant disproportionality (Equity in IDEA, 2016), passed in 2016 but not implemented until 2019 (DOE, 2019). Under these regulations, states are required to use specified methods to calculate whether there is significant disproportionality by race/ethnicity in identification of students with disabilities, educational placements, or disciplinary removals of students with disabilities (Equity in IDEA, 2016). If disproportionality is found to be significant, then school districts are required to review and, where appropriate, revise their policies (Equity in IDEA, 2016). Identified districts need to reserve a portion of their IDEA funds to provide early intervening services to address any significant disproportionality found (DOE, OSEP, 2017). Given the hotly contested backdrop to these regulations and the complexity of the issues regarding disproportionality in special education identification (Ahram et al., 2021; Sullivan & Osher, 2019), technical assistance will be needed to support states and local school districts to comply.

State education agencies (SEAs) should also play an enhanced role in school district accountability, oversight, and technical support, including regular review of district data, disaggregated by race and disability, on suspensions, expulsions, alternative school transfers, and seclusion and restraint. SEAs should hold school districts accountable for discipline practices that violate state nondiscrimination laws and expand the availability of technical assistance for implementation of alternative practices. In addition, they should review the licensure and continuing education requirements of teachers and administrators to align them with the recommendations in this book and consider adding or revising licensure/endorsement requirements for personnel in the role of a discipline dean or comparable position.

5. Expand Section 504 supports.

Because of the well-documented link between childhood trauma and learning, there is a strong basis for considering trauma in all forms as a basis for qualifying students for services under Section 504 (see Chapter 10, this volume). Hoescht and Chee in Chapter 10 suggest that trauma should be clearly recognized as a disability under Section 504 and that qualifying students should be provided with a thorough Section 504 plan that includes accommodations, behavior intervention strategies, and culturally informed practices. Such support is particularly important for Native American youth, given their background of historical trauma and the corresponding high prevalence of trauma in Native communities.

6. Pass comprehensive state laws.

Many states have already passed legislation designed to reduce exclusionary discipline through grade-level restrictions, bans on suspension for certain categories of offenses, and requirements to implement alternatives prior to school exclusion (National Center on Safe and Supportive Learning Environments, n.d.; Rafa, 2019.). To accelerate the pace of change, states should pass holistic discipline reform legislation aimed at preventing districts from substituting other punitive practices for those limited by law. A major role for state-level discipline reform is promoting the use of evidence-supported alternatives to exclusionary discipline, such as restorative practices and trauma-informed approaches (see Chapter 10, this volume). State legislation should require schools to use culturally appropriate practices in school discipline (see Chapter 10) and effectuate strategies specifically focused on disproportionality. Given the link between academic deficits and student behavior (McIntosh et al., 2008), state laws promoting use of evidence-based reading techniques (Gewertz, 2020) are also a key strategy to address the school-to-prison pipeline.

CONCLUSION

Ensuring education is a meaningful pathway to opportunity for all young people requires us to reject the outdated and disproven practices of exclusionary school discipline and policing. We have an opportunity for a hard reset in education and to fundamentally change school practices and pedagogy to appropriately serve students whom the education system has been failing (Ladson-Billings, 2021). We can and must rise to this challenge.

APPENDICES

Assessment of Culturally and Contextually Relevant Supports (ACCReS)

Directions: Please indicate the extent to which you agree with the following statements. Also, consider the following definitions of culture and culturally and contextually relevant supports.

- **Culture:** A shared history and experience, differentiating a group from other groups. Culture may pertain to an individual's race, ethnicity, gender, sexual orientation, exceptionality/disability, socioeconomic status/class, religion, geographic context (e.g., rural, suburban, urban), immigration status, language, and/or nationality.
- **Culturally and contextually relevant supports:** Implementation or action aligned with students' culture and environment to promote success in learning, behavior and development.

	Strongly disagree	Disagree	Somewhat disagree	Somewhat agree	Agree	Strongly agree
	1	2	3	4	5	6
Equitable Classroom Practices						
1. I use explicit instruction when I teach (e.g., clearly describe, model, and practice content with students).						
2. I differentiate instruction to support the different learners I teach.						
3. I provide additional (or more intensive) academic support when a student needs it.						
4. I plan lessons that are designed to actively engage all learners when I teach.						
5. I listen actively to students when they express concerns.						
6. I engage in more positive interactions with students than negative interactions.						
7. I am consistent and fair when it comes to discipline.						
8. I explicitly teach social skills (e.g., ways to ask for help appropriately).						
9. I explicitly teach students about my expectations for classroom behavior.						
10. Each day, I personally greet all my students.						
11. I work to build a positive relationship with each student I teach.						
12. I deliver praise equitably in my classroom.						
13. I actively monitor all parts of the classroom.						

Consideration of Culture and Context

1. Culturally and contextually relevant instruction is important to how I teach.

2. I know how to provide culturally and contextually relevant instruction.

3. I modify the curriculum to be culturally and contextually relevant, when appropriate.

4. I consider students' culture when I decide on the type of instructional support I will provide.

5. I understand that behavior may be context specific (e.g., different behaviors may be more appropriate at home or school).

6. I consider a student's culture when selecting a research-based intervention strategy.

7. I self-assess my cultural biases regularly.

8. I understand that some students are at risk for being disproportionally excluded from the learning environment (e.g., sent to the office, suspended, expelled).

9. I gather information about my students' families (e.g., customs, languages spoken, cultural traditions).

10. I consider students' culture and language when I select assessment tools.

11. I know where to find information about culturally and contextually relevant behavior management practices.

(Continued)

213

(Continued)

	Strongly disagree	Disagree	Somewhat disagree	Somewhat agree	Agree	Strongly agree
	1	2	3	4	5	6

Accessing Information and Support

1. I ask families to help define my classroom expectations.

2. I collect classroom data to inform the equity of my interactions across students (e.g., frequency and distribution of positive interactions).

3. I collect classroom data to inform the equity of my disciplinary actions across students (e.g., evidence of consistent consequences administered).

4. I review academic data for trends that reflect disproportionality (e.g., students of a certain race not achieving in mathematics versus students from other groups).

5. I seek professional development opportunities (e.g., attend conferences, workshops, trainings) to learn about how to engage in culturally and contextually relevant practice.

6. I request the resources (e.g., time, staff, training) I need to implement culturally and contextually relevant instruction.

7. I request the resources (e.g., time, staff, training) I need to implement culturally and contextually relevant behavior support.

214

8. I request to meet with support personnel (e.g., instructional coaches, lead teachers, consultants) to help me consider cultural and contextual factors that might affect how I support students' behavior.

9. I meet with support personnel (e.g., instructional coaches, lead teachers, consultants) to help me to find evidence of disproportionality (e.g., racial, gender) in my classroom data.

10. I talk to administrators in my building about accessing the resources I need to provide culturally and contextually relevant academic supports.

11. I seek the resources (e.g., time, access, translators) I need to partner with families to support students.

Adapted from Fallon, L.M., Cathcart, S.C., & Johnson, A.H., Journal of Psychoeducational Assessment (Vol. 39(7)) pp. 816–831, copyright © 2021 by SAGE Publications

Reprinted by Permission of SAGE Publications

Building Bridges Materials

MEDITATION QUESTIONS

Questions to ask in mediation (after rules are reviewed):

1. Who would like to go first?
2. Can you tell me what happened? (Ask both students.)
3. How do you feel about what happened?
4. What could you do to make things better?
5. What could the other person do to make things better?
6. What are you going to do if you see each other?

THINKING SHEET

1. What did I do?
2. What was my goal (What was I thinking)?
3. How did that work for me (What were the consequences? Did it turn out the way I wanted)?
4. What is a better choice and why?

School Disciplinary Provisions Relating to Students With Disabilities

Core IDEA requirement	• Students with disabilities should receive a free appropriate public education (FAPE) in the least restrictive environment (LRE).
Manifestation determination reviews	• Disciplinary actions constituting a change in placement require a manifestation determination review (MDR) to determine if the behavior was a manifestation of the student's disability. • Change of placement includes suspensions, expulsions, and disciplinary alternative transfers for more than 10 consecutive days or 10 cumulative days if there is a pattern of behavior. • MDR test: Regarding the conduct in question: (1) Was it caused by, or did it have a direct and substantial relationship to, the student's disability, or (2) was the conduct the direct result of the local educational agency's failure to implement the IEP? • If a student's behavior is the result of a disability, the student's educational placement does not change. The school should conduct a functional behavioral assessment (FBA) if one has not already been conducted and create or revise a behavior intervention plan (BIP). • If a student's behavior is not a result of a disability, then disciplinary procedures applicable to general education students apply.
Educational services during suspension or expulsion	• A student suspended or expelled for more than 10 cumulative days in a school year must be provided with the services in their IEP at the school's expense.
Interim Alternative Educational Setting (IAES)	• A student can be transferred to a 45-day IAES placement if (1) the student's offense involved a gun or other specified weapon at school; (2) the student's offense involved the possession, sale, solicitation or use of illegal drugs at school; or (3) the student has inflicted serious bodily injury upon another person while at school.

(Continued)

(Continued)

Students not yet eligible	• Students not yet eligible for special education are entitled to disciplinary protection if school personnel have a specified basis of knowledge about their eligibility. • Parents can request an expedited evaluation if a student not yet eligible is facing expulsion or suspension without the school having a basis of knowledge of a disability.

Source: Individuals With Disabilities Education Act (IDEA) (2016), 20 U.S.C. §1400 et seq.; IDEA Regulations (2017), 34 C.F.R. § § 300.530–300.536.

Notes

Chapter 8

1. We calculated McDonald's omega to evaluate internal consistency due to its superiority to Cronbach's alpha when factor loadings are unequal (Trizano-Hermosilla & Alvarado, 2016). Coefficients > .75 were interpreted to indicate acceptable internal consistency (Reise et al., 2013).

Chapter 10

1. Throughout this paper, the terms *Native American* and *American Indian/ Alaska Native* (AI/AN) are used interchangeably. The majority of Native Americans in San Juan County identify as Diné (Navajo).

2. Through email correspondence, Bloomfield School District indicated these numbers were inaccurate. However, the source of this inaccuracy was not identified (J. Olivas, personal communication, March 26, 2019).

3. Some schools located within the boundaries of the Navajo Reservation are tribally controlled schools funded and/or operated by the Bureau of Indian Education. These schools are not included in this general discussion and present interesting jurisdictional questions of governing law.

4. To qualify under Section 504 (2016), a student must have a physical or mental impairment that substantially limits one or more major life activities, or have a record of such impairment, or be regarded as having such an impairment.

5. Through a grant from the New Mexico Access to Justice Committee, in fall of 2020, the law center partnered with Restorative Solutions, Inc. to provide training on restorative practices to local school districts. For more information on incorporating restorative practices into schools, see http://restorativesolutions.us/.

References

Abramovitz, R., & Mingus, J. (2016). Unpacking racism, poverty, and trauma's impact on the school-to-prison pipeline. In A. J. Carten, A. B. Siskind, & M. P. Greene (Eds.), *Strategies for deconstructing racism in the health and human services* (pp. 245–265). Oxford University Press.

Achilles, G. M., McLaughlin, M. J., & Croninger, R. G. (2007). Sociocultural correlates of disciplinary exclusion among students with emotional, behavioral, and learning disabilities in the SEELS national dataset. *Journal of Emotional and Behavioral Disorders, 15*, 33–45. doi.org/10.1177/10634266070150010401

Adams, C. J., Robelen, E. W., & Shah, N. (2012). Data show retention disparities. *Education Week, 31*(23), 1–18.

Adams, D. L., & Erevelles, N. (2016). Shadow play: Discrit, dis/respectability, and carceral logics. In D. Connor, B. A. Ferri, & S. A. Annamma (Eds.), *DisCrit: Disability studies and critical race theory in education* (pp. 131–144). Teachers College Press.

Adams, R., Reiss, B., & Serlin, D. (Eds.). (2015). *Keywords for disability studies.* NYU Press.

Ahram, R., Voulgarides, C. K., & Cruz R. A. (2021). Understanding disability: High-quality evidence in research on special education disproportionality. *Review of Research in Education, 45*(1), 311–345. doi.org/10.3102/0091732X20985069

Ahranaji, M. (2017). The prisonization of America's public schools. *Hofstra Law Review, 45*, 1097–1117.

Alexander, M. (2012). *The new Jim Crow: Mass incarceration in the age of colorblindness* (rev. ed.). New Press.

Algozzine, B., Wang, C., & Violette, A. S. (2011). Reexamining the relationship between academic achievement and social behavior. *Journal of Positive Behavioral Interventions, 13*(1), 3–16. doi.org/10.1177/1098300709359084

Ali, S. S. (2021, August 7). *Why many districts are struggling over whether to keep officers in schools.* NBC News. www.nbcnews.com/news/us-news/why-many-districts-are-struggling-over-whether-keep-officers-schools-n1275106

Allman, K., & Slate, J. R. (2013). Disciplinary consequences assigned to students with emotional disorder, learning disability, or other health impairment: Effects on their academic achievement. *Journal of Education Research, 7*(1), 83–101.

Alvarez, A., & Milner, H. R. (2018). Exploring teachers' beliefs and feelings about race and police violence. *Teaching Education, 29*(4), 383–394.

American Academy of Pediatrics. (2014). *Adverse childhood experiences and the lifelong consequences of trauma.* cdn.ymaws.com/www.ncpeds.org/resource

/collection/69DEAA33-A258-493B-A63F-E0BFAB6BD2CB/ttb_aces_consequences
.pdf

American Psychological Association. (2016, July). *Racial trauma is real: The impact of police shootings on African Americans.* psychologybenefits.org/2016/07/14/racial-trauma-police-shootings-on-african-americans/

American Psychological Association Task Force on Zero Tolerance Policies. (2008). Are zero tolerance policies effective in the schools? An evidentiary review and recommendations. *American Psychologist, 63,* 852–862. doi.org/10.1037/0003-066X.63.9.852

American Psychiatric Association. (2017, July). *What is cognitive-behavioral therapy?* www.apa.org/ptsd-guideline/patients-and-families/cognitive-behavioral

Americans With Disabilities Act of 1990, 42 U.S.C. § 12101 *et seq.* (2016)

Anderson, K. A. (2018). Policing and middle school: An evaluation of a statewide school resource officer policy. *Middle Grades Review, 4*(2). scholarworks.uvm.edu/cgi/viewcontent.cgi?article=1119&context=mgreview

Annamma, S., & Morrison, D. (2018). DisCrit classroom ecology: Using praxis to dismantle dysfunctional education ecologies. *Teaching and Teacher Education, 73*(1), 70–80. doi.org/10.1016/j.tate.2018.03.008

Annamma, S., Morrison, D., & Jackson, D. (2014). Disproportionality fills in the gaps: Connections between achievement, discipline and special education in the school to prison pipeline. *Berkeley Review of Education, 5*(1), 53–87. doi.org/10.5070/B85110003

Annamma, S. A. (2017). *The pedagogy of pathologization: Dis/abled girls of color in the school-prison nexus.* Routledge.

Annamma, S. A., Connor, D., & Ferri, B. (2013). Dis/ability critical race studies (DisCrit): Theorizing at the intersections of race and dis/ability. *Race Ethnicity and Education, 16*(1), 1–31. doi.org/10.1080/13613324.2012.730511

Annamma, S. A., Connor, D. J., & Ferri, B. A. (2016). Dis/ability critical race studies (DisCrit): Theorizing at the intersections of race and dis/ability. In D. J. Connor, B. A. Ferri, & S. A. Annamma (Eds.), *DisCrit: Disability studies and critical race theory in education* (pp. 9–32). Teachers College Press.

Annamma, S. A., Ferri, B. A., & Connor, D. J. (2012). Disability critical race theory: Exploring the intersectional lineage, emergence, and potential futures of DisCrit in education. *Review of Research in Education, 42*(1), 46–71. doi.org/10.3102%2F0091732X18759041

Annamma, S. A., Ferri, B., & Connor, D. (2018). Disability critical race theory: Exploring intersectional lineage, emergence, and potential futures of DisCrit in education. *Review of Research in Education, 42*(1), 46–71. doi.org/10.3102/0091732X18759041

Annamma, S. A., Handy, T., Miller, A. L., & Jackson, E. (2020). Animating discipline disparities through debilitating practices: Girls of color and inequitable classroom interactions. *Teachers College Record, 122*(5), 1–46.

Annamma, S. A., Jackson, D. D., & Morrison, D. (2017). Conceptualizing color-evasiveness: Using dis/ability critical race theory to expand a color-blind racial ideology in education and society. *Race, Ethnicity and Education, 20*(2), 147–162. doi.org/10.1080/13613324.2016.1248837

Anyon, Y., Jenson, J. M., Altschul, I., Farrar, J., McQueen, J., Greer, E., Downing., & Simmons, J. (2014). The persistent effect of race and the promise of alternatives to suspension in school discipline outcomes. *Children and Youth Services Review*, *44*, 379–386.

Artiles, A. (2011). Toward an interdisciplinary understanding of educational equity and difference: The case of the racialization of ability. *Educational Researcher*, *40*(9), 431–445.

Artiles, A. J. (1998). The dilemma of difference: Enriching the disproportionality discourse with theory and context. *The Journal of Special Education*, *32*(1), 32–36. doi.org/10.1177/002246699803200105

Assistance to States for the Education of Children with Disabilities, 34 C.F.R. Part 300 (2017)

Auerbach, A., Chafouleas, S. M., & Briesch, A. M. (2018). State-level guidance on screening for social, emotional, and behavioral risk: A follow-up study. *School Mental Health*, *11*, 141–147. doi.org/10.1007/s12310-018-9278-z

Austin, R. D. (2009). *Navajo courts and common law: A tradition of tribal self-governance*. University of Minnesota Press.

Babisak, J. (2020). *Police in schools: Guide to alternatives and improved approaches*. Transforming School Discipline Collaborative. bit.ly/TSDCpolicetoolkit

Baglieri, S. (2016). Toward unity in school reform: What DisCrit contributes to multicultural and inclusive education. In D. J. Connor, B. A. Ferri, & S. A. Annamma (Eds.), *DisCrit: Disability studies and critical race theory in education* (pp. 167–179). Teachers College Press.

Bal, A. (2018). Culturally responsive positive behavioral interventions and supports: A process–oriented framework for systemic transformation. *Review of Education, Pedagogy, and Cultural Studies*, *40*(2), 144–174.

Bal, A., Thorius, K. K., & Kozleski, E. (2012). *Culturally responsive positive behavioral support matters*. The Equity Alliance.

Balfanz, R., Byrnes, V., & Fox, J. (2014). Sent home and put off-track: The antecedents, disproportionalities, and consequences of being suspended in the ninth grade. *Journal of Applied Research on Children: Informing Policy for Children at Risk*, *5*(2). Article 13. digitalcommons.library.tmc.edu/childrenatrisk/vol5/iss2/13

Ball, D. L., & Cohen, D. K. (1999). Developing practice, developing practitioners: Toward a practice-based theory of professional education. In G. Sykes & L. Darling-Hammond (Eds.), *Teaching as the learning profession: Handbook of policy and practice* (pp. 3–22). Jossey-Bass.

Barrett, N., McEachin, A., Mills, J. N., & Valant, J. (2017). *What are the sources of school discipline disparities by student race and family income?* Education Research Alliance for New Orleans. educationresearchalliancenola.org/files/publications/111417-Barrett-McEachin-Mills-Valant-What-Are-the-Sources-of-School-Discipline-Disparities-by-Student-Race-and-Family-Income.pdf

Bass, L. (2012). When care trumps justice: The operationalization of Black feminist caring in educational leadership. *International Journal of Qualitative Studies on Education*, *25*(1), 73–87.

Baule, S. M., & Superior, W. I. (2020). The impact of positive behavior intervention support (PBIS) on suspensions by race and ethnicity in an urban school district. *AASA Journal of Scholarship & Practice, 16*(4), 45–56.

Beauboeuf-Lafontant, T. (2002). A womanist experience of caring: Understanding the pedagogy of exemplary Black women teachers. *The Urban Review, 34*(1), 71–86.

Bell, D. (1993). *Faces at the bottom of the well: The permanence of racism.* New York: Basic Books. ISBN 13:9780465068142

Benner, G. J., Kutash, K., Nelson, J. R., & Fisher, M. B. (2013). Closing the achievement gap of youth with emotional and behavioral disorders through multi-tiered systems of support. *Education and Treatment of Children, 36*(3), 15–29.

Beratan, G. D. (2008). The song remains the same: Transposition and the disproportionate representation of minority students in special education. *Race, Ethnicity and Education, 11*(4), 337–354. doi.org/10.1080/13613320802478820

Bergan, J. R., & Kratochwill, T. R. (1990). *Behavioral consultation and therapy.* Plenum.

Black, C. (2016). *Functional behavioral assessments and behavioral intervention plans: A component of the TSDC toolkit for school transformation.* Transforming School Discipline Collaborative. drive.google.com/file/d/1o-5SFz-SsDGT4Thg7IlyszMR2ADOmVut/view

Blake, J., Smith, D., Marchbanks, M., Seibert, A., Wood, S., & Kim, E. (2016). Does student-teacher racial/ethnic match impact black students' discipline risk? A test of the cultural synchrony hypothesis. In R. Skiba, K. Mediratta, & M. Rausch (Eds.), *Inequality in school discipline* (pp. 79–98). Palgrave Macmillan.

Blake, J. J., Butler, B. R., Lewis, C. W., & Darensbourg, A. (2011). Unmasking the inequitable discipline experiences of urban Black girls: Implications for urban educational stakeholders. *The Urban Review, 43*, 90–106. psycnet.apa.org/doi/10.1007/s11256-009-0148-8

Blanchett, W. J. (2010). Telling it like it is: The role of race, class, & culture in the perpetuation of learning disability as a privileged category for the white middle class. *Disability Studies Quarterly, 30*(2).

Blodgett, C., & Lanigan, J. D. (2018). The association between adverse childhood experience (ACE) and school success in elementary school children. *School Psychology Quarterly, 33*(1), 137–146. dx.doi.org/10.1037/spq0000256

Bogdan, R., & Biklen, S. (2003). *Qualitative research for education.* Allyn & Bacon.

Bon, S. C., & Zirkel, P. A. (2014). Time-out and seclusion litigation: A liability nightmare? *The University of Toledo Law Review, 45*, 505–525.

Bonilla-Silva, E. (2007). Color-blind racism. *Race, class, and gender in the United States*, 131–138.

Bradley, R., Doolittle, J., & Bartolotta, R. (2008). Building on the data and adding to the discussion: The experiences and outcomes of students with emotional disturbance. *Journal of Behavioral Education, 17*, 4–23.

Bradshaw, C. P., Mitchell, M. M., O'Brennan, L. M., & Leaf, P. J. (2010). Multilevel exploration of factors contributing to the overrepresentation of Black students in office disciplinary referrals. *Journal of Educational Psychology, 102*, 508–520.

Brady, K. P. (2018). School resource officers and the unsettled legal standard for assessing student excessive force claims. *West's Education Law Reporter*, *359*, 689–710.

Brandenburg, J. E., Holman, L. K., Apkon, S. D., Houtrowd, A. J., Robert, R., & Scholas, M. G. (2020). School reopening during COVID-19 pandemic: Considering students with disabilities. *Journal of Pediatric Rehabilitation Medicine*, 1–7. doi.org/10.3233/PRM-200746

Brantlinger, E., & Danforth, S. (2013). Critical theory perspective on social class, race, gender, and classroom management. In C. M. Evertson & C. S. Weinstein (Eds.), *Handbook of classroom management* (pp. 167–190). Routledge.

Brave Heart, M. Y. H. (2007). The impact of historical trauma: The example of the Native community. In M. Bussey & J. Wise (Eds.), *Trauma transformed: An empowerment response* (pp. 176–193). Columbia University Press. www.jstor.org /stable/10.7312/buss13832.16

Brave Heart, M. Y. H., Chase, J., Elkins, J., & Altschul, D. (2011). Historical trauma among Indigenous peoples of the Americas: Concepts, research, and clinical considerations. *Journal of Psychoactive Drugs*, *43*(4), 282–290. doi:10.1080/02791 072.2011.628913

Brayboy, B. (2006). Toward a tribal critical race theory in education. *The Urban Review*, *37*(5), 425–446. doi.org/10.1007/s11256-005-0018-y

Briesch, A. M., Chafouleas, S. M., & Chaffee, R. K. (2017). Analysis of state-level guidance regarding school-based, universal screening for social, emotional, and behavioral risk. *School Mental Health*, *10*, 147–162. doi.org/10.1007/ s12310-017-9232-5

Briesch, A. M., Chafouleas, S. M., Nissen, K., & Long, S. (2020). A review of state-level procedural guidance for implementing Multitiered Systems of Support for Behavior (MTSS-B). *Journal of Positive Behavior Interventions*, *22*(3), 131–144. doi.org/10.1177/1098300719884707

Briesch, A. M., Chafouleas, S. M., & Riley-Tillman, T. C. (2016). *Direct behavior rating (DBR): Linking assessment, communication, and intervention*. Guilford.

Briesch, A. M., Cintron, D. W., Dineen, J. N., Chafouleas, S. M., McCoach, D. B., & Auerbach, E. (2020). Comparing stakeholders' knowledge and beliefs about supporting students' social, emotional, and behavioral health in schools. *School Mental Health*, *12*, 222–238. doi.org/10.1007/s12310-019-09355-9

Brown, T. (2007). Lost and turned out: Academic, social and emotional experiences of students excluded from school. *Urban Education*, *42*(5), 432–455.

Brown v. Board of Education, 347 U.S. 483 (1954)

Brunner, M. S. (1993). *Reduced recidivism and increased employment opportunity through research-based reading instruction*. U.S. Department of Justice, Office of Justice Programs. www.ojp.gov/pdffiles1/Digitization/141324NCJRS.pdf

Camacho, K., & Krezmien, M. (2018). Individual- and school-level factors contributing to disproportionate suspension rates: A multilevel analysis of one state. *Journal of Emotional and Behavioral Disorders*, *27*(4), 1–12.

Camacho, K. A., & Krezmien, M. P. (2020). A statewide analysis of school discipline policies and suspension practices. *Preventing School Failure: Alternative*

Education for Children and Youth, 64(1), 55–66. doi.org/10.1080/104598
8X.2019.1678010

Canady, M. (2018, November). Understanding at-risk students and what they can teach us about effective prevention programs. *Department of Justice Journal of Federal Law and Practice*, 66(6), 131–140.

Carothers, D., Aydin, H., & Houdyshell, M. (2019). Teacher shortages and cultural mismatch: District and university collaboration for recruiting. *Journal of Social Studies Education Research*, 10(3), 39–63. www.learntechlib.org/p/216455/

Carter, P. L., Skiba, R., Arredondo, M. I., & Pollock, M. (2017). You can't fix what you don't look at: Acknowledging race in addressing racial discipline disparities. *Urban Education*, 52(2), 207–235. doi.org/10.1177/0042085916660350

Carter Andrews, D. J., & Gutwein, M. (2020). Middle school students' experiences with inequitable discipline practices in school: The elusive quest for cultural responsiveness. *Middle School Journal*, 51(1), 29–38.

Cartledge, G., & Kleefeld, J. (2010). *Working together: Building children's social skills through folktales: Grades 3–6*. Research Press.

Carver, P. R., & Tice, P. (2010). *Alternative schools and programs for public school students at risk of educational failure: 2007–08—first look* [NCES 2010-026]. National Center for Education Statistics. permanent.fdlp.gov/gpo8816/2010026.pdf

Castro-Villareal, F., Rodriguez, B. J., & Moore, S. (2014). Teachers' perceptions and attitudes about Response to Intervention (RTI) in their schools: A qualitative analysis. *Teaching and Teacher Education*, 40, 104–112. doi.org/10.1016/j.tate.2014.02.004

Cavendish, W., Connor, D., Gonzalez, T., Jean-Pierre, P., & Card, K. (2020). Troubling "The Problem" of racial overrepresentation in special education: A commentary and call to rethink research. *Educational Review*, 72(5), 567–582. doi.org/10.1080/00131911.2018.1550055

Centers for Disease Control and Prevention. (2019). *About the CDC-Kaiser ACE study*. www.cdc.gov/violenceprevention/childabuseandneglect/acestudy/about.html?CDC_AA_refVal=https%3A%2F%2Fwww.cdc.gov%2Fviolencepreventio n%2Facestudy%2Fabout.html

Chafouleas, S. M., Briesch, A. M., Dineen, J. N., & Marcy, H. M. (2020, October). *Mapping promising alternative approaches to exclusionary practices in U.S. schools*. UConn Collaboratory on School and Child Health. csch.uconn.edu

Chafouleas, S. M., Johnson, A. H., Overstreet, S., & Santos, N. M. (2016). Toward a blueprint for trauma-informed service delivery in schools. *School Mental Health*, 8, 144–162. doi.org/10.1007/s12310-015-9166-8

Chafouleas, S. M., McCoach, D. B., Cintron, D. W., Briesch, A. M., Dineen, J. N., & Volk, D. (2022). *Exploring predictors of social, emotional, and behavioral screening approaches in U.S. public schools* (Manuscript under review).

Charmaz, K. (2006). Constructing grounded theory: A practical guide through qualitative analysis. Thousand Oaks, CA: Sage.

Chicago Public Schools. (2021, August 30). *Student code of conduct*. www.cps.edu
/about/policies/student-code-of-conduct-policy/

Chicago Public Schools. The Ark of the St. Sabina, BUILD, Community Organizing
and Family Issues (COFI), Mikva Challenge, Voices for Youth in Chicago Education (VOYCE). (2021, March). *Report & recommendations*. Whole School
Safety Steering Committee. bit.ly/safetyalternative

Children's Defense Fund. (1975). *School suspensions: Are they helping children?*
Washington Research Project. files.eric.ed.gov/fulltext/ED113797.pdf

Choloewa, B., Amatea, E., West-Olatunji, C. A., & Wright, A. (2012). Examining the
relational processes of a highly successful teacher of African American children.
Urban Education, 47(1), 250–279.

Choloewa, B., Goodman, R., West-Olatunji, C., & Amatea, E. (2014). A qualitative
examination of the impact of culturally responsive educational practices on the
psychological well-being of students of color. *Urban Review, 46*, 574–596.

Chu, S. Y., & Garcia, S. (2014). Culturally responsive teaching efficacy beliefs of
in-service special education teachers. *Remedial and Special Education, 35*(4),
218–232. doi.org/10.1177/0741932513520511

Civil Rights Data Collection. (2020). Civil Rights Data Collection (CRDC) for the
2013–14 school year. www2.ed.gov/about/offices/list/ocr/docs/crdc-2013-14
.html

Clarren, R. (2017, July 24). How America is failing Native American students:
Punitive discipline, inadequate curriculum, and declining federal funding created an education crisis. *The Nation*. www.thenation.com/article/archive/left
-behind/

Coggshall, J. G., Osher, D., & Colombi, G. (2012). Enhancing educators' capacity to
stop the school-to-prison pipeline. In J. S. Kaye, K. R. DeCataldo, & T. A. Lang
(Eds.), *Keeping kids in school and out of court: A collection of reports to inform
the national leadership summit on school-justice partnerships* (pp. 11–127). New
York State Permanent Judicial Commission on Justice for Children.

Cohen, D. K., & Ball, D. L. (2001). Making change: Instruction and its improvement.
Kappan, 83(1), 73–77.

Cohen, J. S. (2020, July 14). *A teenager didn't do her online schoolwork. So a
judge sent her to juvenile detention*. ProPublica. www.propublica.org/article
/a-teenager-didnt-do-her-online-schoolwork-so-a-judge-sent-her-to-juvenile
-detention

Cole, E. R. (2009). Intersectionality and research in psychology. *American Psychologist, 64*(3), 170–180.

Coles, J. A., & Powell, T. (2020). A BlackCrit analysis on Black urban youth and suspension disproportionality as anti-Black symbolic violence. *Race Ethnicity and
Education, 23*(1), 113–133.

Collins, L. W., & Zirkel, P. A. (2017). Functional behavior assessments and behavior intervention plans: Legal requirements and professional recommendations. *Journal of Positive Behavior Interventions, 19*, 180–190. doi
.org/10.1177%2F1098300716682201

230   References

Collins, P. H. (1990). *Black feminist thought: Knowledge, consciousness, and the politics of empowerment.* Routledge.

Comas-Díaz, L. (2016). Racial trauma recovery: A race-informed therapeutic approach to racial wounds. In A. N. Alvarez, C. T. H. Liang, & H. A. Neville (Eds.), *The cost of racism for people of color: Contextualizing experiences of discrimination* (pp. 249–272). American Psychological Association.

Committee for Children. (2018). Recent trends in state legislative exclusionary discipline reform (Policy Brief). www.cfchildren.org/wp-content/uploads/policy-advocacy/exclusionary-policy-brief.pdf

Congressional Research Service. (2018, July 5). *School resource officers: Issues for Congress.* www.everycrsreport.com/files/20180705_R45251_db5492370a04c7e3b39f27ce52416d229a0ac17d.pdf

Connelly, L. M. (2016). Trustworthiness in qualitative research. *Medsurg Nursing,* 25(6), 435.

Connor, D., Gabel, S., Gallagher, D., & Morton, M. (2008). Disability studies and inclusive education: Implications for theory, research, and practice. *International Journal of Inclusive Education, 12,* 441–457.

Connor, D. J., Ferri, B. A., & Annamma, S. A. (Eds.). (2016). *DisCrit: Disability studies and critical race theory in education.* Teachers College Press. ISBN: 978-0-8077.5667-6

Cook, B. G., & Odom, S. L. (2013). Evidence-based practices and implementation science in special education. *Exceptional Children, 79*(3), 135–144. doi.org/10.1177/001440291307900201

Cook, C. R., Coco, S., Zhang, Y., Fiat, A. E., Duong, M. T., Renshaw, T. L., Long, A. C., & Frank, S. (2018). Cultivating positive teacher-student relationships: Preliminary evaluation of the establish–maintain–restore (EMR) method. *School Psychology Review, 47*(3), 226–243.

Cook, C. R., Duong, M. T., McIntosh, K., Fiat, A. E., Larson, M., Pullmann, M. D., & McGinnis, J. (2018). Addressing discipline disparities for Black male students: Linking malleable root causes to feasible and effective practices. *School Psychology Review, 47*(2), 135–152.

Cook, C. R., Frye, M., Slemrod, T., Lyon, A. R., Renshaw, T. L., & Zhang, Y. (2015). An integrated approach to universal prevention: Independent and combined effects of PBIS and SEL on youths' mental health. *School Psychology Quarterly, 30*(2), 166–183. doi.org/10.1037/spq0000102

Cooper, A. J. (1892). *A Voice from the South.* Aldine.

Cooper, C. W. (2009). Parent involvement, African American mothers, and the politics of educational care. *Equity & Excellence in education, 42*(4), 379–394.

Cooper, L. A., Hill, M. N., & Powe, N. R. (2002). Designing and evaluating interventions to eliminate racial and ethnic disparities in health care. *Journal of General Internal Medicine, 17*(6), 477–486.

Cornish, A., & Block, M. (Hosts). (2014, January 17). Ruling may mean bankruptcy for New Orleans school system [Audio podcast episode]. *All things considered.* NPR. www.npr.org/2014/01/17/263494979/ruling-may-mean-bankruptcy-for-new-orleans-school-system

Correia, D. (2015, June 8). *Indian killers: Police violence against Native people in Albuquerque.* La Jicarita. lajicarita.wordpress.com/2015/06/08/indian-killers-police-violence-against-native-people-in-albuquerque/

Costello, B., Wachtel, J., & Wachtel, T. (2013). *The restorative practices handbook for teachers, disciplinarians, and other administrators.* International Institute for Restorative Practices.

The Cowen Institute. (2018). *The state of public education in New Orleans.* Babineau, K., Hand, D., & Rossmeier, V. www.thecoweninstitute.com.php56-17.dfw3-1.websitetestlink.com/uploads/SPENO_2018_Final_-_Single_Page_Spread-1524079672.pdf

Crenshaw, K. (1989). Demarginalizing the intersection of race and sex: A Black feminist critique of anti-discrimination doctrine, feminist theory, and antiracist policies. University of Chicago Legal Forum, 139–167.

Crenshaw, K. (1991). Mapping the margins: Intersectionality, identity politics, and violence against women of color. *Stanford Law Review, 43*(6), 1241–1299.

Crenshaw, K., Gotanda N., Peller, G., & Thomas, K. (Eds.). (1995). *Critical race theory: The key writings that formed the movement.* The New Press.

Crenshaw, K., Ocen, P., & Nanda, J. (2015). *Black girls matter: Pushed out, overpoliced, and underprotected.* Center for Intersectionality and Social Policy Studies, Columbia University.

Cullinan, D., & Kauffman, J. M. (2005). Do race of student and race of teacher influence ratings of emotional and behavioral problem characteristics of students with Emotional Disturbance? *Behavioral Disorders, 30*(4), 393–402. doi.org/10.1177/019874290503000403

Cummings, S. L. (2013). Empirical studies of law and social change: What is the field? What are the questions? *Wisconsin Law Review, 2013,* 171–204.

Curran, F. C., Fisher, B. W., Viano, S., & Kupchik, A. (2019). Why and when do school resource officers engage in school discipline? The role of context in shaping disciplinary involvement. *American Journal of Education, 126*(1), 33–63. doi.org/10.1086/705499

The Data Center. (2016). *The New Orleans youth index 2016.* www.datacenterresearch.org/reports_analysis/the-new-orleans-youth-index-2016/. A. Perry.

Davis, F. (2019). *The little book of race and restorative justice: Black lives, healing, and US social transformation.* Good Books.

Delgado, R., & Stefancic, J. (1998). Critical race theory: Past, present, and future. *Current Legal Problems, 51*(1), 467–491. doi.org/10.1093/clp/51.1.467

Delgado, R., & Stefancic, J. (2001). *Critical race theory: An introduction.* NYU Press.

DeMitchell, T. A., & Cobb, C. D. (2003). Policy responses to violence in our schools: An exploration of security as a fundamental value. *Brigham Young University Education and Law Journal, 2,* 459–484.

Dillon, D. J., Holmes, A. J., Birk, J. L., Brooks, N., Lyons-Ruth, K., & Pizzagalli, D. A. (2009). Childhood adversity is associated with left basal ganglia dysfunction during reward anticipation in adulthood. *Biological Psychiatry, 66*(3), 206–213. doi.org/10.1016/j.biopsych.2009.02.019

Dineen, J. N., Chafouleas, S. M., Briesch, A. M., McCoach, D. B., Newton, S. D., & Cintron, D. W. (2021). Exploring social, emotional, and behavioral screening approaches in U.S. public school districts. *American Education Research Journal.* doi.org/10.3102/00028312211000043

Dixson, A. (2003). "Let's do this!" Black women teachers' politics and pedagogy. *Urban Education, 38*(2), 217–235.

Doane, A. W., & Bonilla-Silva, E. (Eds.). (2003). *White out: The continuing significance of racism.* Psychology Press.

Domzalski, K., & Saias, B. (2021, June 4). A year of activism: Students reflect on their fight for racial justice at school. *Education Week.* edweek.org/leadership/a-year-of-activism-students-reflect-on-their-fight-for-racial-justice-at-school/2021/06

Dunhamn, J., Harris, J., Jarrett, S., Moore, L., Nishida, A., Price, M., Robinson, B., & Schalk, S. (2015). Developing and reflecting on a Black disability studies pedagogy: Work from the National Black Disability Coalition. *Disability Studies Quarterly, 35*(2). dsq-sds.org/article/view/4637/3933

Dunlap, G., Sailor, W., Horner, R. H., & Sugai, G. (2009). Overview and history of positive behavior support. In W. Sailor, G. Dunlap, G. Sugai, & R. Horner (Eds.), *Handbook of positive behavior support* (pp. 3–16). Springer.

Dunn, K. E., Airola, D. T., Lo, W., & Garrison, M. (2012). What teachers think about what they can do with data: Development and validation of the data-driven decision making efficacy and anxiety inventory. *Contemporary Educational Psychology, 38,* 87–98.

D'Zurilla, T. J., & Goldfried, M. R. (1971). Problem solving and behavior modification. *Journal of Abnormal Psychology, 78,* 107–126. dx.doi.org/10.1037/h0031360

Eagle, J., Dowd-Eagle, S., Snyder, A., & Gibbons Holtzman, E. (2015). Implementing a multi tiered system of support (MTSS): Collaboration between school psychologists and administrators to promote systems-level change. *Journal of Educational and Psychological Consultation, 25*(2–3), 160–177.

Earl, L. M. (2008). Leadership for evidence-informed conversations. In L. M. Earl & H. Timperley (Eds.), *Professional learning conversations* (pp. 43–52). Springer.

Edelman, P. (2019). The criminalization of poverty and the people who fight back. *Georgetown Journal on Poverty Law and Policy, 26,* 213–226.

Eid, T., & Goldtooth, D. (2017). Children are sacred: Applying Navajo (Diné) fundamental law to strengthen juvenile justice. *South Dakota Law Review, 62,* 728.

Elliott, S. N., Witt, J. C., Galvin, G. A., & Peterson, R. (1984). Acceptability of positive and reductive behavioral interventions: Factors that influence teachers' decisions. *Journal of School Psychology, 22*(4), 353–360.

Ending the Epidemic of Childhood Trauma. (2019). *United States House of Representatives Committee on Oversight and Reform, 116th Cong* [testimony of Denise O. Shervington]. docs.house.gov/meetings/GO/GO00/20190711/109762/HHRG-116-GO00-Wstate-ShervingtonD-20190711.pdf

Erevelles, N., & Minear, A. (2010). Unspeakable offenses: Untangling race and disability in discourses of intersectionality. *Journal of Literary & Cultural Disability Studies*, 4(2), 127–146.

Equity in IDEA, 34 CFR § § 300.646, 300.646 (2016)

Every Student Succeeds Act, 20 U.S.C. § 6301 (2015)

Ewing, E. (2018). *Ghosts in the schoolyard: Racism and school closings on Chicago's South Side*. University of Chicago Press.

Faircloth, S. C., & Tippeconnic, J. W., III. (2010). *The dropout/graduation rate crisis among American Indian and Alaska Native students: Failure to respond places the future of Native peoples at risk*. The Center for Civil Rights Remedies. bit.ly/graduationcrisis

Falk, M., & Troeh, E. (2017, January 23). *A "no excuses" New Orleans charter school has a change of heart*. WWNO Education Desk. www.wwno.org/post/no-excuses-new-orleans-charter-school-has-change-heart

Fallon, L. M., Cathcart, S. C., DeFouw, E. R., O'Keeffe, B. V., & Sugai, G. (2018). Promoting teachers' implementation of culturally and contextually relevant classwide behavior plans. *Psychology in the Schools*, 55(3), 278–294. doi.org/10.1002/pits.22107

Fallon, L. M., Cathcart, S. C., & Johnson, A. H. (2021). Assessing differential item functioning in a teacher self-assessment of cultural responsiveness. *Journal of Psychoeducational Assessment*, 39(7), 816–831. doi.org/10.1177/07342829211026464

Fallon, L. M., O'Keeffe, B. V., & Sugai, G. (2012). Consideration of culture and context in school-wide positive behavior support: A review of current literature. *Journal of Positive Behavior Interventions*, 14(3), 209–219. doi.org/10.1177/1098300712442242

Family Educational Rights and Privacy Act, 34 C.F.R. § 99 (2000)

Family Educational Rights and Privacy Act Regulations, 34 C.F.R. Part 99, (2016)

Fedders, B. (2018). Schooling at Risk. *Iowa Law Review*, 103(3), 871–923. ilr.law.uiowa.edu/print/volume-103-issue-3/schooling-at-risk/

Feierman, J., Kleinman, R., Lapp., D., Luse, M., Rieser, L., & Schwartz, R. (2012). Stemming the tide: Promising legislation to reduce school referrals to the courts. In J. S. Kaye, K. R. DeCataldo, & T. A. Lang (Eds.), *Keeping kids in school and out of court: A collection of reports to inform the national leadership summit on school-justice partnerships* (pp. 111–127). New York State Permanent Judicial Commission on Justice for Children.

Feldman, M. S., & Almguist, J. (2012). Analyzing the implicit in stories. In J. A. Holstein & J. F. Gubrium (Eds.), *Varieties of narrative analysis* (pp. 207–228). SAGE. doi.org/10.4135/9781506335117

Feldman, M. S., Sköldberg, K., Brown, R. N., & Horner, D. (2004). Making sense of stories: A rhetorical approach to narrative analysis. *Journal of Public Administration Research and Theory*, 14(2), 147–170.

Fenning, P., & Jenkins, K. (2018). Racial and ethnic disparities in exclusionary school discipline: Implications for administrators leading discipline reform efforts. *NASSP Bulletin*, 102(4), 291–302. doi.org/10.1177%2F0192636518812699

Fenning, P., & Johnson, M. (2016). Developing prevention-oriented codes of conduct. *Children's Legal Rights Journal, 36*(2), 107–136. lawecommons.luc.edu/cgi/viewcontent.cgi?article=1123&context=clrj

Fenning, P., & Johnson, M. B. (2019). Supporting policy and practice to address implicit bias in discipline. In G. L. Gullo, K. Capatosto, & C. Staats (Eds.), *Implicit bias in schools: A practitioner's guide* (pp. 123–148). Routledge.

Fenning, P., Pulaski, S., Gomez, M., Morello, M., Maciel, L., Maroney, E., & Maltese, R. (2012). Call to action: A critical need for designing alternatives to suspension and expulsion. *Journal of School Violence, 11*, 105–117.

Fenning, P., & Rose, J. (2007). Overrepresentation of African-American students in exclusionary discipline: The role of policy. *Urban Education, 42*(6), 536–559. doi.org/10.1177%2F0042085907305039

Fenning, P., & Sharkey, J. (2012). Creating equitable school policies to prevent and address ethnic disproportionality in school discipline practices. In A. L. Noltemeyer & C. S. Mcloughlin (Eds.), *Disproportionality in education and special education* (pp. 237–258). Charles C. Thomas Publishers.

Fergus, E. (2016). Social reproduction ideologies: Teacher beliefs about race and culture. In D. Connor, B. Ferri, & S. Annamma (Eds.), *DisCrit-disability studies and critical race theory in Education (disability, culture and equity series)*. Teachers College Press.

Ferguson, A. A. (2001). *Bad boys: Public schools in the making of Black masculinity*. The University of Michigan Press.

Ferri, B., & Connor, D. (2005). Tools of exclusion: Race, disability, and (re) segregated education. *Teachers College Record, 107*(3), 453–474.

Fisher, B. W., & Hennessy, E. A. (2016). School resource officers and exclusionary discipline: A systematic review and meta-analysis. *Adolescent Research Review, 1*, 217–233. doi.org/10.1007/s40894-015-0006-8.

Fixsen, D. L., Naoom, S. F., Blase, K. A., Friedman, R. M., & Wallace, F. (2005). *Implementation research: A synthesis of the literature* [FMHI publication #231]. University of South Florida, Louis de la Parte Florida Mental Health Institute, The National Implementation Research Network. nirn.fpg.unc.edu/sites/nirn.fpg.unc.edu/files/resources/NIRN-MonographFull-01-2005.pdf

Flick, U. W. E. (2009). *An introduction to qualitative research* (4th ed.). SAGE.

Fox, M., Blankenship-Knox, A., & Krimbill, E. M. (2021). Balancing confidentiality and campus security: SROs, FERPA, and students with disabilities. *West's Education Law Reporter, 387*, 429–438.

Freeman, A. D. (1978). Legitimizing racial discrimination through antidiscrimination law: A critical review of Supreme Court doctrine. *Minnesota Law Review, 62*, 1049–1119.

French, B. H., Lewis, J. A., Mosley, D. V., Adames, H. Y., Chavez-Dueñas, N. Y., Chen, G. A., & Neville, H. A. (2020). Toward a psychological framework of radical healing in communities of color. *The Counseling Psychologist, 48*(1), 14–46. doi.org/10.1177/0011000019843506

Frey, K. S., Hirschstein, M. K., & Guzzo, B. A. (2000). Second Step: Preventing aggression by promoting social competence. *Journal of Emotional and Behavioral Disorders, 8*(2), 102–112.

Fronius, T., Darling-Hammond, S., Persson, H., Guckenburg, S., Hurley, N., & Petrosino, A. (2019). *Restorative justice in U.S. schools: An updated research review.* WestEd Justice & Prevention Research Center. wested.org/wp-content /uploads/2019/04/resource-restorative-justice-in-u-s-schools-an-updated-research -review.pdf

Gage, N. A., Whitford, D. K., Katsiyannis, A., Adams, S., & Jasper, A. (2019). National analysis of the disciplinary exclusion of black students with and without disabilities. *Journal of Child and Family Studies, 28*(7), 1754–1764. doi .org/10.1007/s10826-019-01407-7

Gay, G. (2010). *Culturally responsive teaching: Theory, research, and practice* (2nd ed.). Teachers College Press.

Gewertz, C. (2020, February). Reading instruction: A flurry of new state laws. *Education Week.* edweek.org/teaching-learning/reading-instruction-a-flurry-of-new -state-laws/2020/02

Gibbs, G. R. (2018). *Analyzing qualitative data.* SAGE.

Gilliam, W. S., Maupin, A. N., Reyes, C. R., Accavitti, M., & Shic, F. (2016). *Do early educators' implicit biases regarding sex and race relate to behavior expectations and recommendations of preschool expulsions and suspensions* [Research study brief]. Yale University, Yale Child Study Center.

Giroux, H. A. (1981). *Ideology, culture and the process of schooling.* Falmer Press.

Glennon, T. (1995). Race, education, and the construction of a disabled class. *Wisconsin Law Review, 1995*(6), 1237–1337.

Goff, P. A., Jackson, M. C., Leone, D., Lewis, B. A., Culotta, C. M., & DiTomasso, N. A. (2014). The essence of innocence: Consequences of dehumanizing Black children. *Journal of Personality and Social Psychology, 106*(4), 526–545.

González, T. (2015). Socializing schools: Addressing racial disparities in discipline through restorative justice. In D. J. Losen (Ed.), *Closing the school discipline gap: Equitable remedies for excessive exclusion* (pp. 151–165). Teachers College Press.

Gopolan, M., & Nelson, A. (2019). Understanding the racial discipline gap in schools. *AERA Open, 5*(2) 2–26. doi.org/10.1177/2332858419844613

Gordon, B. (1990). The necessity of African American epistemology for educational theory and practice. *Journal of Education, 172*(3), 88–106.

Gorski, P. (2019, April). Avoiding racial equity detours. *Educational Leadership, 76*(7), 56–61.

Gottfredson, D. C., Crosse, S., Tang, Z., Bauer, E. L., Harmon, M. A., Hagen, C. A., & Greene, A. D. (2020). Effects of school resource officers on school crime and responses to school crime. *Criminology & Public Policy, 19*(3), 905–940.

Graham v. Connor. (1989). 490 U.S. 386, 396

Graves, D., & Mirsky, L. (2007). *American Psychological Association report challenges school zero tolerance policies and recommends restorative justice.* Restorative Practices E-Forum. www.iirp.edu/news/american-psychological-association -report-challenges-school-zero-tolerance-policies-and-recommends-restorative -justice

Grayshield, L., Rutherford, J. J., Salazar, S. B., Mihecoby, A. L., & Luna, L. L. (2015). Understanding and healing historical trauma: The perspectives of Native American elders. *Journal of Mental Health Counseling, 37*(4), 295–307.

Green, T. D. (2012). *Black male students' perceptions of student-teacher relationships and its effect on achievement* (Publication No. 1039648405) [Doctoral dissertation, Dowling College, School of Education]. ProQuest. proquest.com /docview/1039648405

Greene, R., & Winkler J. (2019). Collaborative and proactive solutions (CPS): A review of research findings in families, schools, and treatment facilities. *Clinical Child & Family Psychology Review, 22*(4), 549–561. doi.org/10.1007/s10567-019-00295-z

Greene, R. W. (2014). *Lost at school: Why our kids with behavioral challenges are falling through the cracks and how we can help them.* Scribner.

Gregory, A., Allen, J. P., Mikami, A. Y., Hafen, C. A., & Pianta, R. C. (2015). The promise of teacher professional development in reducing racial disparity in classroom exclusionary discipline. In D. J. Losen (Ed.), *Closing the school discipline gap. Equitable remedies for excessive exclusion* (pp. 166–179). Teachers College Press.

Gregory, A., Clawson, K., Davis, A., & Gerewitz, J. (2016). The promise of restorative practices to transform teacher-student relationships and achieve equity in school discipline. *Journal of Educational and Psychological Consultation, 26*(4), 325–353.

Gregory, A., & Evans, K. (2020). *The starts and stumbles of restorative justice in education: Where do we go from here?* National Education Policy Center. nepc .colorado.edu/publication/restorative-justice

Gregory, A., Hafen, C. A, Ruzek, E., Mikami, A. Y., Allen, J. P., & Pianta, R. C. (2016). Closing the racial discipline gap in classrooms by changing teacher practice. *School Psychology Review, 45*(2), 171–191.

Gregory, A., Ruzek, E., DeCoster, J., Mikami, A., & Allen, J. (2019). Focused classroom coaching and widespread racial equity in school discipline. *AERA Open, 5*(4). doi.org/10.1177%2F2332858419897274

Gregory, A., Skiba, R., & Noguera, P. (2010). The achievement gap and the discipline gap: Two sides of the same coin? *Educational Researcher, 39*(1), 59–68.

Gregory, A., Skiba, R. J., & Mediratta, K. (2017). Eliminating disparities in school discipline: A framework for intervention. *Review of Research in Education, 41*(1), 253–278. doi.org/10.3102/0091732X17690499

Gregory, A., & Weinstein, R. S. (2008). The discipline gap and African Americans: Defiance or cooperation in the high school classroom. *Journal of School Psychology, 46*(4), 455–475.

Gunn, J. (2018). *This is a student's brain on trauma.* education.cu-portland.edu/blog /classroom-resources/this-is-a-students-brain-on-trauma/

Gupta-Kagan, J. (2019). Reevaluating school searches following school-to-prison pipeline reforms. *Fordham Law Review, 87,* 2013–2067.

Gutentag, T., Horenczyk, G., & Tatar, M. (2018). Teachers' approaches toward cultural diversity predict diversity-related burnout and self-efficacy. *Journal of Teacher Education, 69*(4), 408–419. doi.org/10.1177/0022487117714244

Guyer, A. E., Nelson, E. E., & Perez-Edgar, K. (2006). Striatal functional alteration in adolescents characterized by early childhood behavioral inhibition. *The Journal of Neuroscience, 26*(24), 6399–6405. dx.doi.org/10.1523 /JNEUROSCI.0666-06.2006

Hainmueller, J. (2012). Entropy balancing for causal effects: A multivariate reweighting method to produce balanced samples in observational studies. *Political Analysis, 20*(1), 25–46.

Hamilton, L., Halverson, R., Jackson, S., Mandinach, E., Supovitz, J., & Wayman, J. (2009). *Using student achievement data to support instructional decision making* [NCEE 2009-4067]. National Center for Education Evaluation and Regional Assistance, Institute of Education Sciences, U.S. Department of Education. ies .ed.gov/ncee/wwc/publications/practice/guides/

Hanson, J. L., Hariri, A. R., & Williamson, D. E. (2015). Blunted ventral striatum development in adolescence reflects emotional neglect and predicts depressive symptoms. *Biological Psychiatry, 78*(9), 598–605.

Harris, B., Ravert, R. D., & Sullivan, A. L. (2017). Adolescent racial identity: Self-identification of multiple and "other" race/ethnicities. *Urban Education, 52*(6), 775–794. doi.org/10.1177/0042085915574527

Harris, C. I. (1995). Whiteness as property. In K. Crenshaw, N. Gotanda, G. Peller, & K. Thomas (Eds.), *Critical race theory: The key writings that formed the movement* (pp. 276–291). The New Press.

Hatch, J. A. (2002). *Doing qualitative research in education settings.* SUNY Press.

Heckman, J. (2016). *The Heckman equation* [Research summary]. heckmanequation .org/www/assets/2017/01/F_Heckman_CBAOnePager_120516.pdf

Henning, K. (2018). The challenge of race and crime in a free society: The racial divide in fifty years of juvenile justice reform. *George Washington Law Review, 86*, 1604–1666.

Hernandez-Melis, C., Fenning, P., & Lawrence, E. (2016). Effects of an alternative to suspension intervention in a therapeutic high school, *Preventing School Failure: Alternative Education for Children and Youth, 60*(3), 252–258.

Hershfeldt, P. A., Sechrest, R., Pell, K. L., Rosenberg, M. S., Bradshaw, C. P., & Leaf, P. J. (2009). Double-check: A framework of cultural responsiveness applied to classroom behavior. *Teaching Exceptional Children Plus, 6*(2), 2–18.

Hill-Collins, P. (2002). *Black feminist thought: Knowledge consciousness and the politics of empowerment.* Routledge.

Hill-Collins, P. (2009). Foreword: Building knowledge and transforming institutions. In B. T. Dill & R. E. Zambrana (Eds.), *Emerging intersections: Race, class and gender in theory policy and practice* (pp. vii–xiv). Rutgers University Press.

Hill, E. (2007, February). *Improving alternative education in California.* Legislative Analyst's Office of Sacramento, California.

Hill, L. A. (2017). Disrupting the trajectory: Representing disabled African American boys in a system designed to send them to prison. *Fordham Urban Law Journal, 45*, 201–239.

Hines, D., & Wilmot, J. (2018). From spirit-murdering to spirit-healing: Addressing anti-Black aggressions and the inhumane discipline of Black children. *Multicultural Perspectives, 20*(2), 62–69.

Hirschfield, P. J. (2008). Preparing for prison? The criminalization of school discipline in the USA. *Theoretical Criminology, 12*(1), 79–101.

Hoge, M., & Rubinstein-Avila, E. (2014). Out of sight, out of mind: A case study of an alternative school for students with emotional disturbance (ED). *Qualitative Research in Education, 3*(3) 295–319. dx.doi.org/10.4471/qre.2014.49

Holden, M., Holden, J. Kuhn, I., Mooney, A., Morgan, C., Pidgeon, N., & Taylor, R. (2001). *Therapeutic crisis intervention* (5th ed.). Cornell Family Life Development Center, Cornell University.

Homer, E. M., & Fisher, B. W. (2020). Police in schools and student arrest rates across the United States: Examining differences by race, ethnicity, and gender. *Journal of School Violence, 19*(2), 192–204.

Horner, R., Sugai, G., & Anderson, C. (2010). Examining the evidence base for School-Wide Positive Behavior Support. *Focus on Exceptional Children, 42*(8), 1–14. doi.org/10.17161/foec.v42i8.6906

Horner, R. H., Sugai, G., Lewis-Palmer, T., & Todd, A. W. (2001). Teaching school-wide behavioral expectations. *Report on Emotional and Behavioral Disorders in Youth, 1*(4), 77–79.

Hussar, B., Zhang, J., Hein, S., Wang, K., Roberts, A., Cui, J., Smith, M., Bullock Mann, F., Barmer, A., & Dilig, R. (2020). *The condition of education 2020* [NCES 2020-144]. U.S. Department of Education, National Center for Education Statistics. nces.ed.gov/pubs2020/2020144.pdf

Idaho State Department of Education (ISDE). (n.d.). *Alternative Schools.* sde.idaho .gov/school-choice/alternative/

Individuals With Disabilities Education Act, 20 U.S.C. § 1400 *et seq.* (2016)

Ingraham, C. L. (2000). Consultation through a multicultural lens: Multicultural and cross-cultural consultation in schools. *School Psychology Review, 29*(3), 320–343.

Institute of Women & Ethnic Studies. (2015). *Emotional wellness and exposure to violence.* static1.squarespace.com/static/59f78bfbf43b558afe23e48a/t/5a84a730 71c10b7697d3c5ad/1518642994026/EWS-Report-2015.pdf

Irvine, J. J. (2012). Complex relationships between multicultural education and special education: An African American perspective. *Journal of Teacher Education, 63*(4), 268–274.

J. W. v. Vallas, 10 Civ. 01925 (E.D. La., 2010). www.splcenter.org/sites/default/files /d6_legacy_files/downloads/case/J.W._complaint070810.pdf

Jackson, D., & Wolforth, S. (2021). *Integrating social & emotional learning within a multi-tiered system of supports to advance equity.* Council of Chief State School Officers. 753a0706.flowpaper.com/CCSSOSELMTSSToolkit

Jackson, K. (2019). The behavioral health care workforce shortage—Sources and solutions. *Social Work Today, 19*(3). www.socialworktoday.com/archive/MJ19p16.shtml

Jacobs, J., Gregory, A., Hoppey, D., & Yendol-Hopper, D. (2009). Data literacy: Understanding teachers' data use in a context of accountability and response to intervention. *Action in Teacher Education, 31*(3), 41–55.

Jajtner, K. M., Mitra, S., Fountain, C., & Nichols, A. (2020). Rising income inequality through a disability lens: Trends in the United States 1981–2018. *Social Indicators Research, 151*(1), 81–114. doi.org/10.1007/s11205-020-02379-8

Jimerson, J. B., & Wayman, J. C. (2015). Professional learning for using data: Examining teacher needs and supports. *Teachers College Record, 117*(4), 1–36.

Joffe-Walt, C. (Host). (2020, July 23). Nice White parents [Audio podcast episodes]. *The New York Times*. nytimes.com/2020/07/23/podcasts/nice-white-parents-serial.html

Johnson, L. (2015). From the anti-slavery movement to now: (RE) examining the relationship between critical race theory and Black feminist thought. *Race, Gender & Class (Towson, Md.)*, 22(3–4), 227–243.

Johnson, M., & Naughton, J. (2019). Just another school?: The need to strengthen legal protections for students facing disciplinary transfers. *Notre Dame Journal of Law, Ethics and Public Policy*, 33(1), 69–107. lawecommons.luc.edu/cgi/viewcontent.cgi?article=1642&context=facpubs

Jones, S. R. (1996). Toward inclusive theory: Disability as social construction. *NASPA Journal*, 33(4), 347–354. doi.org/10.1080/00220973.1996.11072421

Kauffman, J. M., & Landrum, T. J. (2013). *Characteristics of emotional and behavioral disorders in children and youth* (10th ed.). Pearson.

Kaufman, J. S., Jaser, S. S., Vaughan, E. L., Reynolds, J. S., Di Donato, J., Bernard, S. N., & Hernandez-Brereton, M. (2010). Patterns in office referral data by grade, race/ethnicity, and gender. *Journal of Positive Behavior Interventions*, 12(1), 44–54.

Kaufman, M. (2020). *Badges and incidents: A transdisciplinary history of the right to education in America*. Cambridge University Press.

Kautz, T., Heckman, J. J., Diris, R., ter Weel, B., & Borghans, L. (2014, December). *Fostering and measuring skills: Improving cognitive and non-cognitive skills to promote lifetime success*. National Bureau of Economic Research. doi.org/10.3386/w20749

Kazdin, A. E. (1980). Acceptability of alternative treatments for deviant child behavior. *Journal of Applied Behavior Analysis*, 13(2), 259–273.

Kendi, I. X. (2019). *How to be an antiracist*. One World.

Kenney, M. K., & Singh, G. K. (2016). *Adverse childhood experiences among American Indian/Alaska Native children: The 2011–2012 National Survey of Children's Health*. Scientifica. doi.org/10.1155/2016/7424239

Kerig, P. K. (2019). Linking childhood trauma exposure to adolescent justice involvement: The concept of posttraumatic risk-seeking. *Clinical Psychology: Science and Practice*, 26(3). doi.org/10.1111/cpsp.12280

K. C. v. Marshall Cty. Bd. of Educ, WL 364441 (6th Cir. 2019)

Kim, C. Y., Losen, D. J., & Hewitt, D. T. (2010). *The school-to-prison pipeline: Structuring legal reform*. New York University Press.

Kincaid, A. P., & Sullivan, A. L. (2017). Parsing the relations of race and socioeconomic status in special education disproportionality. *Remedial and Special Education*, 38(3), 159–170.

King, J. B., Jr. (2016, September 7). *School resource officers* (dear colleague letter). United States Department of Education. www2.ed.gov/documents/press-releases/secretary-sro-letter.pdf

Kirwin Institute for the Study of Race and Ethinicity. (2017). *State of the science: Implicit bias review*. kirwaninstitute.osu.edu/implicit-bias-training/resources/2017-implicit-bias-review.pdf

Kohli, R., Pizarro, M., & Nevarez, A. (2017). The "new racism" of K-12 schools: Centering critical research on racism. *Review of Research in Education, 41,* 182–202. doi.org/10.3102%2F0091732X16686949

Koonce, J. B. (2012). "Oh, those loud Black girls!": A phenomenological study of Black girls talking with an attitude. *Journal of Language & Literacy Education, 8*(2), 26–46.

Korstjens, I., & Moser, A. (2018). Series: Practical guidance to qualitative research, part 4: Trustworthiness and publishing. *European Journal of General Practice, 24*(1), 120–124.

Krahn, G. L., Walker, D. K., & Correa-De-Araujo, R. (2015). Persons with disabilities as an unrecognized health disparity population. *American Journal of Public Health (1971), 105*(S2), S198–S206. doi.org/10.2105/AJPH.2014.302182

Krezmien, M. P., Leone, P. E., & Achilles, G. M. (2006). Suspension, race, and disability: Analysis of statewide practices and reporting. *Journal of Emotional and Behavioral Disorders, 14,* 217–226. doi.org/10.1177/10634266060140040501

Kupchik, A. (2010). *Homeroom security: School discipline in an age of fear.* NYU Press.

Kupchik, A. (2019, March 11). *Researching the impact of school policing.* End Zero Tolerance. www.endzerotolerance.org/single-post/2019/03/11/research-on -the-impact-of-school-policing

Kupchik, A., & Monahan, T. (2006). The new American school: Preparation for post-industrial discipline. *British Journal of Sociology of Education, 27*(5), 617–631.

Kuppens, S., & Ceulemans, E. (2019). Parenting styles: A closer look at a well-known concept. *Journal of Child and Family Studies, 28*(1), 168–181. doi.org/10.1007 /s10826-018-1242-x

Ladson-Billings, G. (1999). Preparing teachers for diverse student populations. *Review of Research in Education, 24,* 211–244.

Ladson-Billings, G. (2008). Just what is critical race theory and what's it doing in a "nice" field like education? In L. Parker, D. Deyhle, & S. Villenas (Eds.), *Race is . . . race isn't: Critical Race theory and qualitative studies in education* (pp. 7–30). Westview Press.

Ladson-Billings, G. (2009). *The dreamkeepers: Successful teachers of African American children.* Wiley.

Ladson-Billings, G. (2021). I'm here for the hard re-set: Post pandemic pedagogy to preserve our culture. *Equity & Excellence in Education, 54*(1), 68–78. doi.org /10.1080/10665684.2020.1863883

Ladson-Billings, G., & Tate, W. (1995). Toward a critical race theory of education. *Teachers College Record, 97*(1), 47–68.

Lane, K. L. (2009). *Comprehensive, integrated, three-tiered model of prevention: Treatment integrity teacher self-report form.* www.ci3t.org/measures

Lane, K. L., & Menzies, H. M. (2003). A school-wide intervention with primary and secondary levels of support for elementary students: Outcomes and considerations. *Education and Treatment of Children, 26,* 431–451.

Lane, K. L., & Menzies, H. M. (2005). Teacher-identified students with and without academic and behavioral concerns: Characteristics and responsiveness to a school-wide intervention. *Behavioral Disorders, 31,* 65–83.

Lane, K. L., Menzies, H. M., Ennis, R. P., & Oakes, W. P. (2015). *Supporting behavior for school success: A step-by-step guide to key strategies.* Guilford.

Lane, K. L., Oakes, W. P., Buckman, M. M., & Menzies, H. M. (2022). Comprehensive Integrated, Three-Tiered (Ci3T) models of prevention: Prioritizing integrated systems. In C. J. Lemons, S. R. Powell, K. L. Lane, & T. C. Aceves (Eds.), *Handbook of Special Education Research: Research based practices and intervention innovations* (pp. 4–18). Routledge. DOI: 10.4324/9781003156888-2

Lane, K. L., Oakes, W. P., & Menzies, H. M. (2010). Systematic screenings to prevent the development of learning and behavior problems: Considerations for practitioners, researchers, and policy makers. *Journal of Disabilities Policy Studies, 21,* 160–172.

Lane, K. L., Oakes, W. P., & Menzies, H. M. (2014). Comprehensive, integrated, three-tiered models of prevention: Why does my school—and district—need an integrated approach to meet students' academic, behavioral, and social needs? *Preventing School Failure: Alternative Education for Children and Youth, 58,* 121–128. doi.org/gcmc7f

Lane, K. L., & Walker, H. M. (2015). The connection between assessment and intervention: How does screening lead to better interventions? In B. Bateman, M. Tankersley, & J. Lloyd (Eds.), *Enduring issues in special education: Personal perspectives* (pp. 283–301). Routledge.

Lasky, S., Schaffer, G., & Hopkins, T. (2008). Learning to think and talk from evidence: Developing system-wide capacity for learning conversations. In L. M. Earl & H. Timperley (Eds.), *Professional learning conversations* (pp. 95–107). Springer.

Lawson, G., & Welfare, L. E. (2018, November). "An investigation of school resource and safety programs policy and practice in Virginia." Paper presented at *American Society of Criminology*, Atlanta, GA.

Lechner, A., Cavanaugh, M., & Blyler, C. (2016). *Addressing trauma in American Indian and Alaska Native Youth.* Mathematica Policy Research Report. aspe.hhs.gov/system/files/pdf/207941/AIANYouthTIC.PDF

Legette, K. B., Rogers, L. O., & Warren, C. A. (2020, July). *Humanizing student-teacher relationships for black children: Implications for teachers' social-emotional training.* Urban Education. doi.org/10.1177/0042085920933319

Lehr, C., Lanners, E., & Lange, C. (2003, October). *Alternative schools: Policy and legislation across the United States.* Alternative Schools Research Project, Institute on Community Integration, University of Minnesota. files.eric.ed.gov/fulltext/ED502533.pdf

Lehr, C. A., Tan, C. S., & Ysseldyke, J. (2009). Alternative schools: A synthesis of state-level policy and research. *Remedial and Special Education, 30*(1), 19–32. doi.org/10.1177/0741932508315645

Leong, F. T., & Brown, M. T. (1995). Theoretical issues in cross-cultural career development: Cultural validity and cultural specificity. In W. B. Walsh & S. H. Osipow (Eds.), *Handbook of vocational psychology: Theory, research, and practice* (pp. 143–180). Erlbaum.

Leverson, M., Smith, K., McIntosh, K., Rose, J., & Pinkelman, S. (2021). *PBIS cultural responsiveness field guide: Resources for trainers and coaches.* Center on Positive Behavioral Interventions & Supports. bit.ly/pbisculturalresponsiveness

Lewis, A. E., & Diamond, J. B. (2015). *Despite the best intentions: How racial inequality thrives in good schools.* Oxford University Press.

Lincoln, Y. S. (1995). Emerging criteria for quality in qualitative and interpretive research. *Qualitative inquiry, 1*(3), 275–289.

Linton, S. (2005). What is disability studies? *PMLA : Publications of the Modern Language Association of America, 120*(2), 518–522.

Little, J. W. (2012). Understanding data use practice among teachers: The contribution of micro-process studies. *American Journal of Education, 118,* 143–166.

Lopez L., Hart L. H., & Katz, M. H. (2021). Racial and ethnic health disparities related to COVID 19. *Journal of the American Medical Association, 325*(8), 719–720. doi:10.1001/jama.2020.26443.

Losen, D. (2013, January). *National summit on disproportionality.* The Center for Civil Rights Remedies. https://civilrightsproject.ucla.edu/events/2013/closing-the -school-discipline-gap-conference-research-papers/closing-the-school-discipline -gap-research-to-practice

Losen, D. (Ed.). (2015). *Closing the school discipline gap: Equitable remedies for excessive exclusion.* Teachers College Press.

Losen, D., Hodson, C., Ee, J., & Martinez, T. (2014). Disturbing inequities: Exploring the relationship between racial disparities in special education identification and discipline. *Journal of Applied Research on Children, 5*(2), 15. digitalcommons .library.tmc.edu/childrenatrisk/vol5/iss2/15

Losen, D., Hodson, C., Keith, M., Morrison, K., & Belway, S. (2015). *Are we closing the school discipline gap?* The Center for Civil Rights Remedies. civil-rightsproject.ucla.edu/resources/projects/center-for-civil-rights-remedies/school -to-prison-folder/federal-reports/are-we-closing-the-school-discipline-gap /AreWeClosingTheSchoolDisciplineGap_FINAL221.pdf

Losen, D. J. (2011). *Discipline policies, successful schools, and racial justice.* National Education Policy Center. nepc.colorado.edu/publication/discipline-policies

Losen, D. J. (2018). *Disabling punishment: The need for remedies to the disparate loss of instruction experienced by Black students with disabilities.* The Center for Civil Rights Remedies. today.law.harvard.edu/wp-content/uploads/2018/04 /disabling-punishment-report-.pdf

Losen, D. J., & Gillespie, J. (2012). *Opportunities suspended: The disparate impact of disciplinary exclusion from school.* The Civil Rights Project.

Losen, D. J., Martinez, P., & Shin, G. H. R. (2021). *Disabling inequality: The urgent need for race-conscious resource remedies.* The Center for Civil Rights Remedies. civilrightsproject.ucla.edu/research/k-12-education/special -education/disabling-inequity-the-urgent-need-for-race-conscious-resource- remedies

Louisiana Budget Project. (2018, September 13). *New Orleans poverty rate top among U.S. metros.* www.labudget.org/2018/09/new-orleans-poverty-rate-tops -among-u-s-metros/

Louisiana Department of Education. (n.d.). *2015–2016 Louisiana special education data profile.* louisianabelieves.com/docs/default-source/academics/2015-16-special -education-data-profile.pdf?sfvrsn=e1e6971f_7

Love, B. J. (2004). *Brown* plus 50 counter-storytelling: A critical race theory analysis of the "majoritarian achievement gap" story. *Equity & Excellence in Education, 37*(3), 227–246. doi.org/10.1080/10665680490491597

Love, B. L. (2016). Anti-Black state violence, classroom edition: The spirit murdering of Black children. *Journal of Curriculum and Pedagogy, 13*(1), 22–25.

Lynn-Whaley, J., & Gard, A. (2012). Neuroscience behind misbehavior: Reimagining how schools discipline youth. In J. S. Kaye, K. R. DeCataldo, & T. A. Lang (Eds.), *Keeping kids in school and out of court: A collection of reports to inform the national leadership summit on school-justice partnerships* (pp. 26–39). New York State Permanent Judicial Commission on Justice for Children.

Lyons, H. Z., Bike, D. H., Johnson, A., & Bethea, A. (2011). Culturally competent qualitative research with people of African descent. *Journal of Black Psychology, 38*(2), 153–171.

Maggin, D. M., Zurheide, J., Pickett, K. C., & Baillie, S. J. (2015). A systematic evidence review of the Check-In/Check-Out program for reducing student challenging behaviors. *Journal of Positive Behavior Interventions, 17*, 197–208.

Malcolm, K. (2018). School discipline: Is developmental appropriateness required? *Children's Legal Rights Journal, 38*, 169–173.

Mandinach, E. B. (2012). A perfect time for data use: Using data-driven decision making to inform practice. *Educational Psychologist, 47*, 71–85.

Mandinach, E. B., & Gummer, E. S. (2016). What does it mean for teachers to be data literate: Laying out the skills, knowledge, and dispositions. *Teaching and Teacher Education, 60*, 366–376.

Matsuda, M. J., Lawrence, C. R., Delgado, R., & Crenshaw, K. (1993). *Words that wound: Critical race theory, assaultive speech, and the First Amendment.* Westview.

Mavropoulou, S., & Padeliadu, S. (2002). Teachers' causal attributions for behavior problems in relation to perception of control. *Educational Psychology, 22*, 191–202.

May, S., Ard, W.I., Todd, A. W., Horner, R. H., Glasgow, A., Sugai, G., & Sprague, J. R. (2013). *School-wide information system. Educational and Community Supports.* University of Oregon.

Mayer, G. R. (1995). Preventing antisocial behavior in the schools. *Journal of Applied Behavior Analysis, 28*(4), 467–478. doi.org/10.1901/jaba.1995.28-467

Mayes, T. A. (1999). Corporate formation as sacrament. *Legal Studies Forum, 23*, 467–478.

Mayes, T. A. (2003). Persons with autism and criminal justice: Core concepts and leading cases. *Journal of Positive Behavior Interventions, 5*, 92–100.

Mayes, T. A. (2018). Keeping the "I" in the IDEA: A response to a proposal to abandon individualization in special education in favor of rule-based delivery models. *BYU Education & Law Journal, 2018*, 141–157.

Mayes, T. A. (2019). A brief model for explaining dispute resolution options in special education. *Ohio State Journal on Dispute Resolution, 34*, 153–170.

Mayes, T. A., & Zirkel, P. A. (2000). Disclosure of special education students' records: Do the 1999 IDEA regulations mandate that schools comply with FERPA? *Journal of Law and Policy, 8*, 455–479.

McAllister, G., & Irvine, J. J. (2000). Cross cultural competency and multicultural teacher education. *Review of Educational Research*, *70*(1), 3–24. doi.org /10.3102/00346543070001003

McCadden v. City of Flint, 18-12377, 2019 WL 1584548 (E.D. Mich. 2019)

McCall, Z., & Skrtic, T. M. (2009). Intersectional needs politics: A policy frame for the wicked problem of disproportionality. *Multiple Voices for Ethnically Diverse Exceptional Learners*, *11*(2), 3–23.

McCold, P. (2006). The recent history of restorative justice: Mediation, circles, and conferencing. In D. Sullivan & L. Tifft (Eds.), *Handbook of restorative justice: A global perspective* (pp. 23–51). Routledge.

McCurdy, B. L., Mannella, M. C., & Eldridge, N. (2003). Positive behavior support in urban schools: Can we prevent the escalation of antisocial behavior? *Journal of Positive Behavioral Interventions*, *5*(3), 158–170. doi.org/10.1177/10983007030050030501

McIntosh, K., Ellwood, K., McCall, L., & Girvan, E. J. (2018). Using discipline data to enhance equity in school discipline. *Intervention in School and Clinic*, *53*(3), 146–152. doi.org/10.1177/1053451217702130

McIntosh, K., Flannery, K. B., Sugai, G., Braun, D. H., & Cochrane, K. (2008). Relationships between academics and problem behavior in the transition from middle school to high school. *Journal of Positive Behavior Interventions*, *10*(4), 243–255. doi.org/10.1177/1098300708318961

McIntosh, K., Girvan, E., Horner, R., & Smolkowski, K. (2014). Education not incarceration: A conceptual model for reducing racial and ethnic disproportionality in school discipline, *Journal of Applied Research on Children*, *5*(2), 1–22. digitalcommons.library.tmc.edu/childrenatrisk/vol5/iss2/4

McIntosh, K., & Goodman, S. (2016). *Integrated multi-tiered systems of support: Blending RTI and PBIS*. Guilford.

McIntosh, K., Moniz, C., Craft, C. B., Golby, R., & Steinwand-Deschambeault, T. (2014). Implementing school-wide positive behavioural interventions and supports to better meet the needs of indigenous students. *Canadian Journal of School Psychology*, *29*(3), 236–257. doi.org/10.1177/0829573514542217

McLaughlin, K. A., & Sheridan, M. A. (2016). Beyond cumulative risk: A dimensional approach to childhood adversity. *Current Directions in Psychological Science*, *25*(4), 239–245. doi.org/10.1177/0963721416655883

McQuiller, M. V. (2019). Enough is enough: Congressional solutions to curb gun violence in America's K–12 schools. *DePaul Journal for Social Justice*, *12*, 1–21.

Meade, W. (2019). Handcuffs in schools: Do school resource officers fill a role in special education? *Journal of Cases in Educational Leadership*, *22*(1), 73–82.

Medaris, M. L., Campbell, E., & James, B. (1997). *Sharing information: A guide to the Family Educational Rights and Privacy Act and participation in juvenile justice programs*. U.S. Department of Justice, Office of Juvenile Justice and Delinquency Prevention.

Melloy, K. J., & Murry, F. R. (2019). A conceptual framework: Creating socially just schools for students with emotional and behavioral disabilities. *World Journal of Education*, *9*(5), 113–124.

Merkwae, A. (2015). Schooling the police: Race, disability, and the conduct of school resource officers. *Michigan Journal of Race and Law, 21,* 147–181.

Merriam, S. (2009). *Qualitative research: A guide to design and implementation.* Jossey-Bass.

Meyer, M. M., & Behar-Horenstein, L. S. (2015). When leadership matters: Perspectives from a teacher team implementing response to intervention. *Education and Treatment of Children, 38,* 383–402. doi.org/10.1353/etc.2015.0022

Migliarini, V., & Annamma, S. A. (2020). Classroom and behavior management: (Re) conceptualization through disability critical race theory. In R. Papa (Ed.), *Handbook on promoting social justice in education* (pp. 1–22). Springer. doi .org/10.1007/978-3-319-74078-2_95-2

Miller, S. L. (2020). Alternative education in American schools: An overrepresentation of minority placement from the school to the prison pipeline. *International Journal of Organizational Behavior in Education, 8*(1), 1–6.

Miller-Cotto, D., & Byrnes, J. P. (2016). Ethnic/racial identity and academic achievement: A meta-analytic review. *Developmental Review, 41,* 51–70. doi .org/10.1016/j.dr.2016.06.003

Milner, R. H., & Howard, T. (2004). Black teachers, Black students, Black communities, and Brown: Perspectives and insights from experts. *The Journal of Negro Education, 73*(3), 285–297.

Milner, H. R., IV, Cunningham, H. B., Delale-O'Connor, L., & Kestenberg, E. G. (2018). *"These kids are out of control": Why we must reimagine classroom management for equity.* Corwin.

Minnow, M. (1990). *Making all the difference: Inclusion, exclusion, and American law.* Cornell University Press.

Miu, A. C., Bilc, M. I., Bunea, I., & Szentagotai-Tatar, A. (2017). Childhood trauma and sensitivity to reward and punishment: Implications for depressive and anxiety symptoms. *Personality & Individual Differences, 119*(1), 134–140. doi .org/10.1016/j.paid.2017.07.015

Moody, M. (2016). From under-diagnoses to over-representation: Black children, ADHD, and the school-to-prison pipeline. *Journal of African American Studies, 20*(2), 152–163. doi.org/10.1007/s12111-016-9325-5

Monell v. New York City Department of Social Services, 436 U.S. 658 (1978)

Moradi, B., & Grzanka, P. R. (2017). Using intersectionality responsibly: Toward critical epistemology, structural analysis, and social justice activism. *Journal of Counseling Psychology, 64*(5), 500–513. doi.org/10.1037/cou0000203

Morgan, P. L., & Farkas, G. (2016). Evidence and implications of racial and ethnic disparities in emotional and behavioral disorders identification and treatment. *Behavioral Disorders, 41*(2), 122–131. doi.org/10.17988/0198-7429-41.2.122

Morgan, P. L., Farkas, G., Tufis, P. A., & Sperling, R. A. (2008). Are reading and behavior problems risk factors for each other? *Journal of Learning Disabilities, 41*(5), 417–436. doi.org/10.1177/0022219408321123

Morris, E. W. (2005). "Tuck in that shirt!" Race, class, gender, and discipline in an urban school. *Sociological Perspectives, 48*(1), 25–48.

Morris, M. W. (2016). *Pushout: the criminalization of Black girls in schools*. The New Press.

Musgrove, M. (2011, January 21). *A Response to Intervention (RTI) process cannot be used to delay-deny an evaluation for eligibility under the Individuals with Disabilities Education Act (IDEA)* (Memorandum). Office of Special Education and Rehabilitative Services, U.S. Department of Education. www2.ed.gov/policy/speced/guid/idea/memosdcltrs/osep11-07rtimemo.pdf

Musu-Gillette, L., Zhang, A., Wang, K., Zhang, J., Kemp, J., Diliberti, M., & Oudekerk, B. A. (2018). [NCES 2018-036/NCJ 251413]. National Center for Education Statistics. nces.ed.gov/pubsearch/pubsinfo.asp?pubid=2018036

N.M. Code R. § 6.11.2. (2020)

N.M. Stat. Ann. § 22-5-4.3. (2021)

Na, C., & Gottfredson, D. C. (2013). Police officers in schools: Effects on school crime and the processing of offending behaviors. *Justice Quarterly, 30*(4), 619–650.

Nance, J. P. (2019). Implicit racial bias and students' Fourth Amendment rights. *Indiana Law Journal, 94*, 47–102.

National Association of School Psychologists. (2016). *Integrated model of academic and behavioral supports* [Position statement]. https://www.nasponline.org/research-and-policy/policy-priorities/position-statements

National Association of School Psychologists. (2020, August 13). *National organizations call for rigorous training and appropriate use of school resource officers* (Press release). www.nasponline.org/about-school-psychology/media-room/press-releases/national-organizations-call-for-rigorous-training-and-appropriate-use-of-school-resource-officers

National Association of School Psychologists. (2021). *Shortages in school psychology: Challenges to meeting the growing needs of U.S. students and schools* [Research summary]. https://www.nasponline.org/research-and-policy/policy-priorities/critical-policy-issues/shortage-of-school-psychologists

National Association of School Resource Officers. (2012). *To protect and educate: The school resource officer and the prevention of violence in schools*. Canady, M., James, B., & Nease, J. www.nasro.org/clientuploads/resources/NASRO-Protect-and-Educate.pdf

National Association of State Boards of Education. (2019, January). The NASBE Interview. *The State Education Standard*, 45–46.

National Center for Education Statistics. (2017). *Crime, violence, discipline and safety in U.S. public schools*. nces.ed.gov/pubs2017/2017122.pdf

National Center for Education Statistics. (2020a). *Public school district data for the 2018–2019, 2019–2020 school years*. nces.ed.gov/ccd/districtsearch/index.asp

National Center for Education Statistics. (2020b, May). *Students with disabilities*. hnces.ed.gov/programs/coe/indicator_cgg.asp

National Center for Education Statistics. (2020c). *Students with disabilities*. nces.ed.gov/programs/coe/indicator_cgg.asp

National Center on Safe and Supportive Learning Environments. (n.d.). *School discipline laws & regulations by state & category*. safesupportivelearning.ed.gov/discipline-compendium/choose-type/all/all

National Child Traumatic Stress Network. (2017). *Addressing race and trauma in the classroom: A resource for educators.* www.nctsn.org/sites/default/files/resources //addressing_race_and_trauma_in_the_classroom_educators.pdf

National Congress of American Indians. (2018). *Tribal leaders toolkit.* www.ncai.org /Education_Data_Checklist_FINAL_10_2018.pdf

National Education Association. (n.d.). *Implementing racial justice.* www.nea .org/professional-excellence/just-equitable-schools/core-values/implementing -racial-justice

Navajo Courts. (2012). *Peacemaking program of the judicial branch of the Navajo Nation.* www.courts.navajo-nsn.gov//Peacemaking/Plan/PPPO2013-2-25.pdf

Neville, H. A., Coleman, M. N., Falconer, J. W., & Holmes, D. (2005). Color-blind racial ideology and psychological false consciousness among African Americans. *Journal of Black Psychology, 31*(1), 27–45.

Newcomer, J. R., & Zirkel, P. A. (1999). An analysis of judicial outcomes of special education cases. *Exceptional Children, 65,* 469–480.

New Mexico Advisory Council to the U.S. Commission on Civil Rights. (2005). *The Farmington report: Civil rights for Native Americans 30 years later.* www.usccr .gov/pubs/docs/122705_FarmingtonReport.pdf

Newell, M., Kaundinya, P., & Gaona, M. (2020). Theoretical foundations of diversity in school psychology. In K. Kelly, A. Garbacz, & C. Albers (Eds.), *Theories of school psychology* (pp. 22–49). Routledge.

Newell, M., & Kratochwill, T. R. (2007). The integration of response to intervention and critical race theory-disability studies: A robust approach to reducing racial discrimination in evaluation decisions. In S. R. Jimerson, M. K. Burns, & A. M. VanDerHeyden (Eds.), *Handbook of response to intervention: The science and practice of assessment and intervention* (pp. 65–79). Springer Science. doi .org/10.1007/978-0-387-49053-3_5

Newell, M. L., & Chavez-Korell, S. (2017). The evolution of multiculturalism: An interdisciplinary perspective. In E. C. Lopez, S. G. Nahari, & S. L. Proctor (Eds.), Handbook of multicultural school psychology (pp. 3–17). Routledge.

Nickerson, A., & Jimerson, S. R. (2015). *Supporting students experiencing childhood trauma: Tips for parents and educators.* National Association of School Psychologists. bit.ly/nasptrauma

Noguera, P. (2003). Schools, prisons and social implications of punishment: Rethinking disciplinary practices. *Theory into Practice, 42*(4), 341–350.

Nowicki, J. M. (2018). *K–12 education: Discipline disparities for black students, boys, and students with disabilities.* Report to Congressional Requesters [GAO-18-258]. U.S Government Accountability Office.

Obidah, J., Jackson-Minot, M., Monroe, C., & Williams, B. (2004). Crime and punishment: Moral dilemmas in the inner-city classroom. In V. Siddle-Walker & J. R. Snarey (Eds.), *Race-ing moral formation: African American perspectives on care and justice* (pp. 111–129). Teachers College Press.

Ogbu, J. U. (1985). Research currents: Cultural-ecological influences on minority school learning. *Language Arts, 62*(8), 860–869.

Ogbu, J. U. (1987). Variability in minority school performance: A problem in search of an explanation. *Anthropology & Education Quarterly, 18*(4), 312–334.

Okonofua, J. A., Paunesku, D., & Walton, G. M. (2016). Brief intervention to encourage empathic discipline cuts suspension rates in half among adolescents. *Proceedings of the National Academy of Science*, 113(9), 5221–5226.

Orgoványi-Gajdos, J. (2016). *Teachers' professional development on problem solving: Theory and practice for teachers and teacher educators*. Sense.

Osher, D., Fisher, D., Amos, L., Katz, J., Dwyer, K., Duffey, T., & Colombi, G. D. (2015). *Addressing the root causes of disparities in school discipline: An educator's action planning guide*. National Center on Safe Supportive Learning Environments. safesupportivelearning.ed.gov/addressing-root-causesdisparities-school-discipline

P.B. v. Pastorek. (2010). Case No. 10 Civ. 04049. (E.D. La., 2010). www.splcenter.org/seeking-justice/case-docket/pb-et-al-v-pastorek

P.P. v. Compton Unified School District, 135 F.Supp.3d 1098 (C.D. Cal. 2015)

Paskus, L., & Furlow, B. (2015). *Native youth face higher suicide risk*. New Mexico in Depth. nmindepth.com/2015/05/26/native-american-youth-face-higher-suicide-risk/

Pearson v. Callahan, 555 U.S. 223 (2009)

Perry, B. L., & Morris, E. W. (2014). Suspending progress: Collateral consequences of exclusionary punishment in public schools. *American Sociological Review*, 79(6), 1067–1087.

Perzigian, A. B., Afacan, K., Justin, W., & Wilkerson, K. L. (2017). Characteristics of students in traditional versus alternative high schools: A cross-sectional analysis of enrollment in one urban district. *Education and Urban Society*, 49(7), 676–700. doi.org/10.1177/0013124516658520

Petrosino, A., Guckenburg, S., & Fronius, T. (2012). 'Policing schools' strategies: A review of the evaluation evidence. *Journal of Multidisciplinary Evaluation*, 8(17), 80–101.

Phi Delta Kappa. (2018, May). *PDK poll of the public's attitudes toward the public schools: School security results*. pdkpoll.org/assets/downloads/3PDKPoll2018_School-Security-Report_FINAL-x.pdf

Phinney, J. S. (1991). Ethnic identity and self-esteem: A review and integration. *Hispanic Journal of Behavioral Sciences*, 13(2), 193–208. doi.org/10.1177/07399863910132005

Polanco-Roman, L., Danies, A., & Anglin, D. M. (2016). Racial discrimination as race-based trauma, coping strategies, and dissociative symptoms among emerging adults. *Psychological trauma: Theory, Research, Practice and Policy*, 8(5), 609–617. doi.org/10.1037/tra0000125

Polat, N. (2010). A comparative analysis of pre- and in-service teacher beliefs about readiness and self-competency: Revisiting teacher education for ELLs. *System*, 38(2), 228–244. doi.org/10.1016/j.system.2010.03.004

Polit, D. F., & Beck, C. T. (2014). *Essentials of nursing research: Appraising evidence for nursing practice* (8th ed.). Wolters Kluwer/Lippincott Williams & Wilkins.

Ponterotto, J. G., & Park-Taylor, J. (2007). Racial and ethnic identity theory, measurement, and research in counseling psychology: Present status and future directions. *Journal of Counseling Psychology*, 54(3), 282–294. doi.org/10.1037/0022-0167.54.3.282

Postsecondary National Policy Institute. (2020, November 17). *Native American students in higher education.* pnpi.org/native-american-students/

Powers, K., Potthoff, S., Bearinger, L., & Resnick, M. (2003). Does cultural programming improve educational outcomes for American Indian youth? *Journal of American Indian Education, 42*(2), 17–49. www.jstor.org/stable/24398758

Prasse, D. (n.d.). *Why adopt an RtI model?* www.rtinetwork.org/learn/what/whyrti

Proctor, S. L., & Meyers, J. (2014). Best practices in primary prevention in diverse schools and communities. In P. Harrison & A. Thomas (Eds.), *Best practices in school psychology: Foundations* (pp. 33–47). National Association of School Psychologists.

Proctor, S. L., & Owens, C. (2019). School psychology graduate education retention research characteristics: Implications for diversity initiatives in the profession. *Psychology in the Schools, 56*(6), 1037–1052. doi.org/10.1002/pits.22228

Quintana, S. M., Troyano, N., & Taylor, G. (2001). Cultural validity and inherent challenges in quantitative methods for multicultural research. In J. G. Ponterotto, J. M. Casas, L. A. Suzuki, & C. M. Alexander (Eds.), *Handbook of multicultural counseling* (pp. 604–630). SAGE.

Racial Wealth Divide Initiative, Prosperity Now. (2016). *The racial wealth divide in New Orleans.* prosperitynow.org/files/resources/Racial_Wealth_Divide_in_New _Orleans_OptimizedforScreenReaders.pdf

Rafa, A. (2019, January). *The status of school discipline in state policy.* Education Commission of the States. www.ecs.org/the-status-of-school-discipline-in-state-policy/

Rappaport, M. (2014). *Building Bridges: An alternative to school suspension.* Bridges, LLC.

Rappaport, M. (2018). *Building more bridges.* CreateSpace.

Rappaport, M., & Coleman, S. L. (2016). *The suspension question: Bridging the gap between prevention, intervention, and suspension.* CreateSpace.

Redfield, S. E., & Nance, J. P. (2016). *School-to-prison pipeline: Preliminary report.* American Bar Association.

Reed, K. N., Fenning, P., Johnson, M., & Mayworm, A. (2020). Promoting statewide discipline reform through professional development with administrators. *Preventing School Failure: Alternative Education for Children and Youth, 64*(2), 172–182. doi.org/10.1080/1045988X.2020.1716674

Reid, D. K., & Knight, M. G. (2006). Disability justifies exclusion of minority students: A critical history grounded in disability studies. *Educational Researcher, 35*(6), 18–23. doi.org/10.3102/0013189X035006018

Reise, S. P., Bonifay, W. E., & Haviland, M. G. (2013). Scoring and modeling psychological measures in the presence of multidimensionality. *Journal of Personality Assessment, 95*(2), 129–140. doi.org/10.1080/00223891.2012.725437

Restorative Justice Colorado. (2021). *Restorative practices in schools.* rjcolorado.org /restorative-justice/restorative-practices-in-schools

Reynolds, C. R., & Kamphaus, R. W. (2015). *Behavior assessment for children: Third edition* (BASC-3) [Assessment Instrument]. Pearson.

Richardson, F. C., & Fowers, B. J. (1997). Critical theory, postmodernism, and hermeneutics: Insights for critical psychology. In D. Fox & I. Prilleltensky (Eds.), *Critical psychology: An introduction* (pp. 265–283). SAGE.

Robert Wood Johnson Foundation. (2015). *Menominee Nation.* www.rwjf.org/en /library/articles-and-news/2015/10/coh-prize-menominee-wi.html

Robert Wood Johnson Foundation. (2019). *Building a Culture of Health: San Juan County, New Mexico.* www.rwjf.org/en/cultureofhealth/what-were-learning /sentinel-communities/san-juan-county-new-mexico.html

Roberts, M. (2010). Toward a theory of culturally relevant critical teacher care: African American teachers' definitions and perceptions of care for African American students, *Journal of Moral Education, 39*(4), 449–467.

Rogers, D., & Webb, J. (1991). The ethic of caring in teacher education. *Journal of Teacher Education, 42*(3), 173–181. doi.org/10.1177/002248719104200303

Rothstein, R. (2015). The racial achievement gap, segregated schools, and segregated neighborhoods: A constitutional insult. *Race and Social Problems, 7,* 21–30. doi .org/10.1007/s12552-014-9134-1

Rothstein, R. (2017). *The color of law: A forgotten history of how our government segregated America.* Liveright.

Rumberger, R., & Losen, J. (2016). *The high cost of harsh discipline and its disparate impact.* The Center for Civil Rights Remedies. escholarship.org/uc /item/85m2m6sj

Rumberger, R. W. (2015). *Student mobility: causes, consequences, and solutions.* National Education Policy Center. nepc.colorado.edu/publication/student-mobility

Ryan, J. B., Katsiyannis, A., Counts, J. M., & Shelnut, J. C. (2018). The growing concerns regarding school resource officers. *Intervention in School and Clinic, 53,* 188–192. doi.org/10.1177/1053451217702108

Sailor, W., Skrtic, T. M., Cohn, M., & Olmstead, C. (2021). Preparing teacher educators for statewide scale-up of multi-tiered systems of support (MTSS). *Teacher Education and Special Education, 44*(1), 24–41. doi.org/10.1177%2F0888406420938035

Salazar, D. J., Clauson, S., Abel, T. D., & Clauson, A. (2019). Race, income, and environmental inequality in the U.S. states, 1990–2014. *Social Science Quarterly, 100*(3), 592–603. doi.org/10.1111/ssqu.12608

Sarker, S., Lau, F., & Sahay, S. (2000). Using an adapted grounded theory approach for inductive theory building about virtual team development. *ACM SIGMIS Database: The DATABASE for Advances in Information Systems, 32*(1), 38–56.

Sawchuk, S. (2020, June 26). More school districts sever ties with police. Will others follow? *Education Week.* www.edweek.org/leadership/more-school-districts -sever-ties-with-police-will-others-follow/2020/06

Sawchuk, S., Schwartz, S., Pendharkar, E., & Najarro, I. (2021, June 4). Defunded, removed, and put in check: School police a year after George Floyd. *Education Week.* www.edweek.org/leadership/defunded-removed-and-put-in-check-school -police-a-year-after-george-floyd/2021/06

Schiff, M., & Bazemore, G. (2012). "Whose kids are these?" Juvenile justice and education partnerships using restorative justice to end the "school-to-prison pipeline." In J. S. Kaye, K. R. DeCataldo, & T. A. Lang (Eds.), *Keeping kids in school and out of court: A collection of reports to inform the national leadership summit on school-justice partnerships* (pp. 68–82). New York State Permanent Judicial Commission on Justice for Children.

Schulte, A. C., Stevens, J. J., Elliott, S. N., Tindal, G., & Nese, J. F. T. (2016). Achieve-ment gaps for students with disabilities: Stable, widening, or narrowing on a state-wide reading comprehension test? *Journal of Educational Psychology, 108*, 925–942.

Section 504 of the Rehabilitation Act of 1973, 29 U.S.C. § 794 (2016)

Section 504 Regulations, 34 C.F.R. Part 104 (2017)

Seelau, R. (2012). Regaining control over the children: Reversing the legacy of as-similative policies in education, child welfare, and juvenile justice that targeted Native American Youth. *American Indian Law Review, 37*(1), 63–108. www .jstor.org/stable/41940641

Shakespeare, T. (2006). The social model of disability. In L. J. Davis (Ed.), *The Dis-ability Studies Reader* (2nd ed, pp. 197–204). Taylor & Francis.

Sharkey, J., & Fenning, P. (2012). Rationale for designing school contexts in support of proactive discipline. *Journal of School Violence, 11*(2), 95–104.

Shaver, E. A., & Decker, J. R. (2017). Handcuffing a third grader?: Interactions between school resource officers and students with disabilities. *Utah Law Re-view, 2017*, 229–282.

Shedd, C. (2015). *Unequal city: Race, schools, and perceptions of injustice*. Russell Sage Foundation.

Simon, J. (2007). *Governing through crime: How the war on crime transformed American democracy and created a culture of fear*. Oxford University Press.

Simonsen, B., Fairbanks, S., Briesch, A., Myers, D., & Sugai, G. (2008). Evidence-based practices in classroom management: Considerations for research to prac-tice. *Education and Treatment of Children, 31*(3), 351–380. www.jstor.org /stable/42899983

Siwatu, K. O. (2007). Preservice teachers' culturally responsive teaching self-efficacy and outcome expectancy beliefs. *Teaching and Teacher Education, 23*(7), 1086–1101. doi.org/10.1016/j.tate.2006.07.011

Siwatu, K. O., Putman, S. M., Starker-Glass, T. V., & Lewis, C. W. (2015). The Culturally Responsive Classroom Management Self-Efficacy Scale: De-velopment and initial validation. *Urban Education, 52*(7), 862–888. *doi .org/10.1177/0042085915602534*

Skiba, R., & Williams, N. (2014). *Are Black kids worse? Myths and facts about racial differences in behavior*. The Equity Project, Indiana University. www.justice4all .org/wp-content/uploads/2016/04/Are-Black-Kids-Worse-Myths-and-Facts -About-Racial-Differences-in-Behavior.pdf

Skiba, R. J. (2002). Special education and school discipline: A precarious balance. *Behavioral Disorders, 27*(2), 81–97.

Skiba, R. J., Arredondo, M. I., Gray, C., & Rausch, M. K. (2016). What do we know about discipline disparities? New and emerging research. In R. Skiba, K. Medi-ratta, & M. Karega (Eds.), *Inequality in school discipline: Research and practice to reduce disparities* (pp. 21–38). Palgrave.

Skiba, R. J., Chung, C. G., Trachok, M., Baker, T. L., Sheya, A., & Hughes, R. L. (2014). Parsing disciplinary disproportionality: Contributions of infrac-tion, student, and school characteristics to out-of-school suspension and expulsion. *American Educational Research Journal, 51*(4), 640–670. doi. org/10.3102/0002831214541670

Skiba, R. J., Horner, R. H., Chung, C.-G., Rausch, M. K., May, S. L., & Tobin, T. (2011). Race is not neutral: A national investigation of African American and Latino disproportionality in school discipline. *School Psychology Review, 40*(1), 85–107.

Skiba, R. J., Michael, R. S., Nardo, A. C., & Peterson, R. L. (2002). The color of discipline: Sources of racial and gender disproportionality in school punishment. *The Urban Review, 34*(4), 317–342. doi.org/10.1023/A:1021320817372

Skiba, R. J., Simmons, A. B., Ritter, S., Gibb, A. C., Rausch, M. K., Cuadrado, J., & Chung, C. G. (2008). Achieving equity in special education: History, status, and current challenges. *Exceptional Children, 74*(3), 264–288.

Smedley, A., & Smedley, B. D. (2005). Race as biology is fiction, racism as a social problem is real: Anthropological and historical perspectives on the social construction of race. *The American Psychologist, 60*(1), 16–26. doi .org/10.1037/0003-066X.60.1.16

Smedley, B. D., Stith, A. Y., & Care, C. (Eds.). (2003). *Unequal treatment: Confronting racial and ethnic disparities in health care.* National Academies Press. doi .org/10.17226/12875

Solórzano, D. G., & Yosso, T. J. (2002). Critical race methodology: Counter-storytelling as an analytical framework for education research. *Qualitative Inquiry, 8*(1), 23–44.

Song, S. Y., Wang, C., Espelage, D. L., Fenning, P. A., & Jimerson, S. R. (2020). COVID-19 and school psychology: Adaptations and new directions for the field. *School Psychology Review, 49*(4), 431–437, doi.org/10.1080/2372966X.2020.1852852

Soodak, L. C., & Podell, D. M. (1994). Teachers' thinking about difficult-to-teach students. *Journal of Educational Research, 88*, 44–51.

Southern Poverty Law Center. (2010, July 8). *SPLC sues to protect children in New Orleans school after first-grader handcuffed.* www.splcenter.org/news/2010/07/08 /splc-sues-protect-children-new-orleans-school-after-first-grader-handcuffed

Spillane, J. P. (2012). Conceptualizing the data-based decision-making phenomena. *American Journal of Education, 118*, 113–141.

Staats, C. (2015–2016). Understanding implicit bias: What educators should know. *American Educator, 29*, 29–43. www.aft.org/sites/default/files/ae _winter2015staats.pdf

Stanard, C. (2016). *A DisCrit narrative case study: How are the cards stacked in alternative school for African American students with disabilities?* [Unpublished doctoral dissertation]. Kennesaw State University. digitalcommons.kennesaw .edu/speceddoc_etd/2/

Stanford, S., & Muhammad, B. (2018). The confluence of language and learning disorders and the school-to-prison pipeline among minority students of color: A critical race theory. *American University Journal of Gender, Social Policy & the Law, 26*, 691–718.

Stecker, P. M., Fuchs, L. S., & Fuchs, D. (2005). Using curriculum-based measurement to improve student achievement: A review of research. *Psychology in the Schools, 42*, 795–819.

Stecklow, W. (2021, January–February). Qualified immunity: Is the end near? *New York State Bar Association Journal, 93*(1), 22–25. nysba.org/app/uploads /2020/12/Journal_JanFeb_2021_web1.pdf

Steinberg, M., & Lacoe, J. (2017). What do we know about school discipline reform? Assessing the alternative to suspensions and expulsions. *Education Next, 17*(1), 44–52.

Stephen C. v. Bureau of Indian Education, No. CV-17-08004-PCT-SPL, 2018 WL 1871457 (D. Ariz. March 29, 2018)

Stephens, N. M., Fryberg, S. A., Markus, H. R., Johnson, C. S., & Covarrubias, R. (2012). Unseen disadvantage: How American universities' focus on independence undermines the academic performance of first-generation college students. *Journal of Personality and Social Psychology, 102*(6), 1178.

Stephens, N. M., Townsend, S. S., & Dittmann, A. G. (2019). Social-class disparities in higher education and professional workplaces: The role of cultural mismatch. *Current Directions in Psychological Science, 28*(1), 67–73.

Stephens, N. M., Townsend, S. S., Markus, H. R., & Phillips, L. T. (2012). A cultural mismatch: Independent cultural norms produce greater increases in cortisol and more negative emotions among first-generation college students. *Journal of Experimental Social Psychology, 48*(6), 1389–1393.

Stevenson, H. C., Jr. (Ed.). (2003). *Playing with anger: Teaching coping to African American boys through athletics and culture.* Greenwood.

Stutzman Amstutz, L., & Mullet, J. (2005). *The Little Book of Restorative Discipline for Schools.* Intercourse, Pennsylvania: Good Books.

Substance Abuse and Mental Health Services Association. (2014). *SAMHSA's concept of trauma and guidance for a trauma-informed approach.* ncsacw.samhsa.gov /userfiles/files/SAMHSA_Trauma.pdf

Sullivan, A. L., Klingbeil, D. A., & Van Norman, E. R. (2013). Beyond behavior: Multilevel analysis of the influence of sociodemographics and school characteristics on students' risk of suspension, *School Psychology Review, 42*(1), 99–114. doi. org/10.1080/02796015.2013.12087493

Sullivan, A. L., & Osher, D. (2019). IDEA's double bind: A synthesis of disproportionality policy interpretations. *Exceptional Children, 85*(4), 395–412. doi.org/10.1177/0014402918818047

Sullivan, A. L., Sadeh, S., & Houri, A. K. (2019). Are school psychologists' special education eligibility decisions reliable and unbiased? A multi-study experimental investigation. *Journal of School Psychology, 77*, 90–109. doi.org/10.1016 /j.jsp.2019.10.006

Sullivan, A. L., Weeks, M., Kulkarni, T., Nguyen, T., Kendrick-Dunn, T. B., & Barrett, C. (2020). Historical foundations of health disparities: A primer for school psychologists to advance social justice. *Communiqué, 49*(2), 30–32.

Superville, D. R. (2020, August 17). The police in schools debate needs more nuance, ed groups say. *Education Week.* www.edweek.org/education/the-police -in-schools-debate-needs-more-nuance-ed-groups-say/2020/08

Swenson, S., & Ryder, R. (2016, August 1). *Inclusion of behavioral supports in IEPs* [Dear colleague letter]. U.S. Department of Education. sites.ed.gov/idea/files/dcl -on-pbis-in-ieps-08-01-2016.pdf

Terrades, V., & Khan, S. H. (2018). Will it ever end? Preventing mass shootings in Florida and the U.S. *Suffolk Law Review, 51,* 505–534.

Teske, S. C., Huff, B., & Graves, C. (2012). Collaborative role of courts in promoting outcomes for students: The relationship between arrests, graduation rates, and school safety. In J. S. Kaye, K. R. DeCataldo, & T. A. Lang (Eds.), *Keeping kids in school and out of court: A collection of reports to inform the national leadership summit on school-justice partnerships* (pp. 128–141). New York State Permanent Judicial Commission on Justice for Children.

Theriot, M., & Dupper, D. (2010). Student discipline problems and the transition from elementary to middle School. *Education and Urban Society, 42*(2), 205–222. doi .org/10.1177/0013124509349583

Theriot, M. T. (2009). School resource officers and the criminalization of student behavior. *Journal of Criminal Justice, 37*(3), 280–287.

Tillman, L. (2002). Culturally sensitive research approaches: An African American perspective. *Educational Researcher, 31*(9), 3–12.

Tillman, L. (2004). African American principals and the legacy of Brown. *Review of Research Education, 28,* 101–146.

Title VI of the Civil Rights Act of 1964, 42 U.S.C. 2000d (1964)

Torres, E. M., Ehrhart, M. G., Beidas, R. S., Farahnak, L. R., Finn, N. K., & Aarons, G. A. (2018). Validation of the Implementation Leadership Scale (ILS) with supervisors' self-ratings. *Community Mental Health Journal, 54*(1), 49–53.

Townsend, B. (2000). The disproportionate discipline of African American learners: Reducing school suspensions and expulsions. *Exceptional Children, 66*(3), 381–391.

Tracy, S. J. (2010). Qualitative quality: Eight "big-tent" criteria for excellent qualitative research. *Qualitative Inquiry, 16*(10), 837–851.

Transforming School Discipline Collaborative. (2016). *TSDC's model student code of conduct: An interdisciplinary approach to transforming school discipline.* isbe. net/documents/tsdc-model-code-conduct.pdf

Trent, S. C., Artiles, A. J., & Englert, C. S. (1998). From deficit thinking to social constructivism: A review of special education theory, research and practice. *Review of Research in Education, 23*(1), 277–307. doi.org/10.3102%2F0091732X023001277

Trizano-Hermosilla, I., & Alvarado, J. M. (2016). Best alternatives to Cronbach's alpha reliability in realistic conditions: Congeneric and asymmetrical measurements. *Frontiers in Psychology, 7,* 769. doi.org/10.3389/fpsyg.2016.00769

United Way. (2016). *Study of financial hardship Louisiana update.* Louisiana Association of United Ways. www.unitedforalice.org/Attachments/AllReports/16UW%20 ALICE%20Report_LAUpdate_3.21.17_Lowres.pdf

U.S. Census Bureau. (2010). *Quick Facts: San Juan County, New Mexico.* www .census.gov/quickfacts/fact/table/sanjuancountynewmexico,nm/PST045217

U.S. Census Bureau. (2020). *Quick Facts: San Juan County, New Mexico.* www.census .gov/quickfacts/sanjuancountynewmexico

U.S. Department of Education. (2018). *40th annual report to Congress on the implementation of the Individuals with Disabilities Education Act.* www2.ed.gov /about/reports/annual/osep/2018/parts-b-c/index.html

U.S. Department of Education, Office for Civil Rights. (2012). *Civil rights data collection*. ocrdata.ed.gov

U.S. Department of Education, Office for Civil Rights. (2014a). *Civil rights data collection*. ocrdata.ed.gov

U.S. Department of Education, Office for Civil Rights. (2014b, March). *Civil rights data collection data snapshot: School discipline* (Issue Brief No. 1). www2 .ed.gov/about/offices/list/ocr/docs/crdc-discipline-snapshot.pdf

U.S. Department of Education, Office for Civil Rights. (2016). *Parent and educator resource guide to section 504 in public elementary and secondary schools.* www2.ed.gov/about/offices/list/ocr/docs/504-resource-guide-201612.pdf

U.S. Department of Education, Office for Civil Rights. (2018). *Civil rights data collection*. ocrdata.ed.gov

U.S. Department of Education, Office for Civil Rights. (2019). *2015–2016 civil rights data collection: School Climate and Safety.* www2.ed.gov/about/offices/list/ocr /docs/school-climate-and-safety.pdf

U.S. Department of Education, Office for Civil Rights. (2020). *Protecting students with disabilities: Frequently asked questions about Section 504 and the education of children with disabilities.* www2.ed.gov/about/offices/list/ocr/504faq .html

U.S. Department of Education, Office for Civil Rights. (2021, June). *An overview of exclusionary discipline practices in public schools for the 2017–2018 school year.* Civil Rights Data Collection. ocrdata.ed.gov/assets/downloads/crdc-exclusionary -school-discipline.pdf

U.S. Department of Education, Office of Special Education Programs. (2017, March). *IDEA Part B regulations significant disproportionality (equity in IDEA): Essential questions and answers.* sites.ed.gov/idea/files/significant-disproportionality -qa-03-08-17-1.pdf

U.S. Government Accountability Office. (2018). *K–12 education: Discipline disparities for Black students, boys, and students with disabilities.* www.gao.gov/assets /gao-18-258.pdf

Valencia, R. R. (Ed.). (1997). *The evolution of deficit thinking: Educational thought and practice.* Routledge.

Valencia, R. R. (2010). *Dismantling contemporary deficit thinking: Educational thought and practice.* Routledge.

Vaught, S. E. (2009). The color of money: School funding and the commodification of Black children. *Urban Education, 44*(5), 545–570. doi.org /10.1177/0042085908318776

Vavrus, F., & Cole, K. (2002). "I didn't do nothin'": The discursive construction of school suspension. *The Urban Review, 34*(2), 87–111.

Velasquez, A., West, R. E., Graham, C., & Osguthorpe, R. (2013). Context and implications document for: Developing caring relationships in schools: A review of the research on caring and nurturing pedagogies. *Review of Education, 1*(2), 162–190. doi.org/10.1002/rev3.3015

Villegas, A. M. (1988). School failure and cultural mismatch: Another view. *The Urban Review, 20*(4), 253–265.

Vincent, C. G., Cartledge, G., May, S., & Tobin, T. J. (2009). *Do elementary schools that document reductions in overall office discipline referrals document reductions across all student races and ethnicities?* (Evaluation Brief). Center on Positive Behavioral Interventions and Supports. pbis.org/evaluation/evaluationbriefs/default .aspx

Vincent, C. G., Randall, C., Cartledge, G., Tobin, T. J., & Swain-Bradway, J. (2011). Toward a conceptual integration of cultural responsiveness and school-wide positive behavior support. *Journal of Positive Behavior Interventions, 13*(4), 219–229. doi.org/10.1177/1098300711399765

VOYCE. (n.d.). *Rethinking Safety Campaign.* voyceproject.org/initiatives/rethinking -safety-campaign/

Wachtel, T. (2013). Defining restorative. *International Institute of Restorative Practices*, 1–12.

Wagner, M., Kutash, K., Duchnowski, A. J., Epstein, M. H., & Sumi, W. C. (2005). The children and youth we serve: A national picture of the characteristics of students with emotional disturbances receiving special education. *Journal of Emotional and Behavioral Disorders, 13*(2), 79–96. doi.org/10.1177/106342660501 30020201/

Walker, H. M., Forness, S. R., & Lane, K. L. (2014). Design and management of scientific research in applied school settings. In B. Cook, M. Tankersley, & T. Landrum (Eds.), *Advances in learning and behavioral disabilities* (Vol. 27, pp. 141–169). Emerald.

Walker, H. M., Nishioka, V. M., Zeller, R., Severson, H. H., & Feil, E. G. (2000). Causal factors and potential solutions for the persistent underidentification of students having emotional or behavioral disorders in the context of schooling. *Assessment for Effective Intervention, 26*, 29–39.

Walker, V. S. (2013). Ninth annual *Brown* lecture in education research: Black educators as educational advocates in the decades before *Brown v. Board of Education. Educational Researcher, 42*(4), 207–222.

Watts, I. E., & Erevelles, N. (2004). These deadly times: Reconceptualizing school violence by using critical race theory and disability studies. *American Educational Research Journal, 41*(2), 271–299. doi.org/10.3102/00028312041002271

Weisburst, E. K. (2019). Patrolling public schools: The impact of funding for school police on student discipline and long-term education outcomes. *Journal of Policy Analysis and Management, 38*(2), 338–365.

Welsh, R. O., & Little, S. (2018). The school discipline dilemma: A comprehensive review of disparities and alternative approaches. *Review of Educational Research, 88*, 752–794.

Whitaker, A., Torres-Guillén, S., Morton, M., Jordan, H., Coyle, S., Mann, A., & Sun, W.-L. (2019). *Cops and no counselors: How the lack of school mental health staff is harming students.* American Civil Liberties Union.

The White House. (2021, July 23). *Fact sheet: How the Biden-Harris administration is advancing educational equity.* www.whitehouse.gov/briefing-room /statements-releases/2021/07/23/fact-sheet-how-the-biden-harris-administration -is-advancing-educational-equity/

Whitford, D. K. (2017). School discipline disproportionality: American Indian students in special education. *Urban Review*, *49*, 693–706. doi.org/10.1007/s11256-017-0417-x

Whitford, D. K., Gage, N. A., Katsiyannis, A., Counts, J., Rapa, L. J., & McWhorter, A. (2019). The exclusionary discipline of American Indian and Alaska Native (AI/AN) students with and without disabilities: A Civil Rights Data Collection (CRDC) National Analysis. *Journal of Child and Family Studies*, *28*(12), 3327–3337. doi.org/10.1007/s10826-019-01511-8

Wiggin, L. (2016). Education connection: The effects of race, culture, and special education on minority disproportionality in the juvenile justice system. *Children's Legal Rights Journal*, *36*(1), 66–70.

Wiley, A. L., Tankersley, M., & Simms, A. (2012). Teachers' causal attributions for student problem behavior: Implications for school-based behavioral interventions and research. In B. G. Cook, M. Tankersley, & T. J. Landrum (Eds.), *Advances in learning and behavioral disabilities* (Vol. 25, pp. 279–300). Emerald Group.

Williams, P. (1987). Spirit-murdering the messenger: The discourse of finger pointing as the law's response to racism. *University of Miami Law Review*, *42*(1), 127–157. repository.law.miami.edu/umlr/vol42/iss1/8/

Wilson, M. A. F., Yull, D. G., & Massey, S. G. (2020). Race and the politics of educational exclusion: Explaining the persistence of disproportionate disciplinary practices in an urban school district. *Race, Ethnicity and Education*, *23*(1), 134–157. doi.org/10.1080/13613324.2018.1511535

Woolfolk, A. E., Rossoff, B., & Hoy, W. K. (1990). Teachers' sense of efficacy and their beliefs about managing students. *Teaching and Teacher Education*, *6*, 137–148.

Wordlow v. Chicago Bd. of Educ. No. 16-cv-8040, 2018 WL 6171792 (N.D. Ill. Nov. 26, 2018)

Wright, J. P., Morgan, M. A., Coyne, M. A., Beaver, K. M., & Barnes, J. C. (2014). Prior problem behavior accounts for the racial gap in school suspensions. *Journal of Criminal Justice*, *42*, 257–266. doi.org/10.1016/j.jcrimjus.2014.01.001

Yazan, B. (2015). Three approaches to case study methods in education: Yin, Merriam, and Stake. *The Qualitative Report*, *20*(2), 134–152. doi.org/10.46743/2160-3715/2015.2102

Yazzie, R. (1994). Life comes from it: Navajo justice concepts. *New Mexico Law Review*, *24*, 175.

Yazzie, R. (1996). "Hozho Nahasldii"—We are now in good relations: Navajo restorative justice. *Saint Thomas Law Review*, *9*, 117–124.

Yosso, T. J. (2005). Whose culture has capital? A critical race theory discussion of community cultural wealth. *Race ethnicity and education*, *8*(1), 69–91.

Zhang, D. Katsiyannis, A., & Herbst, M. (2004). Disciplinary exclusions in special education: A 4-year analysis. *Behavior Disorders*, *29*(4), 337–347.

Zimmer-Gembeck, M. J., Chipuer, H. M., Hanisch, M., Creed, P. A., & McGregor, L. (2006). Relationships at school and stage-environment fit as resources for adolescent engagement and achievement. *Journal of Adolescence*, *29*, 911–933.

Zirkel, P. A. (2011). The remedial authority of hearing and review officers under the Individuals with Disabilities Education Act: An update. *Journal of the National Association of Administrative Law Judiciary, 31,* 1–43.

Zirkel, P. A. (2019a). An empirical analysis of recent case law arising from school resource officers. *Journal of Law and Education, 48,* 305–333.

Zirkel, P. A. (2019b). School resource officers and students with disabilities: A disproportionate connection? *Exceptionality, 27,* 1–16. doi.org/10.1080/0936283 5.2019.1579725

Zirkel, P. A., & Clark, J. H. (2008). School negligence case law trends. *Southern Illinois Law Review, 32,* 345–363.

Zirkel P. A., & Fossey, R. (2018). Liability for student suicide: An update of the case law. *West's Education Law Reporter, 354,* 628–636.

Index

About the Editors and Contributors

EDITORS

Pamela Fenning, PhD, ABPP is a professor and co-director of the School Psychology program at Loyola University Chicago School of Education. She is a licensed clinical and school psychologist in Illinois. Her research focuses on MTSS interventions at the high school level, racial bias in exclusionary discipline practice and policy, evaluation of state-level discipline reform, and school-based supports for military youth.

Miranda Johnson, JD, MPA, is a clinical professor at Loyola University Chicago School of Law and the director of Loyola's Education Law and Policy Institute. She has represented parents and students in school discipline, special education, and bullying cases in administrative proceedings and state and federal courts. Her research focuses on law and policy reform to reduce the use of exclusionary school discipline practices and replace them with proactive and positive supports.

Chapter 2

Markeda Newell, PhD, is interim dean of the Loyola University Chicago School of Education and an associate professor of school psychology. The focus of her research is on the development, implementation, and evaluation of multicultural and consultation competence among school psychologists. She is specifically interested in identifying the fundamental knowledge and skills school psychologists need to serve students who represent a range of racial/ethnic, linguistic, economic, and cultural backgrounds.

Emma Healy, MEd, is a licensed school psychologist and doctoral student in the School Psychology program at Loyola University Chicago. Her research focuses on dismantling the school-to-prison pipeline, alternatives to suspension programs, and culturally sensitive tools used in the assessment of children. She has been trained in school, outpatient, and community-based mental health settings and looks forward to using equity-based practices in her work with children and families.

Chapter 3

Patrice Leverett, PhD, is a nationally certified school psychologist and an assistant professor of school psychology at the University of Nevada–Las Vegas. Prior to completing her doctoral degree, she served as a special education teacher and school psychologist. Leverett's research interests include the design and evaluation of culturally responsive interventions, student advocacy, the impacts of intersectionality on educational outcomes, and ultimately increasing diversity and retention in higher education.

Chapter 4

Amy E. Fisher, PhD, is a postdoctoral scholar in the Schubert Center for Child Studies at Case Western Reserve University. Her research focuses on issues of equitable education in policy and practice with a focus on racism and ableism in the K–12 education system. Her current projects are centered on bridging research, policy, and practice to center equitable education.

Benjamin W. Fisher, PhD, is an assistant professor of criminology and criminal justice at Florida State University. His research centers on school criminalization, with a particular focus on racial equity in school safety, security, and discipline.

Chapter 5

Angelina N. Nortey, PhD, is a licensed psychologist and nationally certified school psychologist. Her primary research interests are in school discipline and early career school psychologists' social justice needs, with an emphasis in qualitative methodology. Her research relies on Black feminist and critical theories to explore issues of race and disability in the school setting. She is the founder and clinical director of Sage Wellness and Consulting. Nortey has extensive experience working within and consulting with public, public charter, and private schools.

Chapter 6

Kristen Pearson, PhD, is a licensed child psychologist, certified school psychologist, and assistant professor of psychiatry in the Tulane University School of Medicine. She specializes in the assessment and treatment of children with emotional and behavioral disorders and uses a relationship and strengths-based approach grounded in connecting the home, school, and community. Pearson's experience includes psychoeducational assessment, treatment, and consultation in schools and therapeutic settings for students with significant mental health concerns.

Laura Marques, PhD, is a licensed child and school psychologist in Louisiana and Texas. She specializes in assessment and treatment of childhood disorders, including trauma- and stressor-related disorders and disruptive behavior disorders in youth. Her experiences include working in schools and therapeutic settings to implement evidence-based interventions for youth with severe and complex mental health needs. Marques holds a faculty appointment at Tulane University School of Medicine and serves as faculty for the Tulane Early Childhood Mental Health Consultation program. She also provides assessment, therapy, and consultation in her private practice located in Austin, Texas.

Monica Stevens, PhD, specializes in treating disruptive behavior disorders and uses her experience with relationship-based assessment and interventions to treat the underlying causes of these issues. Stevens has extensive experience addressing the impact of trauma on children and their families. While at Tulane, Stevens has practiced in various community agencies, including those that serve the needs of very young children. She also has experience working with adolescents with severe psychiatric conditions in the hospital and school setting.

Elizabeth Marcell Williams, EdD, is the founding CEO of the Center for Resilience (CfR), the only therapeutic day treatment in Louisiana for children with significant behavioral health needs. She assumed this role after overseeing CfR's nonprofit transition from the state-run New Orleans Therapeutic Day Program (NOTDP), a partnership among the Recovery School District of Louisiana, Orleans Parish School Board, and Tulane University Medical School. Williams has over 20 years of experience as a special education leader. She has served as a director of special education for a New Orleans charter school network and consulted with schools and districts around the country to develop high-quality special education programming.

Chapter 7

Sandra M. Chafouleas, PhD, is a board of trustees distinguished professor in the Neag School of Education at the University of Connecticut. Chafouleas is the author of more than 150 publications, regularly serves as a national presenter and invited speaker, and is the recipient of multiple national and university awards for her scholarship and mentoring. She previously worked as a school psychologist and school administrator in a variety of settings supporting the needs of children experiencing social, emotional, and behavioral challenges.

Amy Briesch, PhD, is an associate professor in the Department of Applied Psychology at Northeastern University. Her primary research interests involve the development of feasible and psychometrically sound measures for the assessment of student behavior in multitiered systems of support. Briesch has authored over 80 peer-reviewed articles and three books focused on school-based behavioral assessment and intervention.

Kathleen Lynne Lane, PhD, is a Roy A. Roberts distinguished professor in the Department of Special Education at the University of Kansas and associate vice chancellor for Research. Lane's research interests focus on designing, implementing, and evaluating comprehensive, integrated, three-tiered (Ci3T) models of prevention to (a) prevent the development of learning and behavior challenges and (b) respond to existing instances, with an emphasis on systematic screening. She is president of the Council for Exceptional Children Division for Research (CEC-DR) and coeditor of *Remedial and Special Education*. Dr. Lane has coauthored 11 books and published 211 refereed journal articles and 42 book chapters.

Wendy Peia Oakes, PhD, is an associate professor at the Mary Lou Fulton Teachers College at Arizona State University. Her work focuses on practices that improve educational access and outcomes for young children with and at risk for emotional and behavioral disorders. Oakes serves as an associate editor for *Remedial and Special Education* and coeditor for an annual special issue of *Education and Treatment of Children*. She served as the president of the Council for Exceptional Children (CEC)–Council for Children With Behavioral Disorders and is currently president-elect for the CEC–Division for Research.

Chapter 8

Lindsay Fallon, PhD, BCBA-D, is an associate professor of school psychology in the College of Education and Human Development at University of Massachusetts Boston. Her research examines consideration of culture and context in support of youth behavior. She is also very interested in training and interventions for educators to be more equitable and just in their interactions with youth.

Margarida Veiga, MEd, LICSW, BCBA, is a doctoral candidate in school psychology in the College of Education and Human Development at the University of Massachusetts Boston. Her research interests include supporting staff training to ensure intervention integrity, promoting treatment integrity of evidence-based interventions, and developing practices aimed at incorporating cultural humility into behavior analytic interventions.

Chapter 9

Emma Healy's biography appears under Chapter 2.

Michelle Rappaport, MSW, LCSW, is the award-winning author of *Building Bridges: An Alternative to Suspension* (Rappaport, 2014). She has worked in the field of special education for 30 years and specializes in working with at-risk youth who are frequently in crisis. In 2017, she was awarded School Social Worker of the Year by the Illinois Association of School Social

Workers. Rappaport works as an office intervention social worker with high school students in a public therapeutic day school. She is a popular speaker at nationally recognized education, social work, and discipline conferences. Her Building Bridges program provides an alternative to suspensions by helping students gain insight into their maladaptive patterns of behaviors and avoid future crises. Her website is https://www.buildingbridgesbook.com/.

Carly Tindall-Biggins, PhD, is a school psychologist for Maine Township High School District 207 and is currently completing a postdoctoral clinical training experience. As a doctoral student in school psychology at Loyola University Chicago, she participated on several research teams examining topics such as racial disproportionality in school discipline practices and school psychologists' familiarity and experience in responding to occurrences of identity-based harassment. Her dissertation examined the ways in which youth are empowered through participatory action research experiences.

Chapter 10

Heather Hoechst, JD, MA, is an attorney and child welfare team leader at the Native American Disability Law Center in Farmington, New Mexico. Her practice focuses on the education civil rights of Native American children with disabilities, with a particular interest in the intersection of race and disability in the school discipline context. She represents students and families in New Mexico, Colorado, Arizona, and in Bureau of Indian Education schools. Hoeshst also represents Native American children protected by the Indian Child Welfare Act as guardian ad litem in the San Juan County District Court. She has lived in the Four Corners since 2016.

Donald Chee worked as an advocate at the Native American Disability Law Center in Farmington, New Mexico, from 2018 until July 2021. A member of the Navajo Nation, he has an extensive background in community health education and American Indian Studies.

Chapter 11

Thomas Mayes, JD, MEd, is the general counsel for the Iowa Department of Education. Before joining the department, he was staff attorney for the Iowa Court of Appeals, a staff attorney in Iowa Legal Aid's Waterloo office, and law clerk to Justice James H. Carter of the Supreme Court of Iowa. He previously served as president of the National Council of State Education Attorneys. He was also appointed to the state's Children's Justice State Council and is a certified child welfare law specialist.

Perry A. Zirkel, PhD, JD, LLM, is university professor emeritus of education and law at Lehigh University, where he formerly was dean of the College of Education and the Iacocca chair in education. He has presented in every state in the United States and written more than 1,600 publications on various aspects of school law, with an emphasis on legal issues in special education. Past president of the Education Law Association and cochair of the Pennsylvania special education appeals panel from 1990 to 2007, he is the author of the monograph *The Legal Meaning of Specific Learning Disability* (2006, Council for Exceptional Children); the more recently published books, *A Digest of Supreme Court Decisions Affecting Education* (2009, Education Law Association) and *Student Teaching and the Law* (2009, Rowman & Littlefield); and the two-volume reference *Section 504, the ADA and the Schools* (2011, LRP Publications). He provides a monthly special education legal update and shares his publications at https://perryzirkel.com/.